The Controlling Concept

Cornerstone of Performance Management

A Practical Guide to Effective Management Control

The Controlling Concept

Cornerstone of Performance Management

A Practical Guide to Effective Management Control

HORVÁTH & PARTNERS
MANAGEMENT CONSULTANTS

Vahlen
World Scientific

Published by

World Scientific Publishing Co. Pte. Ltd.

5 Toh Tuck Link, Singapore 596224

USA office: 27 Warren Street, Suite 401-402, Hackensack, NJ 07601

UK office: 57 Shelton Street, Covent Garden, London WC2H 9HE

and

Verlag Franz Vahlen GmbH

Wilhelmstraße 9, 80801 München, Germany

British Library Cataloguing-in-Publication Data
A catalogue record for this book is available from the British Library.

© 2020 Verlag Franz Vahlen GmbH together, The Controlling Concept: Cornerstone of Performance Management. Published by arrangement with Verlag Franz Vahlen GmbH.

This edition is jointly published by World Scientific Publishing Co. Inc. and Verlag Franz Vahlen GmbH.
This edition is distributed worldwide by World Scientific Publishing Co. Inc. except Germany, Austria and Switzerland.

THE CONTROLLING CONCEPT
Cornerstone of Performance Management

ISBN 978-981-121-864-4 (hardcover)
ISBN 978-981-121-865-1 (ebook for institutions)
ISBN 978-981-121-866-8 (ebook for individuals)

For any available supplementary material, please visit
https://www.worldscientific.com/worldscibooks/10.1142/11778#t=suppl

Desk Editor: Karimah Samsudin

Preface

We are delighted that our tried-and-tested "Controllingkonzept" book is now available in English under the title of "The Controlling Concept", making it accessible to an even larger readership. This version is the translation of the 8th edition of the German book. A Chinese edition has also been available since May 2018, sitting alongside the German and English version.

The 1st edition of this book was published by Prof. Dr. Dr. h.c. mult. Péter Horváth, Professor Emeritus at University of Stuttgart and founder of Horváth & Partners, together with associates from Horváth & Partners, and released in German-speaking countries back in 1990. Since then, the book has continued to be developed further based on the latest developments within corporate practice, cutting-edge scientific findings in different management disciplines, and the very latest developments in IT. This edition therefore replicates the state of the art in controlling. The book is targeted at controllers and managers of larger companies, who wish to create a controlling system that complies with both current as well as future company management requirements.

We would like to thank Prof. Horváth, who supervised this edition organisationally and played a key role in shaping its content, as well as the many colleagues from Horváth & Partners contributing to this edition. We would also like to give particular thanks to René Linsner, Frank Poschadel, Christian Huck and Christina Seez, who all made a massive contribution to bringing the English version to life.

Stuttgart, January 2019   *Dr. Uwe Michel*

Member of the Managing Board

Horváth & Partners Management Consultants

Objectives and structure of the book

How does a company align itself with its objectives and ensure success in the long term? All companies have to face these challenges all the time. The challenges have become even greater given the increasing level of volatility and global uncertainty in recent years. The task for management is to direct the company and to adapt to changes in the corporate environment by way of suitable corporate strategies, structures and processes. Controlling primarily supports management in this task by providing suitable controlling information and processes.

But how is an effective controlling system structured?

By using a wide range of successful consultancy projects regarding the structure and improvement of controlling systems as the basis, Horváth & Partners has developed the "House of Controlling" (see **Fig. 1**). This covers the central components of an effective controlling system and has proven itself in practice time and time again.

This book provides a detailed description of the components of the "House of Controlling", illustrating the key findings in a manner that is easy to understand for readers. In addition, specific structural principles for managers and controllers as well as practical examples enable implementation in small- and medium-sized enterprises as well, thus contributing to the distribution of effective controlling systems in all sectors and through companies of all sizes.

This book is specifically designed for practitioners who have experience in dealing with managerial issues, but who require structural know-how for the purpose of a modern controlling system.

The book therefore has the following objectives in mind:

- Readers should become familiar with and understand the central components and design features of an effective controlling system ("House of Controlling").
- Readers should learn how to deal with the various terms, tasks and tools involved in controlling.
- After having read this book, readers should know how an effective controlling system is structured and which design features need to be observed in particular. They should therefore be able to adapt the knowledge they have obtained to the special characteristics of a company.

This will generally involve replicating the latest practical and scientific findings on controlling and illustrating numerous examples from corporate practice. The general practice-oriented controlling system is always at the forefront of this. This does not involve a detailed scientific approach unlike individual controlling problems.

The structure of the book is aligned with the components of the "House of Controlling" by Horváth & Partners:

To begin with, Chapter 1 clarifies the term "controlling", general controlling tasks and an understanding of the role and skills of the controller. This provides the basis for illustrating the components and design features of an effective controlling system in the subsequent chapters.

Objectives and structure of the book

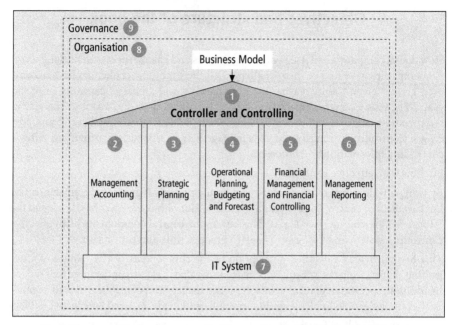

Fig. 1: Structure of the book based on the "House of Controlling" by Horváth & Partners

Chapters 2 to 7 describe the individual components of an effective controlling system. All chapters are structured identically to each other. The objectives of the chapter are indicated in the first section. The second section in each chapter illustrates the need to take the component into account as part of an effective controlling system. The third section describes the central design features and the special characteristics to be noted. The fourth section makes use of a practical example to illustrate and supplement the knowledge blocks developed. Each chapter is concluded by way of a summary of the most important findings in the form of structural checklists for managers and controllers. These checklists are based on diverse consultancy experience with regard to the structure and improvement of controlling systems in practical situations.

Chapters 8 and 9 describe the legal, information-related and organisational framework of a controlling system.

Chapter 10 offers a concluding outlook on current and future developments for controlling and controllers.

Overall, the new edition of these proven guidelines aims to provide an illustration of the "state-of-the-art" controlling technique.

Contents

Contents

Controlling as the Foundation of Performance Management

Introductory Remarks

How can a company be orientated towards a performance goal and manage to ensure that this goal is reached?

Only when the company is able to master this increasingly demanding challenge will its continued existence be secured. But that in itself is not really an answer, because it does not tell us how to master the challenge of performance orientation. This is why successful performance management concepts have been developed all around the world, in academia and in business practice, over the past century.

This book takes a close look at the concept of Controlling, which – while based on US role models – was originally developed in Germany and has since spread and proven itself in Europe as well as America and Asia.

As in other fields, there are various approaches in the concepts for corporate performance management, which sometimes overlap. In many cases, companies have individual solutions which are made up from a mixture of different concepts. Internationalisation and globalisation mean that such "best practices" are communicated and copied all around the world.

One particular problem we find here is the "wording". Although English has become the lingua franca of the business world, there are still frequent communication problems. This makes it even more important to define terms clearly and also to distinguish clearly between them.

This is especially important for the "Controlling Concept" as the word "Controlling" has become a part of the German language; in English, it does not always carry the same meaning as it does in German.

For this reason, we would like to provide a brief explanation of the most important, commonly used specialist terms in Controlling, and shed light on the relationships between them. We are well aware that some things might be described differently in textbooks and in business practice. We believe we should begin by explaining three concepts and defining how they relate to one another:

- Accounting, which is broken down into Financial and Management Accounting
- Performance Measurement/Performance Management
- Controlling/Management Control

Controlling as the Foundation of Performance Management

In literature and in business practice, the term *"accounting"* is used in two ways. First, it is used as an umbrella term to describe all the processes and procedures used to collect and process financial data. Usually, accounting is then broken down into *financial accounting* and *management accounting*. In the narrower sense, accounting is also used to describe financial accounting, which comprises bookkeeping (today more commonly called accounting) and balance sheets.

The task of *management accounting* is to provide management with information from accounting to support the decision-making process.

Performance measurement is a set of tasks which deal with the definition and measurement of performance. Performance measurement is an essential element of operationalising corporate targets.

Performance management is a term which is used in a wide variety of ways. We interpret the term in a very broad sense. We see performance management as all the decisions and activities of management which foster the efficient and effective achievement of corporate goals.

Some authors equate performance measurement with performance management. We do not. For us, performance measurement is the measurement of performance whereas performance management consists of the all-embracing management task of ensuring a good or service is actually produced.

In general, *management control* is seen as the process of planning, managing and monitoring.

Controlling, as described in this book, is a function which integrates the process-based aspects of management control and the topics of performance measurement and management accounting (cf. **Figure 1**).

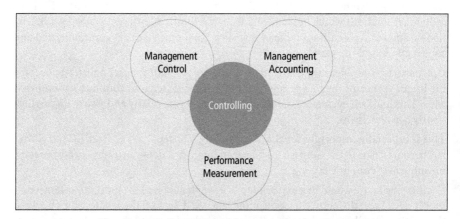

Figure 1: Controlling: Integrative support function

Now, who are the persons in charge of this function?

In English and American English, *accountants* are the people who are responsible for accounting and balance sheets.

Management accountants (sometimes also called cost accountants in English) are in charge of management accounting.

The controller is responsible for providing all the necessary support for management through systems and information (also including management accounting) – they are the main character of our book (cf. **Figure 2**).

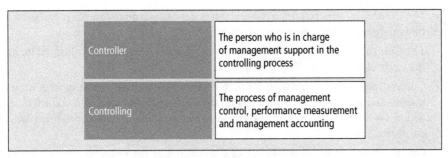

Figure 2: Controller/Controlling

Due to their close involvement in performance management, the controller is referred to as a *business partner* to the manager. (The name *"management accountant"*, which is still common in some places [UK, USA], does not do sufficient justice to the actual role of the controller.)

In our book, *managers* are the people who are responsible for decision-making in the company.

Figure 3 shows an overall view of how we understand the roles and the people playing them in this book:

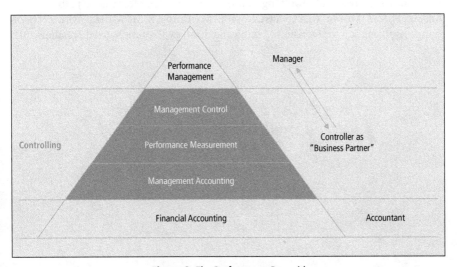

Figure 3: The Performance Pyramid

Financial accounting supplies the basic data from accounting and balance sheets for management accounting. Management accounting and performance measurement are the sole responsibility of the controller. Management control, in the sense of process design and information supply, also falls under the remit of the controller. Performance management operates using Controlling as its foundation.

Thus, we can summarise as follows:

- The Controlling process comprises and integrates management control, performance measurement and management accounting.
- The Controller is the person in charge of management support designing and using the Controlling process ("business partner").
- Controlling lays the foundation for performance management in the form of information and processes. We see this as all the leadership and management activities which are needed to produce the company's goods and services congruent with corporate goals.
- On the whole, we see this concept of Controlling as the essential cornerstone of performance management.

This book is a practical guide for managers and controllers on how the Controlling Concept can increase the performance of their organisations.

Further reading

Bragg S. M., The Controller's Function – The Work of the Managerial Accountant, 4. ed., Hoboken, N. J. 2011.

Chapman, C. S. (Ed.), Controlling Strategy – Management, Accounting, and Performance Measurement, Oxford 2005.

Desroches, D., Lawson, R., Evolving Role of the Controller, Montvale, NJ 2013.

Kaplan, R. S., Atkinson, A. A., Matsumura, E. M., Young, S. M., Management Accounting – Information for Decision Making and Strategy Execution, 6. ed., London 2012.

1 Nature and Structure of Controlling

1.1 Chapter objectives

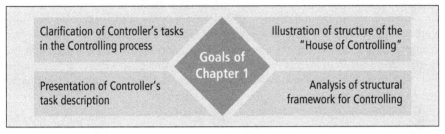

Clarification of Controller's tasks in the Controlling process

Illustration of structure of the "House of Controlling"

Goals of Chapter 1

Presentation of Controller's task description

Analysis of structural framework for Controlling

Fig. 1.1: Chapter objectives

In this introductory chapter we will first develop a common understanding of the term *Controlling*, of the general tasks of Controlling, and of the roles and competences of controllers. The main objective of the chapter is to provide the reader with an initial overview of the main components of an effective Controlling system.

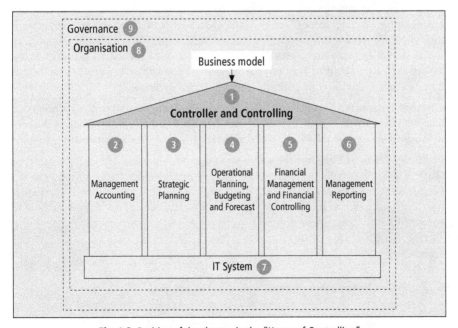

Governance 9

Organisation 8

Business model

1

Controller and Controlling

2	3	4	5	6
Management Accounting	Strategic Planning	Operational Planning, Budgeting and Forecast	Financial Management and Financial Controlling	Management Reporting

IT System 7

Fig. 1.2: Position of the chapter in the "House of Controlling"

1.2 Introduction

Over the years, Controlling has developed continually in business practice and has become an indispensable management support function for any modern company. Nevertheless, there are still considerable differences of opinion about the term Controlling. In many cases, Controlling is often taken erroneously to mean control, but Controlling is much more than that. Controlling is a cross-functional performance management concept tasked with the performance-based coordination of planning, control and the provision of information. Hence, the controller is the "economic conscience" of the company.

In recent decades Controlling has become strongly rooted in nearly all industries; nowadays, Controlling departments can be found not only in classical industrial companies but also in retail, financial services providers, or public authorities. However, alongside the universal necessity for coordinating planning, information provision and control, there are often further specific reasons for setting up a Controlling function in the respective field. These reasons also explain why Controlling functions in different industries sometimes have very individual characteristics.

1.3 Tasks of Controlling

In principle, we must differentiate between Controlling as a function ("controller service", "controllership") and the controller as the executor of that function. As a matter of fact, in terms of performance management, Controlling is a core task of management. To a certain extent, every manager performs some Controlling functions. Thus, Controlling as a process and mindset is created jointly by managers and controllers in a team and forms a type of "intersection". In this, the controller is involved in the management processes of target-setting, planning and performance management by supporting decision-making through the provision of information and the creation of transparency, as well as being a planning facilitator. As a result, the controller is partially responsible for enabling the manager to take timely, target-based decisions.

Together, managers and controllers share responsibility for the Controlling process (see Chapter 8 for details of the Controlling process). **Fig. 1.3** shows Controlling as the area of intersection between the tasks of the manager and those of the controller.

Primarily, Controlling is not the name of a position or person, but rather a remit or scope of tasks carried out by different people, or by management itself, without a specific person actually having to hold the title of "controller". Above all, in small companies the Controlling function is frequently executed by management itself or by the head of accounting.

Is there a controller mission statement in your company?

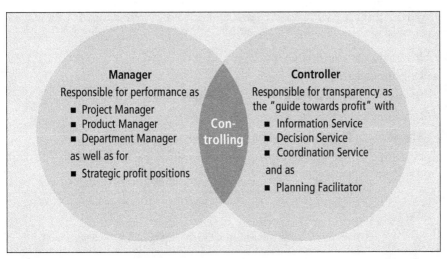

Fig. 1.3: Controlling as intersection between managers and controllers (International Controller Association [ICV] e. V. o. J., p. 3)

The tasks, the self-image and the responsibility of the controller are described very concisely and succinctly in the Controller Mission Statement from the International Group of Controlling (IGC) (cf. **Fig. 1.4**). The current version of the mission statement explicitly emphasises the controller's joint responsibility for target achievement. On the one hand, this joint responsibility stems from the fact that controllers are responsible for the accuracy of the information they collect and prepare; on the other hand, it can be derived from the fact that controllers, by designing and accompanying the management processes of target-setting, planning and performance management, make a significant contribution to management's ability to make decisions in time and with an eye on corporate objectives. However, responsibility for the decisions actually taken, as expressed in the adoption of plans, still remains with management.

Controller Mission Statement

Controllers design and accompany the management process of target setting, planning and performance management, and share responsibility for target achievement.

This means:

Controllers ensure the transparency of business results, finance, processes and strategy and thus contribute to higher economic effectiveness.

Controllers co-ordinate secondary goals and the related plans in a holistic way and organize a reporting system which is future-oriented and covers the enterprise as a whole.

Controllers moderate and design the controlling process of defining goals, planning and management control so that every decision maker can act in accordance with agreed objectives.

Controllers provide the necessary services relating to the provision of data and information.

Controllers develop and maintain the controlling systems.

Fig. 1.4: Controller Mission Statement of the International Group of Controlling (IGC 2013)

In general, through coordination, controllers help solve problems caused by the increasing impact of these environmental factors:

- Increasing dynamism and volatility
- Ongoing globalisation
- Changes in value creation owing to new technologies
- Increasingly shorter product life cycles
- The spread of digitisation across all organisations

Controlling enables corporate management to face these challenges head-on with innovative solutions, instead of relying on old, outdated remedies.

Which concrete strategic and operative challenges does your company face?

However, Controlling is not merely a service to enable management to "cover their backs" with the information it provides. It is also an idea which all employees in a company should take to heart. This idea consists of two aspects. First, acting, and taking personal responsibility for one's actions, to further the company's bottom line and in line with corporate planning; and second, thinking outside of one's specific remit and embracing the concept of interface management. Thus, Controlling is not only carried out by controllers but ideally on the spot by the member of staff directly affected. In this way, Controlling is increasingly transitioning into self-Controlling; more than ever, controllers are undertaking "missionary work" to spread the underlying idea behind Controlling.

1.4 Role and job description of the controller

Now that we have discussed the tasks of Controlling, let us turn to the controller as a person and their position in the organisation. As already mentioned, on the one hand, controllers support management, but on the other hand, they also have decentralised (local) activities in that they spread the word about the idea of controlling among employees. Through their involvement in the planning process and the attendant need for information supply, they provide direct support for corporate management. That being said, controllers are active on all tiers of the hierarchy and in all corporate functions. Accordingly, we are starting to see a differentiated Controlling organisation among larger companies, one which is made up of both central and local controllers.

At this stage, however, we do not want to discuss organisational details – that is the subject of Chapter 8. At the moment, it is enough to say that alongside the performance management model and the claim to leadership of the management, the tasks and position of the controller depend heavily on the size of the company. Thus, for small and mid-sized enterprises it is typical for the controller to be a "Jack-of-all-trades" and not only deal with purely Controlling tasks, while large companies often employ specialists for sub-sections of Controlling in their finance and business functions.

Hence, one way of further defining the tasks of controllers and their position within the leadership structure of a company is to take a look at the respective job description.

Is there a job description for the controllers in your company?

Fig. 1.5 shows the job description of the head of controlling in a mid-sized company. The job description provides information about the rank and chain of command/line of reporting of the controller and their precise fields of activity, competences and powers. Hence, it is particularly suited to clarifying the framework of the controller's activities and to clearly document the position of the controller.

Job description	Mittelstand GmbH
1.0 Job title Head of Controlling	**2.0 Rank** Head of Department
3.0 Goal • To develop and implement procedures that help the company to make enough profit • To support the company's executives by acting as an analyser, adviser and economic supervisor so that they can all undertake controlling themselves	
4.0 Job title of direct supervisor: Managing Director **4.1 Holder of the post also follows specialist instructions from** –	
5.0 Holder of the post gives specialist instructions to • Head of Cost Accounting • Head of Planning and Reporting • Employees in the Controlling department	
6.0 The holder of the post is represented by • Managing Directors, in relation to financial, administrative and business-related matters • Head of Administration department	
7.0 The holder of the post represents Head of Administration department	
8.0 Special powers (Special rights and powers that are not associated with rank and therefore exceed the scope of the general authorisation guidelines should be listed here) • Joint power of representation • Banking authorisation • Representative of the suggestion scheme (commercial sector)	

9.0 Description of the specialist activities that the holder of the post in particular has to carry out (independently)

- Management consulting
- Responsibility for reporting and management information systems
- Compiling budgets and monthly results
- Variance and benchmark analyses
- Performing, interpreting and commenting on comparisons of targets and actual figures
- Compiling forecasts
- Checking product costings and setting target prices
- Overseeing internal and external reporting
- Carrying out efficiency analyses and investment appraisals
- Financial planning
- Assisting with/carrying out strategic planning
- Analysing processes and developing countermeasures
- Standardising and improving controlling tools
- Project management

Note to the holder of the post:
Your duties as specified in the competencies in the job description are binding. You are obliged to act and make decisions accordingly. You must inform your direct supervisor immediately in the event of major deviations.

			I have been provided with the job description.
Date:	Date:	Date:	Date:
Direct supervisor:	Head of Department:	HR Department:	Post holder's signature:

Fig. 1.5: Job description of a controller

For the following sections it is important to bear in mind the picture of Controlling within the management system of the company. Based on these underlying tasks of controllers – coordinator of planning, control and information supply – we can derive all their fields of activity and consolidate them in a cohesive and meaningful framework.

1.5 The "House of Controlling" – Building blocks of an effective controlling system

Based on the aforementioned definition of Controlling, the controller's remit covers tasks relating to planning, control and information supply. In the following section, this framework will serve as the basis for deriving the building blocks of a comprehensive and effective Controlling system.

In order to illustrate both the basic idea and the necessity of Controlling, we will first look at the following classical questions that should be asked in a company (cf. **Fig 1.6**). If you are able to answer all of these questions with a definitive "yes", then feel free to put this book back down again, as your Controlling function is top of the line. If not, then perhaps you should read on.

1.5 The "House of Controlling" – Building blocks of an effective controlling system

Do you know precisely which of your products makes money and where you take a loss?

Do you know the specific impacts of the measures you take on your bottom line?

Do you know what your earnings are purely based on business principles, i.e. without balance sheet or tax distortions?

Does your planning define ambitious targets and allocate resources accordingly?

Do you receive timely information about whether you are still congruent with the plan or if you are deviating in any way?

Is the need for decision-making escalated in a timely fashion and are appropriate measures initialised when needed?

Can you implement your corporate strategy in concrete earnings and action plans?

Are you aware of the factors which drive up overheads?

Fig. 1.6: Eight examples of questions on the necessity and basic concept of Controlling

Every company has a specific strategy which they pursue by appropriately designing their operative processes and creating a suitable organisational structure. The Controlling system is embedded in this organisation. When it comes to the tasks, organisation and instruments involved, Controlling must form a cohesive entity, and must deliver a complete system. In this sense, a Controlling system comprises all the components necessary for executing each and every aspect of the Controlling function.

In all, the Controlling system and its components serve management as management utilises the planning system by creating concrete plans, and to do so processes the information extrapolated by controllers from their information network to finalise decision-making.

For this reason, an effective Controlling system must comprise all components required to guarantee the supply of target-orientated information. This helps management's decision-making, as management is ultimately responsible for shaping the entire value chain appropriately to suit the changing environment.

How is the "House of Controlling" structured in your company?

Thus, an effective controlling system must consist of the following elements in order to be able to complete the tasks of a planning and control system and of an information supply system (cf. **Fig. 1.7**):

- **Block 1: Management Accounting** (cf. Chapter 2): First of all, it is vital that corporate management is supplied with the information necessary to objectively prepare for and take the right decisions. Here, the first important step is to determine precisely what information is needed, to gather that information and to present it in an appropriate format. The most important source of information within the information supply system is (internal) management accounting. Management accounting regularly calculates actual values and compares them with target values to gain information about the real degree to which operative targets are being achieved. This comparison of actual values with targets (target-actual comparison) and the analysis of the deviations form the basis for further performance management measures by corporate management. Effective management accounting consists of cost and profit accounting, investment appraisal and financial statements.

- **Block 2: Strategic planning** (cf. Chapter 3): Frequently, controlling systems are set up purely with the aim of improving the efficiency of operations. Clarity concerning overall company strategy and the strategy of the individual business areas (divisions) is a prerequisite for this perspective. As the general conditions for the strategic management of companies are characterised by growing dynamism, internationalisation and complexity, aspects of strategic management and strategic planning are becoming increasingly important. The most important support activities for strategic management and strategic planning lie in coordinating and managing the strategy process and in supplying management with the information necessary for decision-making. At the centre of this are preconceived developments which represent both opportunities and risks for the company and thus a "potential for success". The aim of strategic planning is to ensure the competitiveness and earning power of a company in the long term.

- **Block 3: Operative planning, budgeting and forecasting** (cf. Chapter 4): In contrast to strategic planning, during operative planning controllers deal with developments which have already manifested themselves in the present through costs and activities. Budgeting is the transfer of operative plans into numbers and figures. Regular forecasts are created in order to facilitate ongoing monitoring and management of target achievement in the quantified operative plans during the year. A forecast is the projection of planned values throughout the year (e.g. projected annual earnings). This projection forms the basis for deviation analyses and enables the early initiation of reactions and counter-measures.

- **Block 4: Financial planning and performance management** (cf. Chapter 5): Alongside securing the earning power and the economic production of goods and services of a company, the second most important factor for securing the viability and thus existence of a company is to ensure its financial strength, i.e. liquidity. To this end, financial planning and performance management is dedicated to ensuring the company's day-to-day solvency, to securing short- and mid-term financing and to guaranteeing long-term liquidity.

- **Block 5: Management reporting** (cf. Chapter 6): In many companies there is an organisational separation between the collection of information (e.g. in management accounting) and the use of that data. For this reason, there must be a transfer of information in the form of a suitable reporting system between the points of information creation and information use. Here it is important that we transfer such information in the form of appropriate key performance indicators (KPIs) as it will support the planning and control work of corporate management. This means that first we must select the most important information, then consolidate it into suitable KPIs, and finally prepare and present it in a suitable form tailored to the needs of individual recipients.

1.5 The "House of Controlling" – Building blocks of an effective controlling system

- **Block 6: IT system** (cf. Chapter 7): Instruments of data processing and modern IT have become an integral and indispensable part of management reporting for companies today. The use of modern IT both improves the quality of the information supplied and of planning and control and makes the processes involved far easier (e. g. through automated data preparation, IT-based planning models or automated reporting systems). The biggest challenge here is digitisation.

- **Block 7: Organisation** (cf. Chapter 8): Generally, Controlling organisation is seen as the combination of the organisational and operational structures in Controlling. When creating the organisational and operational structures, we should ask ourselves the following questions: Which fields of activity should be assigned to a Controlling department? At which level in the company organisation should Controlling activities take place? In which order do Controlling processes take place? How are the Controlling activities integrated into the processes and procedures of the other corporate functions?

- **Governance** (cf. Chapter 9): In order to exercise direction, coordination and monitoring, it is necessary to have a regulatory framework which ensures that rules and regulations are adhered to and that risks can be countered. This adherence to rules and regulations is vital and is known as compliance.

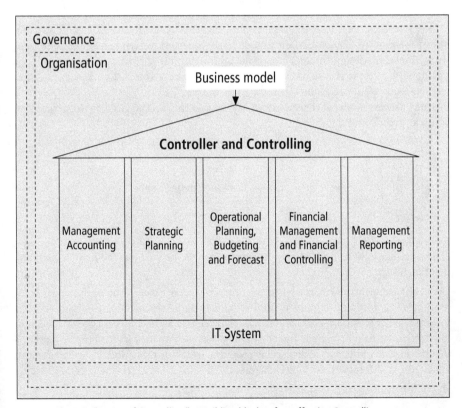

Fig. 1.7: "House of Controlling" – Building blocks of an effective Controlling system

The Horváth & Partners "House of Controlling" comprises all the necessary building blocks of an effective Controlling system (cf. **Fig. 1.7**).

When designing the "House of Controlling", the following questions must be answered for each individual component:

- What are the tasks?
- How should the processes be designed?
- Which interfaces and touchpoints must be considered?
- Which instruments are used and where?
- Who is involved and how?
- How is this embedded in the organisation?
- What IT support is planned?

During the course of this book we will provide a detailed description of each element in the House of Controlling and its main characteristics, and create design checklists for managers and controllers.

1.6 The "House of Controlling" and its context factors

The previous section summarised the central elements of an effective Controlling system in the form of the "House of Controlling". Now, however, we have to ask the question: How should we design the specific details of those building blocks, i.e. how should we breathe life into the House of Controlling? The answer to this is that there is no "one" controlling system which suits all companies. Rather, the House of Controlling depends on the business model of the specific company and the situation and environment that company finds itself in.

What sort of business model does your company have?

The starting point for the "House of Controlling" is the business model of a company (cf. **Fig. 1.7**).

As everyone seems to be bandying the term "business model" about, and everybody understands it in a different way, first of all we should define what the term actually means. The description of a business model developed at the University of St. Gallen in Switzerland is so simple, clear and convincing that we have used its structure as the basis for the explanations and information provided here (for more details, see Gassmann et al. 2013). This model has four elements which form a "magic triangle" (cf. **Fig. 1.8**):

1. Who are our target customers?
2. What benefits do we offer our customers?
3. Which value chain do we use to produce our goods and services?
4. How do we generate a financial return?

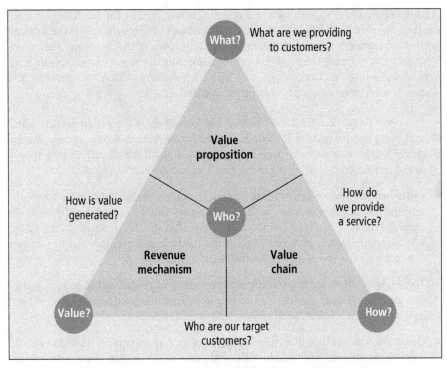

Fig. 1.8: Structure of a business model (Gassmann et al. 2013, p. 6)

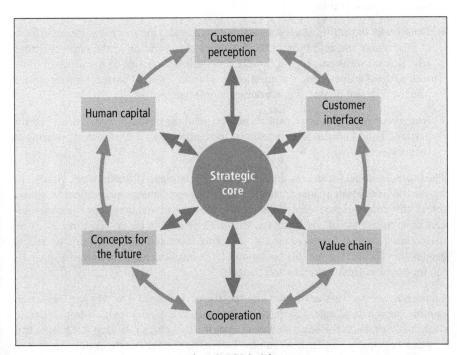

Fig. 1.9: 7C Principle

Another approach to appraising a business model is offered by the 7C Principle developed by Horváth & Partners (cf. **Fig. 1.9**). At the heart of this principle is the strategic core of the company which comprises the basic decisions of the company. These decisions concern defining the product portfolio, selecting the target customers and markets, and utilising the core competences. The other elements "circle" the strategic core and their correlations must be investigated and defined.

- *Customer perception*: Customer perception focuses on those design aspects which take place in particular in the minds of the customers, in their perception. This includes market-related value proposition, positioning on the market and the type of brand utilisation including the instruments of communication used.

- *Customer interface*: The customer interface consists of those decisions which determine the direct interaction with the customer. This includes sales channels, the earnings model (i.e. clarification of precisely what the customer is willing to pay for), customer loyalty concepts (e.g. via contracts, bonus programmes or personal relationship) and the design of the customer service.

- *Value Chain*: The value chain addresses the method of producing the good or service and looks at the core services and service level, existing (production) locations and how they are networked, and (production) procedures used.

- *Cooperation partners*: Within this dimension of the business model we define who the company cooperates with and how that cooperation takes place. Alongside working together with suppliers, both alliances and affiliations (including M&A activities) play an important role.

- *Concepts for the future*: At the core of this design field is the analysis of the main focus of innovation, the definition of the dynamics of innovation in the sense of timing (e.g. first mover versus early follower), and decisions relating to the depth of innovation, thereby answering the question of whether external partners are integrated into the different phases of the innovation process.

- *Human capital*: The human capital component of the business model focuses on the personnel and knowledge structures of the company, as well as aspects relating to corporate culture.

The business model influences the House of Controlling in different ways. Firstly, the business model, strategy and strategic planning complement one another. In simple terms, this can be described as follows. The business model describes the customer-centric architecture of the business; the strategy and strategic planning focus on maintaining competitiveness and ask questions about the company's unique selling proposition (USP). Against this background, the business model also forms the basis for, for example, financial plans and budgets.

Changes in the market due to company-specific environmental factors (e.g. new competitors, new technologies, changes in customer behaviour) make it imperative to continually evaluate the business model and, if necessary, to develop it. Only in this way can a company prepare itself in time for changes and maintain or develop its own competitive position.

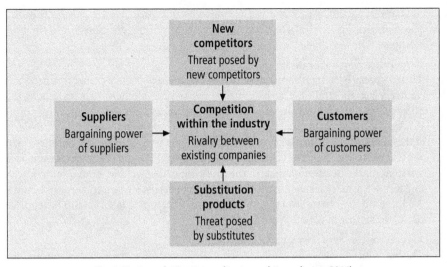

Fig. 1.10: Porter's Five Forces (Porter and Heppelmann 2014)

Do you systematically map the factors which affect the environment your company operates in (e. g. using 5 Forces)?

Thus, the design of the House of Controlling is also heavily dependent upon the company-specific environmental factors. We can use Porter's Five Forces (Porter and Heppelmann 2014) to systematically map a company's environment. This can help companies to describe and understand their own environment based on five competitive forces (cf. **Fig. 1.10**). These forces influence the profitability of a company. The stronger the forces are, the more difficult it is for a company to be profitable in its industry.

Each individual competitive force has a different impact on the company and, in the final analysis, on the House of Controlling.

- **Competition from existing and new companies and from substitutes:**
  The intensity of competition describes how strong the rivalry is within a market or an industry. If competition between the existing companies is intense or if it becomes more intense due to new entrants or substitute products, corporate management must think about expanding or changing their portfolio (entirety of all products and services) or about changing the technologies they use (equipment, procedures and methods for producing the goods and services).
  Here, the impacts of the portfolio on Controlling are manifold: Controlling must design the concept for information supply and reporting which enables the company to take decisions on streamlining or expanding their products and services. The broader and deeper the portfolio is, the more complex this task becomes.
  For their part, the technologies used affect above all the cost estimation proce-

dure and reporting. Additionally, the controller must use investment appraisal and planned earnings analyses to provide the basis for taking decisions on technology changes.

- **Bargaining power of customers:**
  The customer is defined as all current and potential buyers of a company's products and services (portfolio). The bargaining power of customers also influences the competitive situation on the marketplace. Customers with high bargaining power can have a strong influence on the price and sales conditions.
  If the customer is a critical success factor for the company, this should be reflected in the Controlling system. In such a case, the reporting system in particular should have a strong market focus and contain the most important market-related information and KPIs (e.g. market share, sales figures, customer structure, customer satisfaction). Additionally, this has a strong impact on the calculation of (short-term) lower price limits for setting negotiation parameters.

- **Bargaining power of suppliers:**
  The bargaining power of suppliers is another competition force. It determines how much influence suppliers have on prices and other sales conditions.
  Due to the big lever of lower purchasing prices, the Controlling system must also include procurement Controlling. Above all, the aim here is to support supplier selection. In terms of procurement management, it is important to manage supplier relations and identify problems as early as possible.

1.7 What comes next

Now that we have described the principles of an effective Controlling system, the rest of this book will breathe life into the "House of Controlling", i.e. we will present the individual building blocks. To do so, we will identify the most important features and characteristics and use real-world examples to illustrate them.

1.8 Design checklist for managers and controllers

Create clarity about your company's business model!

Develop a controller mission statement together with job and competence descriptions for your controllers and your controlling function which are tailored to your company's specific situation!

Define the building blocks of the "House of Controlling" in your company with a brief description for each one!

 Clarify which strategic and operative challenges exist for your company and think about how the controlling function can help you overcome them.

Further reading

If you would like to find out more about the tasks of Controlling and the role and competences of the controller, we recommend the following publications:

Gleich, R. (Ed.) (2015), Moderne Controllingkonzepte, Zukünftige Anforderungen erkennen und integrieren, Freiburg/Munich 2015.

or

IGC International Group of Controlling (2015), Controller-Kompetenzmodell, Leitfaden für die moderne Controller-Entwicklung mit Muster-Kompetenzprofilen, Freiburg/Munich 2015.

2 Management Accounting

2.1 Chapter objectives

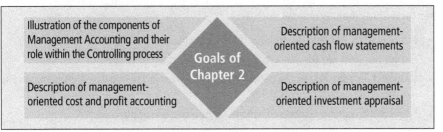

Illustration of the components of Management Accounting and their role within the Controlling process

Goals of Chapter 2

Description of management-oriented cash flow statements

Description of management-oriented cost and profit accounting

Description of management-oriented investment appraisal

Fig. 2.1: Chapter objectives

The objective of this chapter is to acquaint the reader with the three central components of effective management accounting: management-orientated cost and profit accounting, investment appraisal, and the cash flow statement. At the end of the chapter, the reader should be able to understand and apply the functions and tasks covered by these three components.

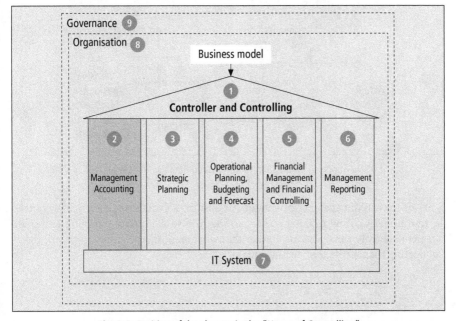

Governance 9

Organisation 8

Business model

1

Controller and Controlling

| 2 | 3 | 4 | 5 | 6 |

Management Accounting | Strategic Planning | Operational Planning, Budgeting and Forecast | Financial Management and Financial Controlling | Management Reporting

IT System 7

Fig. 2.2: Position of the chapter in the "House of Controlling"

2.2 Introduction

The primary objective of Accounting is to supply information. The intended recipients of this supplied information are individuals within the company and external to it; therefore, a distinction is drawn between Management Accounting (internal) and Financial Accounting (external). Management Accounting is the controller's primary information-related instrument, and is used to plan, control and coordinate processes within the company. By contrast, Financial Accounting is responsible for presenting the company's financial situation to parties outside the company.

However, internal Management Accounting related to Controlling continues to encounter some traditional problems, such as:

- Management Accounting focuses on bookkeeping.
- It does not provide adequate management-orientated information.
- Rather than supporting the process of making decisions, it is used after the fact to justify for decisions already made.
- Formal accuracy is prioritised over the data's fitness for purpose.
- The focus is on costing, whereas performance measurement and revenue accounting are given insufficient attention.

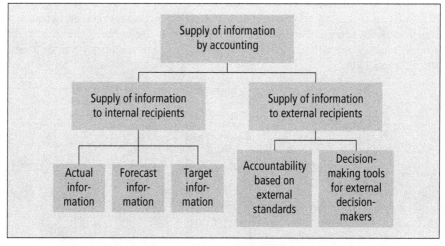

Fig. 2.3: The supply of information through accounting (Horváth et al. 2015, p. 243)

State-of-the art Management-orientated Accounting solves these problems. In contrast to traditional Costing-orientated Accounting, it also comprises planning and management control considerations. Rather than documenting the past, it gives priority to supporting management in decision-making.

How consistent are the functions of internal and external accounting in your company?

Management Accounting represents the Controller's most important tool. It can be compared to a well-tuned piano – which can similarly be useless if:

- it is not operated by an accomplished pianist (the Controller);
- it is used to create music (information) that no one (Management) wants to hear;
- in an orchestra, it is not harmoniously integrated, so that its contribution is not in tune with the instruments around it (planning and control).

The following constitutes a presentation of effective Management Accounting.

Is the controller the "single source of truth" in your company?

2.3 The design for effective Management Accounting

Effective Management Accounting comprises three components: cost and profit accounting, investment appraisal, and the cash flow statement. These are addressed in more detail below.

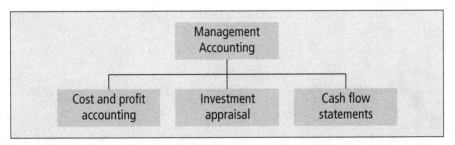

Fig. 2.4: Components of effective Management Accounting

2.3.1 Cost and profit accounting

A distinction can be made between the planning, measurement and control phases within the corporate performance management cycle. Various design-related decisions must be made in each of these phases. Acquisition, analysis and processing of information required to support managers in their responsibilities fall within the purview of cost and profit accounting. In addition, management-orientated accounting must be able to monitor whether management decisions are implemented successfully, with clear target values derived for all decisions made. By comparing actual with plan figures and analysing possible deviations, a need or opportunity for intervention can be recognised.

To fulfil these tasks, specific requirements must be set for the underlying cost and profit accounting system. These requirements should be future-focused, decision-orientated, flexible, cost-efficient, current and reliable.

A focus on the future is the top priority for cost and profit accounting. Information relating only to the past is not sufficient for company management purposes, as the steps it enables are reactive, rather than proactive. Existing Management Accounting systems are aligned exclusively to record effectively incurred costs and their allocation to cost units. They are thus focused entirely on the past. At the same time, missing plan values limit effective corporate performance management, as there is no benchmark available for assessing current development.

Furthermore, supporting management requires decision-orientated cost and profit accounting that is able to support pending decisions with relevant information. The only figures relevant for decision-making are those that could be affected by that decision. If, for example, there is a question of accepting an additional order but capacities are not yet fully utilised, only those additional costs created by the order are relevant to the decision. In general, only variable costs are relevant in such cases. Fixed costs, such as depreciation, have been incurred in any case, and remain unaffected by the pending decision. In decision-making situations of this type, a management-orientated profitability analysis system must therefore designate all costs as fixed or variable. Full costing systems are often unsuitable for determining this type of decision-relevant information, due to their lack of transparency about the cost structure.

In the context of a continually and increasingly dynamic environment, it is important for cost and profit accounting to demonstrate flexibility. However, this flexibility reaches its limit with respect to appropriate, cost-efficient cost and profit accounting capabilities. That is to say, differentiation and refinement must determine the point where the benefits of more precise information are outweighed by the costs of providing that information.

Are the terms, ratios, variables, indicators and calculation methods used in your company clearly and uniformly documented?

Finally, timeliness and reliability are essential features of the cost and profit accounting system. Historical numbers should therefore not be used as a single basis for management decisions. In concert with these numbers, consistent and harmonised guidelines on allocation and charging are the basis for reliable information.

These requirements have profited in a fundamental differentiation between costing systems with respect to the timing and the extent of allocation and charging (cf. **Fig. 2.5**).

The necessary link to the future aspects in cost and profit accounting is achieved through the use of standard costing systems. Direct costing systems, in which only certain elements of the total costs are allocated to the cost units, are used to obtain appropriate information for supporting operative tasks, and to guarantee flexibility. Depending on which elements of the total costs are allocated to the cost units, a distinction is made in the literature between types of direct costing systems: one-level direct costing, multi-level fixed cost calculation, and costing with relative direct costs.

Time reference Scope of cost assignment	Actual costing	Normal costing	Standard costing
Full costing	Actual costing on a full-cost basis	Normal costing on a full-cost basis	Standard costing on a full-cost basis
Direct costing	Actual costing on a direct-cost basis	Normal costing on a direct-cost basis	Standard costing on a direct-cost basis

Fig. 2.5: Traditional costing systems

Activity-based costing has become established as an additional evolutionary step in costing. This has arisen from needs currently posed by cost management with respect to German companies' indirect costs. Today, the potential of activity-based costing is often associated with the tried-and-tested standard costing and contribution margin costing, and the two are frequently attuned to each other.

It must be noted that – despite what the abbreviated name may suggest – traditional costing systems do not only record and settle costs, but output as well. A profit and loss account cannot ultimately provide the operating profit as an important control parameter for the controller is not without consideration of the output side. Full costing is always, therefore, an accounting system for costs, output and profit.

Are all the aspects of your company allocated by cause?

However, in theory and in practice, results accounting has a long way to go before it attains the level of refinement that costing has attained. Limits come primarily from the allocation of output (or, synonymously, revenue) to specific decisions, which as a minimum cannot be made on a "causation principle" basis. Consider, for example, the allocation of revenue from a specific product to a common tool machine. A cross-comparison of revenue objects (= products or services) that provides important conclusions relating to the actual net revenue of a product or service on different submarkets causes fewer difficulties. Revenue accounting can be performed with both plan data and actual data (cf. **Fig. 2.6**).

Revenue object					
	A	B	C	D	E
Unit price (for one product type)	100.00	110.00	110.00	115.00	100.00
+ Surcharge for freight (5 % of the unit price)	5	5.5	5.5	5.75	5
+ Surcharge for non-returnable packaging	7			7	
+ Minimum order surcharge (3 % of unit price + surcharges)	3.15	3.68	3.47	3.62	3.36
= Gross revenue (per unit)	108.15	126.18	118.97	124.37	115.36
./. Functional discount (15 % of the gross revenue)		18.93			17.30
./. Commission (8 % of the gross revenue)	8.65		9.52	9.65	
./. Discount (2 % of the gross revenue ./. functional discount)					
./. Special direct costs for distribution	3.50	9.70	4.20	12.30	8.20
= Net revenue (per unit)	93.84	95.40	102.87	99.63	87.90

Fig. 2.6: Cross-comparison of revenue objects

The most frequently used costing systems are presented in the following: full costing, using the example of standard costing; traditional direct costing; and activity-based costing systems.

2.3.1.1 Full costing systems

Standard costing systems determine the costs of a future accounting period for planning purposes. Planned costs are costs that are determined in advance, subject to rational action.

Standard costing is used to determine and specify the costs of an accounting period. At the end of an accounting period, comparing costs actually incurred with planned costs enables effective cost control. Determining and analysing deviations that have occurred provides the basis for corporate performance management. This provides information about any corrective actions needed in order to achieve the original objectives. As standard costing only fulfils its control function if the actual figures are also determined alongside the target figures, this always includes actual costs. If standard costing is performed on the basis of full costs, all indirect costs are distributed across all cost units.

Specifying planned costs requires hypotheses concerning the relationships between the amount of the costs and their key determining factors. Operating levels are considered to be the most important cost factor in standard costing. The level of utilisation of available resources for output creation is understood as an operating level. In the variance analysis, attempts are then made to trace the determining factors for cost deviations.

Are plan(target)-actual comparisons possible in your company and do you carry out variance analyses?

The primary objective of standard costing is to predict the expected effective costs. The starting point for planning should therefore not represent cost-minimal consumption, but the costs actually to be expected based on the stated starting situation. Accordingly, the expected consumption rates are assessed using the expected procurement prices rather than fixed prices. Price deviations are therefore fully included in this costing. Standard costing as forecast costing is therefore used predominantly to prepare for decision-making. It enables the prediction of future profitability based on a comparison between forecast costs and revenue. As a planning tool, it provides management with information about the impact of different alternative courses of action.

The two most important systems – inflexible and flexible standard costing – are briefly addressed and assessed as follows. Both are based on a cost planning differentiated by cost element, cost centre and cost unit, aligned with the other sub-plans within operational planning (e. g. the sales/revenue plan). Cost planning therefore primarily comprises:

- breaking down cost specifications for the cost centre,
- setting out appropriate reference figures for each cost centre,
- determining deviations between target and actual figures,
- performing deviation analyses to determine the causes of deviations, and
- allocating the deviations to the relevant areas of responsibility (cost centres).

Inflexible standard costing:

In **inflexible standard costing,** planned costs are determined at a certain level of planned utilisation, and kept constant over time, i. e. not adapted to the actual level of utilisation.

Inflexible standard costing does not make any distinction between fixed and variable costs, and does not take into account any fluctuations in the level of utilisation. This means the target costs cannot be determined within inflexible standard costing. Inflexible standard costing is therefore not suitable for the purposes of cost control.

It must be noted that inflexible standard costing creates an initial foundation for cost centre-based cost control. It still does not enable true and ongoing cost control and only provides meaningful results if the level of utilisation remains unchanged.

Flexible standard costing:

> In **flexible standard costing**, a distinction is made in the cost centre between fixed and variable cost components. It is also characterised by the fact that a cost centre's costs are planned for a specific level of utilisation. For the purpose of management control, however, the actual level of utilisation realised is considered within the accounting period. The planned costs adapted to the level of utilisation are referred to as target costs for the degree of utilisation actually achieved. These can be compared with the actual costs, based on the cost element, cost centre and cost unit.

With respect to its structure, flexible standard costing differs only slightly from inflexible standard costing. For each cost centre, one activity type (production hours, machine hours, etc.) is defined, and the planned level of utilisation (planned activity) is specified. Consumption analyses and technical calculations are applied in order to determine consumption rates. These consumption rates relate to the planned level of utilisation, and are used as a quantity structure to calculate the planned costs differentiated by cost element. The planned figures are assessed using fixed prices.

Are quantity and price structures secured in such a way that they can serve as the basis for calculating values?

This amount is split into fixed and proportional costs by means of cost breakdown. The target costs can be calculated using the actual level of utilisation. Comparing the calculated target costs with the actual costs gives the deviation in consumption. It shows the extent to which deviations from the accepted (targeted) consumption occurred.

In flexible standard costing, costs of an activity (planned full cost rate) are determined by dividing the total plan costs by the planned level of utilisation. They form the basis for planned costs calculations, and are not adapted to changes in levels of utilisation.

Multiplying the actual level of utilisation with the planned full cost rate gives the allocated standard costs. The difference between these and the target costs is referred to as the utilisation level deviation, and identifies the insufficient allocation of fixed costs (e. g. insufficient coverage of existing fixed costs in the case of under-utilisation).

Ongoing cost control is the most important objective of flexible standard costing, and is achieved by identifying and analysing deviations. In this process, a distinction must be drawn between the following fundamental types of deviation:

- price deviations,
- quantity deviations,
- consumption deviation, and
- utilisation level deviation.

Price deviations arise from differences between cost prices (e.g. actual procurement prices) and planned prices. Price deviations do not have an effect in the narrower system of standard costing accounting, as planned prices are generally used overall. The influence of prices is "absorbed" before the consumption data is included in the costing, by working with price difference costs.

	Actual costs (relating to actual prices)	€ 86,437
–	Actual costs (relating to planned prices)	€ 81,750
=	**Price deviation**	**€ 4,687**

As the stated planned costs and actual costs relate to the total costs of the cost centre, and therefore consist of several cost elements, it is not possible to state the actual price and planned price as a single figure in each case.

In the event of **quantity deviations**, a differentiation is made between a consumption deviation and a utilisation level deviation. The **consumption deviation** (ΔV) represents the additional or reduced costs for which the cost centre manager is responsible for time and/or materials consumption. It is the difference between the actual and target costs. The cause of this deviation may be due to the cost-efficiency of the consumption (higher level of material consumption), changes to production procedures (procedural deviations or non-compliance with the expected manufacturing times stated in the production plan), or quality changes in the product, etc.

	Actual costs (relating to planned prices)	€ 81,750
–	Target costs	€ 79,800
=	**Consumption deviation**	**€ 1,950**

The **utilisation level deviation** (ΔUL) represents the deviation for which the cost centre manager is not responsible. It is the difference between the allocated planned costs and the target costs. In practical terms, it is the uncovered fixed costs (idle costs) or the additional expenses to cover fixed costs, depending on whether the actual level of utilisation is below or above the planned level of utilisation.

	Target costs	€ 79,800
–	Allocated planned costs	€ 70,200
=	**Utilisation level deviation**	**€ 9,600**

In this process, the "actual level of utilisation" is represented by the planned working hours spent for the actual production quantity.

The previous statements on flexible standard costing are summarised in **Fig. 2.7**.

2 Management Accounting

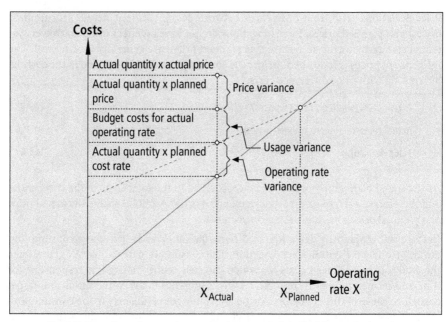

Fig. 2.7: Target/actual comparison and variance analysis in flexible standard costing

Fig. 2.8 provides an additional summary of the differences in the variance analysis for inflexible and flexible standard costing.

For more in-depth understanding, the following goes into further detail on the fundamental selected aspects of cost breakdown, direct cost planning, and indirect cost planning within flexible standard costing.

Cost breakdown:

Cost breakdown is the split of overall costs of one cost element into fixed and variable components, based on the level of utilisation. The result of the cost breakdown results in a statement of which parts of a cost element are fixed, and which are variable.

This fact is generally expressed by the variator. The variator is generally an expression of the cost change in the event of a change to the level of utilisation. In flexible standard costing, the variator usually states how much the planned costs for a planned level of utilisation will change if the degree of utilisation changes by 10 %. This model requires the variator to be stated in numerical values from 0 to 10. In accordance with this definition, fixed costs have the variator 0 and completely variable costs have the variator 10. All values between 0 and 10 are semi-variable (mixed) costs. For example, variator 6 shows that the "electric power" cost element for the production cost centre is 60 % variable (electric power for machine drive) and 40 % fixed (electric power for heating).

The variator is needed in order to convert the planned costs (of the planned level of utilisation = 100 %) into the target costs for a certain level of utilisation.

		Standard costing	
Base data		**Inflexible**	**Flexible**
Planned operating rate	10,000 units		
Planned costs fixed	EUR 120,000.00	120,000.00	40,000.00
Planned costs variable			80,000.00
Planned cost rate	Planned costs variable / planned operating rate = Planned costs per unit	12.00	8.00
Actual costs	EUR 100,000.00	100,000.00	100,000.00
Actual operating rate	7,000 units		
Budget costs	Fixed costs / Actual operating rate × planned cost rate / Total budget costs		40,000.00 / 56,000.00 / 96,000.00
Usage variance	Actual costs – budget costs		**4,000.00**
Allocated planned costs	Actual operating rate × planned cost rate	84,000.00	
Operating rate variance	Budget costs - allocated planned costs		**12,000.00**
Quantity variance	Actual costs – allocated planned costs / Usage variance + operating rate variance	**16,000.00**	**16,000.00**

Fig. 2.8: Deviations analysis for inflexible and flexible standard costing

2 Management Accounting

Planning the costs:

Cost planning is used for all key cost elements and all cost centres. In the area of production, costs are predominantly planned on an output-related basis. In the area of administration and sales, more or less structured planned cost budgets are specified, in which contingencies and temporary conditions should not be considered. The key steps that need to be completed before the cost centre plans are available are:

- Clear segmentation of cost centres (criteria: dedicated area of responsibility and precise key figures for cost causation).
- Defining appropriate planning periods.
- Estimating revenue as a basis for cost planning.
- Determining normal operating conditions.
- Setting out appropriate planned reference figures for the different cost elements in the different cost centres (e.g. labour costs, production time and product units).
- Utilisation level planning (often also referred to as reference figure planning). This step in particular must be performed in coordination with sales and production capacity planning. The planned degree of utilisation has a direct impact on the level of deviations. As such, it must be carefully defined.
- Planning and specifying direct and indirect costs.

Do you differentiate consistently between direct costs and overheads in your company?

Planning the direct costs:

> **Direct material costs** are raw materials (which may also include auxiliary materials) that are processed and/or formed in-house; finished products from affiliated companies or profit centres of the company itself; and finished products delivered from external companies.

Direct material is physically consumed by the product and can therefore be unambiguously allocated to the respective cost unit. Planned direct net material quantities are the starting point for planning. These include quantities that need to be effectively included in the cost object (finished product) assuming that product design and characteristics of consumed materials are "as planned". It must be possible to easily determine this figure using design drawings, bills of materials, etc. In addition, scrap quantities as incurred for each cost unit in the event of as-scheduled production must also be taken into account when specifying a plan figure.

Precise analysis is also possible here. The planned gross direct material costs can therefore be determined as a basis for plan calculation and ongoing controlling of direct material costs as follows:

  Planned net direct material quantities

+ Scrap quantities (planned)

= Planned gross direct material quantities

× Plan price

= **Planned gross direct material costs**

In the standard costing system, the direct material costs for each cost unit are checked for consumption deviations by means of a target/actual cost comparison on a regular basis.

  Actual direct material quantity × planned price

− Target direct material quantity × planned price

= **Consumption deviations direct material**

Cost unit-related controlling can result in significant additional work for recording actual data. Under some circumstances, it may also be useful to control direct material consumption on a cost centre-specific basis.

Where consumption deviations are found, a distinction can be made between the following causes:

- Order-related direct material consumption deviations, for instance as a result of unscheduled product design (special request from the customer);
- Material input quantity deviations, for example in the steel or rubber industries;
- Unplanned material properties in the raw materials; or
- Fluctuations in cost-efficiency within the company.

The respective cost centre manager must take responsibility for these direct material consumption deviations.

> **Direct labour costs** are the costs of work performed, which may be directly allocated to production activities and the manufactured products.

The planning, allocation and control of direct labour costs are differentiated by product (cost unit) and the routings defined in the course of production planning. The objective of direct labour costs planning is to determine in advance the labour costs incurred for a calculation unit (cost unit) for each work process. These costs may be incurred by an as-scheduled work process, by normal or planned performance levels on the part of the employees completing the work, and by planned labour rates.

Even if the direct labour elements in the planned calculation cannot be allocated directly to the cost units, they are still settled by the production cost centre and included in their calculation rates. This is because effective labour cost control is only possible through settlement of this type. Not only is direct production labour proportionally considered at planned labour times (reference figures), but a range of other indirect costs are taken into consideration, as well. It is therefore useful to summarise all production time-dependent costs in a single calculation rate.

2 Management Accounting

The planned direct labour costs are calculated as follows:

Planned direct labour costs = planned working time × planned labour cost rate.

The target direct labour costs for each cost centre must be determined for cost control.

Target direct costs	=	Actual output quantities for the different cost units
	×	Planned working time for each work process and cost unit
	×	Planned direct labour cost rate for each work process and cost unit

In most cases, controlling the direct labour costs comprises a performance level analysis. This process determines the average performance level for a cost centre or worker.

Average performance level: Actual working time × 100/planned working time

If the average performance level deviates significantly from 100, the expected times must be validated. The differences between the target direct labour costs, based on the actual output quantities on the one hand and the actual direct labour costs on the other, must in particular be traced to the following root causes (whereby the consequences are often reflected as "additional salary elements" in cost calculations):

- Direct labour cost deviation resulting from unscheduled series volumes;
- It may be that a worker's performance level is below the guaranteed minimum salary for the corresponding performance level;
- Design changes resulting in changes to the product (order-specific additional salary elements);
- Changes in raw material quality may result in different processing times;
- Interruptions in operation, or machine failure requiring cost centre-related additional salary elements;
- Additional salary elements due to incorrect work times in the routing, if there are no precise standard times available.

Alongside planning of direct material and direct labour costs, special direct costs for manufacturing and sales are planned specifically, and checked at the end of the accounting period.

Planning the indirect costs:

Indirect costs must be split into cost elements in such a way that planning for each indirect cost type is enabled, with the aid of one or several appropriate reference figures.

> **Indirect costs** change depending on the level of utilisation of a cost centre, although they cannot be directly allocated to the created product units. For example, the consumption quantity of operating supplies such as oil or power supply may depend upon a machine's runtime. However, direct allocation to the manufactured products is not possible for these commodities.

Accordingly, there must be an evaluation of which indirect costs react in a fixed or variable manner with respect to the cost centre's level of utilisation.

The planning of depreciation is another relevant example. The level of depreciation to be planned is determined by the effective causes of depreciation as well as the influence of repairs and maintenance services on the systems. If usage and related wear on a system is caused by expiry of a term (ageing), depreciation represents fixed costs. However, if the wear is due to usage, the level of depreciation is based on the degree of system utilisation. If the causes of depreciation are not certain during cost planning, the overall depreciation can be separated into a fixed utilisation level portion and a variable utilisation level portion. In practice, it is often not possible to separate wear into time-related and use-related categories. In this case, depreciation must be considered to be a fixed cost.

Indirect costs have become increasingly important over recent years. For example, the indirect costs portion of product costs in the machinery manufacturing sector have increased from around 30 % in the 1960s to more than 60 % today. Predominantly production-related standard costing prevents both source-specific indirect cost planning and the satisfactory management of indirect costs-related activities. Focusing on direct costs and the proportional amount of indirect costs has been sufficient for straightforward calculation and management decisions for decades. However, the questions faced today are significantly more complex.

There are many current and important questions that can no longer be answered with the help of planned cost information:

- If the number of product variants is increased or lowered, what impact will that have on costs and a company's result?
- How can fixed indirect costs be lowered in the long term?
- How much does it cost to perform a process, such as completing an order or providing a customer with support?

Answers to these questions, and new approaches to recording, planning, managing and allocating indirect costs, can only be found through activity-based costing, which is presented in detail in the section that follows the next one.

2.3.1.2 Direct costing systems

> Unlike full costing systems, in **direct costings** the total incurred, or planned, costs are not allocated to cost objects.

Fundamental considerations lie behind this:

Only the portion of the costs that is actually incurred from creating the output can be allocated to the cost object according to causation.

The remaining portion of the costs is not caused by a specific cost object. Instead these costs are incurred from overall readiness for operation. These fixed costs are not allocated, and instead the entire block is treated as costs for the period.

The separation of costs into variable and fixed costs, or direct and indirect costs, is therefore essential for direct costings. To reiterate: The criterion for distinguishing between fixed and variable is the capability to influence the cost amount if a cost factor changes. The portion of costs that remains unchanged when a cost factor changes comprises fixed costs, while the remainder comprises variable costs. Although a huge number of cost factors exists, the cost factor of the level of utilisation is generally used as a basis for this distinction. When distinguishing between direct and indirect costs, the criterion is the ability to allocate the costs to a reference figure.

Direct costing is widely used in its most important form of incremental costing systems. Incremental costing can be developed to create a short-term profit and loss account (one-level direct costing and multi-level direct costing) by including output and/or revenue. Relative direct costing developed by *Riebel* is less common; under this principle, all of a company's costs are considered to be direct costs, but with different reference figures.

The costs are broken down in cost-element accounting, though sometimes this is only completely done in cost centre accounting. In contrast to full costing, in internal cost allocation only the variable indirect costs are passed on to the direct cost centres, and passed on to the cost objects from there.

Marginal costing using the example of standard costing:

This system exists under many names (variable costing, marginal costing, and proportional costing). If marginal costing is created on the basis of planned values, it is referred to as marginal standard costing.

Marginal standard costing is standard costing on a direct cost basis. In it, cost planning corresponds to that of flexible standard costing, which itself includes the separation of costs into fixed and variable components in cost centre accounting. It differs from flexible standard costing in the allocation of planned costs to cost centres and cost objects. While in flexible standard costing all costs are passed on to the end cost centres, and from there to the cost objects, in internal cost allocation only the proportional costs are passed on in marginal standard costing.

As the fixed costs are not allocated in marginal standard costing, the utilisation level deviation shown for flexible standard costing does not apply!

In many companies, marginal standard costing is successfully used in the production area, as the three requirements essential for it to function are met:

- A distinction between proportional and fixed cost centre costs can be made.
- Reference figures (monthly) at which the proportional costs also actually behave in this way can be planned and settled.
- Meaningful target/actual comparisons can be performed.

If the existing environment does not correspond to these premises, complex and costly marginal standard costing does not bring any fundamental, practical benefits. Currently, although noteworthy proportional cost portions are only to be found in production areas, indirect costs associated with production continue to grow (in relative and absolute terms) in indirect production areas. This renders marginal standard costing insufficient. Activity-based costing systems provide solutions in this respect (see below).

Single-level direct costing:

> **Single-level direct costing** is also known as the contribution margin calculation. It can be performed on the basis of planned figures and on the basis of actual figures. "Direct" means that only the varying costs directly associated with the utilisation level are allocated to the product (i.e. the variable costs). The difference between the revenue for a product and the variable costs is referred to as the (unit) contribution margin. This specifies the contribution a product's revenue is able to make towards covering the fixed costs and achieving profit.

In accordance with the basic principles of direct costing, net result can only be determined for the overall company.

The net result is determined as follows (cf. also **Fig. 5.6**):

	Quantities of product sold × product revenue
−	Quantities of product sold × variable unit costs
=	Total of product contribution margins
−	Fixed costs for the period
=	**Net result for the period**

	Products			Total
	A	**B**	**C**	
Sales quantity	20,000	15,000	5,000	
Product revenue (in €)	6	7.5	12	
Sales revenue (in €)	120,000	112,500	60,000	292,500
– variable sales costs (in €)	20,000	15,000	5,000	40,000
– variable manufacturing costs (in €)	40,000	45,000	25,000	110,000
– variable materials costs (in €)	20,000	22,500	10,000	52,500
Contribution margin (in €)	40,000	30,500	20,000	90,000
– minus fixed costs (in €)				65,000
= Profit (in €)				25,000

Fig. 2.9: Example of single-level direct costing

One point of criticism for one-level direct costing is the undifferentiated allocation of fixed costs into the result as a block. An increasing fixed cost portion of overall costs means that there is a constant decrease in the costs that can be allocated to the product, making accounting less meaningful.

2 Management Accounting

Multi-level direct costing:

In this process, an attempt is made to obtain differentiated contribution margins by splitting the fixed cost block into different fixed cost layers. A company's fixed costs are allocated to those figures regarded as the root-cause for the costs arising. Here, they can only be allocated in as far as they are assigned directly for individual reference figures without any general allocation.

The following are usually selected as reference figures:

• Products (product and product groups),
• Company units (workplace, cost centre, and business functions).

The following applies with respect to product-related fixed costs. In principle, no fixed costs are allocated to the output units (e.g. products). However, it should be possible to control the contribution of the fixed costs arising from one product type in this type's contribution margin. The fundamental structure of the fixed cost contribution calculation is provided in **Fig. 2.10**.

	Products			
	A	B	C	Total
Sales quantity	20,000	15,000	5,000	
Product revenue (in €)	6	7.5	12	
Sales revenue (in €)	120,000	112,500	60,000	292,500
– Variable sales costs (in €)	20,000	15,000	5,000	40,000
– Variable manufacturing costs (in €)	40,000	45,000	25,000	110,000
– Variable materials costs (in €)	20,000	22,500	10,000	52,500
Contribution margin I (in €)	40,000	30,500	20,000	90,000
– Fixed product costs (e.g. advertising and distribution costs)	4,000	6,000	7,000	17,000
Contribution margin II (in €)	36,000	24,000	13,000	73,000
– Fixed product group costs (e.g. tool costs)	10,250		10,000	20,250
Contribution margin III (in €)	49,750		3,000	52,750
– Fixed area costs (e.g. depreciation of buildings, and heating costs)	12,500		2,500	15,000
Contribution margin IV (in €)	37,250		500	37,750
– Fixed company costs (e.g. salaries of company management)				12,750
= Profit (in €)				25,000

Fig. 2.10: Example of fixed cost contribution calculation

A profitability statement based on a multi-level contribution margin calculation is of significant importance in practice. In the context of rising market pressure and competition, companies increasingly need tool sets that enable them to make external market success transparent, and allow analysis of this success as well as that of customer and product segments. The margin contribution calculation has become an important management instrument in this respect, and supports both operational and strategic management needs for the purpose of a strong focus on the market. At a strategic level, forward-looking strategy formulation that anticipates customer needs is the basis for securing the company's success in the long term. Among others, Balanced Score Card (BSC) and portfolio analysis are concepts that are pre-eminently well suited to implementing strategy. The contribution margin calculation is an effective tool for supporting both concepts, in the sense of a market segment calculation. The market segment calculation provides valuable information for customer and financial perspectives for the BSC. For the portfolio analysis, the market segment calculation provides the basic data for product and customer segments. At an operational management level, external market success can be presented transparently with the aid of the contribution margin calculation, as it provides insight into sales, cost and contribution margin structures in both the product and customer dimension.

The success of products and customers becomes clear, and information can also be derived for short-term corporate management purposes, such as for determining short-term minimum pricing in the event that production capacities are temporarily not being fully utilised.

Break-Even Analysis:

In times of fluctuations in levels of utilisation and business activity, it is important that management quickly receives clear information about correlations to results. **Break-Even Analysis** (BEA) serves this purpose. It is an instrument widely used by controllers in their communication with management. It highlights, in a clear format, the effects of changes in prices, costs and quantities on the result (cf. *Coenenberg, Fischer, Günther* 2012, pp. 313 et seqq). In this process, a Break-Even Analysis builds on the concept of the contribution margin calculation.

> The **Break-Even Point (BEP)** provides information as to where precisely the sales revenue corresponds to the total of fixed and variable costs, and therefore where a result of zero is achieved.

The typical applications for Break-Even Analysis are as follows:

- Gaining information as to how a change in the proportional or fixed costs and the price affects the quantity to be sold, at which no losses are made or at which a certain target profit is achieved. Information can also be gained about changes in profit at constant volumes and changes in costs/prices.
- Gaining information about which cost and/or price changes will result in achieving the Break-Even Point.
- Gaining information as to how opposing price and quantity changes affect the profit.
- Gaining information as to how procedural changes (e. g. higher fixed costs and lower variable costs) affect the Break-Even Point and/or profit.

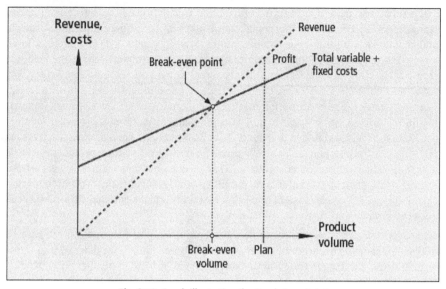

Fig. 2.11: Graph illustrating the Break-Even Point

2.3.1.3 Activity-based costing

Activity-based costing as a Controlling methodology was conceived out of the necessity to develop an effective Controlling system specifically for the adequate consideration of overheads. It supports strategic product and production decisions, and indicates potentials for the optimisation of corporate processes.

Are the overheads allocated by cause in your company?

The traditional cost element and cost centre accounting provide the basis whereby an in-depth analysis, transformation, and restructuring of, for example, the cost centre and cost object accounting is mandatory when activity-based costing is introduced.

As already outlined in the above sections (cf. e.g. the section relating to the planning of overheads), many important questions can no longer be answered using traditional accounting instruments. The following six questions are examples of this:

- What are the ten factors that dictate 80 % of the volume of overheads for a product, product area, or company?
- Which departments are involved in these, and to what extent?
- Which adjustment levers need to be turned in order to gain control of overheads in the medium term?

- Is it known how staff and cost requirements will change if the number of new product launches changes, or if changes are made to products, or if the number of variants changes, or if the number of parts is reduced?
- How expensive is an (exotic) variant if the complexity costs are considered?
- What does a sales order from different regions cost?

One important step in answering the above questions is the introduction of activity-based costing, with which the following objectives are associated:

- Making the overhead functions more transparent from a cost perspective, and therefore making them manageable;
- Identifying cross-functional processes (main processes) and their determinants (cost drivers) and making them assessable from a cost perspective;
- Analysing sub-processes in individual cost centres and departments, and consolidating them on main process level;
- Identifying inefficiencies and potential savings, defining measures, improving cost estimation, and supporting strategic decisions.

Approach for process analysis and activity costs calculation:

The following approach has been proven for process analyses and activity costs calculation (cf. the following steps in particular for *Mayer* 1991, pp. 85 et seqq.):

- Stating hypotheses relating to main processes and cost drivers,
- Deriving sub-processes and activity cost drivers based on cost centre and department task analysis,
- Capacity and cost allocation, and
- Aggregation to final main processes and calculation of cost rates.

The first step is taken as part of a top-down analysis, while steps 2 to 4 follow a bottom-up process. A little practical example is provided to explain the above procedural steps.

Hypotheses relating to main processes and cost drivers:

A preliminary main process structure was compiled as the first step. Proceeding from industry process models, company planning and other targets, an attempt is made to state hypotheses relating to main processes and cost determinants (cost drivers). Industry process models can be found in the literature. Alternatively, they are sometimes provided by business associations as examples. For this reason, the development of hypotheses is important in enabling the targeted analysis of cost centres with respect to sub-processes and cost drivers in the second step.

Proposals for new main processes, or changes to main processes, may arise again in the course of this. **Fig. 2.12** illustrates the principle of main process consolidation.

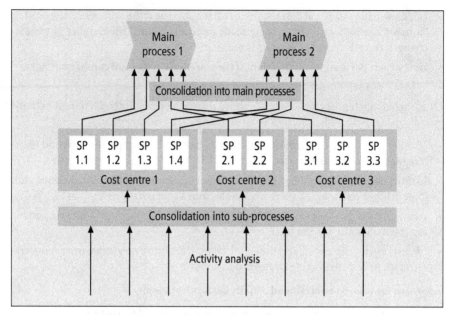

Fig. 2.12: The principle of aggregation to main processes

Process-SE cost centre 5501: Production Planning			Planned/full year: Responsible:	2016 Mayer	
Cost element	Quantity	Price	Prop	Fixed	Total
Salaries	11 pers.	60,000		660,000	660,000
Social security contributions			200,000	200,000	
Office supplies			50,000		50,000
Phone			30,000		30,000
Imputed			50,000	50,000	100,000
IT costs					
Imp. building costs	400 m²	100		40,000	40,000
Imp. amortisation				20,000	20,000
Sum			130,000	970,000	1,100,000

Fig. 2.13: Example cost centre: "5501 Production Planning"

Process-SE cost centre 5504: Quality assurance			Planned/full year: 2016 Responsible: Mayer		
Cost element	Quantity	Price	Prop	Fixed	Total
Salaries	10 pers.	55,000		550,000	550,000
Social security contributions				160,000	160,000
Office supplies			30,000		30,000
Phone			20,000		20,000
Tools			120,000		120,000
Test equipment					
Imp. building costs	200 m²	100		20,000	20,000
Imp. amortisation				100,000	100,000
Sum			170,000	830,000	1,100,000

Fig. 2.14: Example cost centre: "5504 Quality Assurance"

Task analysis for sub-processes definition, as well as capacity and cost allocation:

Task analysis is generally performed using surveys in the cost centre, while empirical data is also often referred to (e. g. data from an overhead costs value analysis). Once the tasks for a cost centre have been determined, they are aggregated into sub-processes. As the output created in these areas is predominantly very heterogeneous, it is appropriate to define several sub-processes for each cost centre. Once this is complete, the sub-processes must be divided into fixed-quantity processes and variable-quantity processes based on the cost centre output. In activity-based costing, the terms "output quantity related" (oqr) and "output quantity neutral" (oqn) are used to describe processes. **Fig. 2.15** describes the analysed "5501 Production Planning" cost centre, the original structure of which is shown in **Fig. 2.13**. The department manager has been identified as an output quantity neutral process. In contrast, the sub-processes "change work places setup" and "supervising production" are output quantity related. The latter is dependent, for example, on the number of variants. A total of 100 of these arose in the last year. Six employees supported the process, in such a way that the costs totalled 600,000 €/100 variants (see **Figs. 2.15** and **2.16**). Here, the "5504 Quality Assurance" cost centre is shown before and after the sub-processes are analysed.

For logical reasons, the previous year's figures are used as the basis for planning when introducing activity-based costing. Here, an attempt is generally made to divide cost centre costs based on the number of employees assigned to each sub-process (as shown for example in **Fig. 2.15** and **2.16**); other variables may also be applicable.

Example cost centre: 5501 Production Planning										
Sub-processes		Process drivers		Cost allocation	Process costs				Process cost rate	
No.	Name	Type (number of…)	Quantity	Base	oqr	oqn	total		pqr	total
1	Change work	Product changes	200	4 MY	400,000	40,000	440,000		2,000	2,200
	Places setup									
2	Supervising	Variants	100	6 MY	600,000	60,000	660,000		6,000	6,600
	Production									
3	Manage department			1 MY		100,000				
				11 MY			1,100,000			

Fig. 2.15: Example: Sub-processes for the "5501 Production Planning" cost centre

Example cost centre: 5504 Quality Assurance

Sub-processes		Process drivers		Cost allocation	Process costs			Process cost rate	
No.	Name	Type (number of…)	Quantity	Base	oqr	oqn	total	pqr	total
1	Change in inspection plans	Product changes	200	2 MY	200,000	50,000	250,000	1,000	1,250
2	Ensuring product quality	Variants	100	6 MJ	600,000	150,000	750,000	6,000	7,500
3	Participation in quality assurance meeting			1 MJ		100,000			
4	Run department			1 MJ		100,000			
				11 MJ			1,100,000.–		

Fig. 2.16: Example: sub-processes for "5504 Quality Assurance" cost centre

2 Management Accounting

Main process consolidation:

As outlined earlier, the individual sub-processes for the considered cost centres need to be pooled to create a limited number of main processes (cf. **Fig. 2.17**). The "5501/1 change in work plans" and "5501/2 supervising production" sub-processes (cf. **Fig. 2.15**) now become, together with the "5504/1 change in inspection plans" and "5504/2 ensuring product quality" sub-processes (cf. **Fig. 2.16**), the main processes of "execute product changes" and "supervise variants" (cf. **Fig. 2.17**). The cost-relevant result of main process consolidation may be as follows (cf. **Fig. 2.18**).

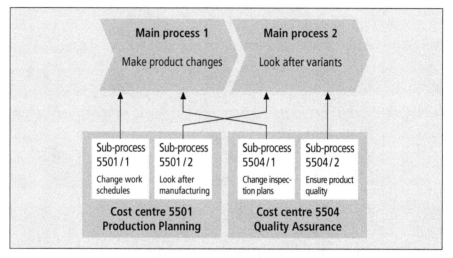

Fig. 2.17: Example: main process consolidation

Main processes	Cost driver	Number	Process costs	Process cost rate	% cost volume
1. Execute product changes	Number of product changes	200	690,000	3,450	33 %
2. Supervise variants	Number of variants	100	1,410,000	14,100	67 %

Fig. 2.18: Example: main processes, cost drivers, and related cost rates

The "execute product changes" main process, which in terms of cost is dependent upon the number of product changes, arose a total of 200 times in the accounting period.

Process costs were 690,000 €, based on the sum of costs incurred by the main process and all entailed sub-processes. Therefore the process cost rate amounts to 3,450 € (process costs/quantity of processes).

The cost sum of 2.1 million € is based on the combined cost sums of cost centres 5501 and 5504. The total sum is differentiated according to processes, rather than cost centres.

The business functions/processes matrix:

The business functions/processes matrix is a tried and tested tool for converting a business function perspective into a process perspective (cf. **Fig. 2.19**). If it is used within a top-down analysis, it serves as an initial, rough assessment of the main processes assumed in the hypothesis with costs and quantities. However, it can also be used within a bottom-up analysis, in which it summarises the results of the process analysis in the functional areas' cost centres. The matrix is made up of functional areas in the rows, and main processes in the columns. The breakdown of functional areas' resources, and costs to the main processes, is visible in the rows. The columns show cost and quantity data for the main processes.

Utilisation as a cost planning and management control instrument:

If activity-based costing is used as a cost management instrument, a distinction can be made between three levels where impact occurs:

- When activity-based costing is introduced, the task analysis may identify uneconomic procedures (idle times or poor performance) or organisational weak points. Savings potentials are often associated with this, which it is essential to exploit.

- Activity-based costing can be permanently integrated into annual planning. This is achieved through consistent planning and management of quantity-based overhead costs (process quantity × process cost rate). If under-utilisation is then identified in the comparison between the actual process quantity and actual costs, this should in turn be incorporated into the next annual planning process.

- Once various cost determinants (cost drivers) are known, long-term cost reduction measures can be agreed upon in the early phases of product development, in collaboration with the development department.

Utilisation as part of cost object accounting:

Activity-based costing differs in principle in the allocation of overhead costs to individual cost objects.

The questions outlined above cannot be answered using traditional cost accounting systems. Here, overheads are allocated to production cost centres via internal cost allocation and referred to the cost object via their reference unit; otherwise, they are charged to the cost object using a percentage-based surcharge on the material or production costs (for example, materials overheads or sales overheads).

A modern activity cost calculation method is now based on the actual dependencies in the causation of overhead costs. Process-based cost calculation should be performed parallel to existing cost accounting, in order to gain accurate information about the individual product results. With the aid of activity-based costing according to the cost causation principle, supposedly profitable "exotic products" (when applying traditional cost calculation methods) generally prove to result in significant losses. In contrast, the standard products that are often less popular among sales departments (fast sellers) are the big winners, as they have only minimal requirements for planning, scheduling and management control processes. This is because, if costs are estimated for top sellers according to the cost causation principle with the support of activity-based costing, it often becomes clear that the overhead rates are much too high. As a result, in reality, these products contribute much more towards corporate profitability than many companies assume on the basis

Costs in € / Capacity in MY	1. Bid processing	2. Engineering	3. Procurement	4. Manufacturing
Procurement — 6 / 1,200,000		1 / 200,000	4.8 / 960,000	
Product Management — 3 / 900,000	0.8 / 240,000	1 / 300,000		0.2 / 60,000
Engineering — 3 / 750,000		2.5 / 625,000		
Manufacturing — 5 / 500,000		0.7 / 70,000		4 / 400,000
Sales/Marketing — 4 / 640,000	3 / 630,000	0.5 / 105,000		
Quality Assurance — 3 / 300,000		0.5 / 50,000	0.5 / 50,000	1 / 100,000
Materials Management — 3 / 600,000			1.9 / 380,000	
Administration — 4 / 480,000	0.4 / 48,000	0.2 / 24,000	0.5 / 60,000	0.2 / 24,000
Man-years / Total process costs — 31 / 1,200,000	4.2 / 918,000	6.4 / 1,374,000	7.7 / 1,450,000	5.4 / 584,000
Cost drivers / Cost driver quantity	Tenders / 15	Orders / 10	Positions / 100	Number of FA / 20
Process cost rate	61,200	137,400	14,500	29,200

Fig. 2.19: Example: business functions/processes matrix (based on *Gleich* 2001, p. 42 et seq.)

of their incorrect cost information. Precise cost information based on the cost causation principle is now an important foundation for additional short-, medium- and long-term sales, production, and investment decisions, as well as for strategic decisions relating to product ranges and prices. The most important objective here should be to allocate the increasing overheads to their point of origin, or to work towards the avoidance of many of these overhead costs in the first place. This may be achieved if, for example, the number of processes is being reduced, or processes are made more cost-efficient and leaner.

In order to provide product and customer results in a way that is differentiated and more focused on the cost causation principle, process costs are also included in periodic cost object accounting or multi-stage contribution costings. Examples of this include customer-specific process costs, such as costs for order processing, marketing costs, costs of distribution channels, etc. However, the required economic efficiency of management accounting must always be considered in this process.

5. Assembly, final testing	6. Order picking, dispatch	7. Invoicing	8. Managing the company	9. Remaining overheads	Total	Remaining overheads
					5.8	0.2
					1,160,000	40,000
0.2	0.2	0.2	0.2		2.8	0.2
60,000	60,000	60,000	60,000		640,000	60,000
0.5					3	0
25,000					750,000	0
0.3					5	0
30,000					500,000	0
					3.5	0.5
					735,000	105,000
0.7	0.3				3	0
70,000	30,000				300,000	0
	1				2.9	0.1
	200,000				580,000	50,000
0.2		1.4	0.5		3.4	0.6
24,000		100,000	60,000		408,000	72,000
1.9	1.5	1.6	0.7	0	29.4	1.6
200,000	290,000	228,000	120,000	0	5,273,000	297,000
Vehicles	Vehicles	Invoices			29.4	1.6
10	10	15	0	0	5,273,000	297,000
20,900	29,000	15,200	120,000	0		

2.3.1.4 Income statement

The income statement has been mentioned at various points in the remarks above. Due to its significant importance in practice, periodic cost object controlling will again be explicitly addressed as short-term profitability analysis instrument in the following.

The income statement is generally used for the ongoing control of a company's economic efficiency. The key goal of an income statement is to understand cost structures and analyse sources of income by relating the costs in the period to the revenue of the period.

In principle, a distinction can be made between the following alternative methods of determining results:

- the total cost method and
- the cost of sales method

The **total cost method** contrasts the total output with the total costs for the period (see **Fig. 2.20**).

2 Management Accounting

If the revenue and production for the period are identical, the total output corresponds to the revenue for the period. However, if there is a deviation between the two figures, the sales revenue must be adjusted to reflect inventory increases or reductions, evaluated at production cost, and possibly any capitalised internal activities. This is necessary in order to ensure that the output and costs for the period remain comparable.

	Revenue
+/–	Inventory increases/reductions
+	Capitalised internal activities
=	Total output
–	Material costs
–	Personnel costs
–	Amortisation
=	Net income

Fig. 2.20: Income statement in accordance with the total cost method

The **cost of sales method** contrasts the sales revenue for products and services sold in the period with their production costs plus the overhead costs that are not considered as production costs.

Whilst in the total cost method, costs are typically structured by primary cost element, the cost of sales method regularly includes a secondary cost structure. (cf. **Fig. 2.21**).

	Revenue
–	Production costs for the products and services sold
=	Gross profit
–	Research and development costs
–	Administrative costs
–	Sales costs
=	Net income

Fig. 2.21: Income statement in accordance with the cost of sales method

The cost of sales method results in a pure sales result. This enables a horizontal sub-division of the earnings by product, product group, customer group, industry, regions, etc. Furthermore, an additional vertical differentiation of the cost blocks is also possible, such as between production costs and sales costs. This means that the concept of multi-level contribution costing can be integrated within the framework of the cost of sales method with great success. An additional advantage of the cost of sales method can also be seen in the recording of gross profit, which can be used as an indicator of operating profitability (cf. *Coenenberg* 2007, pp. 157/160)

Although the presented structures, based on primary and secondary costs, are very typical for the cost of sales and total cost methods, they are not necessarily associated with the configuration of accounting methodology. An alternative structuring of costs can therefore also be performed in the total cost method. However, adequate cost centre accounting, which allocates the individual costs to the functional areas, is required in order for costs to be represented by functional area.

Which method to choose for the income statement depends upon such factors as analytical requirements or quality of the cost centre accounting. Companies who use direct costing tend to use the cost of sales method, due to the greater value of information. However, vertical differentiation between cost blocks, as well as horizontal structuring, varies greatly from company to company due to differing analytical needs. The total cost method tends to be used by companies who deploy full cost accounting systems and have less highly developed cost centre accounting.

Yet, consistency between financial and management accounting is also becoming increasingly important for companies. Despite the existing right to choose between the cost of sales and total cost methods in statutory financial accounting, the cost of sales method is becoming increasingly important as a form of P&L statement, especially at large, market-listed companies. Horváth & Partners carried out a study that examined business reports from a total of 140 businesses listed in the DAX, MDAX, SDAX, and TecDAX with respect to the application of the cost of sales and total cost methods. This study showed that 54.3 % of the companies considered already apply the cost of sales method. Accordingly, the total cost method – which dominates financial accounting in Germany – is on the decline. This study also identified a correlation between accounting standards and the decision to apply the cost of sales and total cost methods. In relation to this, it found that financial accounting in accordance with international accounting standards represents a significant driver for the application of the cost of sales method. However, the preparation of financial statements in accordance with the German Commercial Code (HGB) continued to entail application of the total cost method in most cases. Overall, a trend in the direction of the cost of sales procedure can be identified in financial statutory accounting. In the interests of harmonising financial and management accounting, this implies that the cost of sales method is of greater importance in management accounting. In this context, systems of direct costing and contribution costing will also become even more relevant in guaranteeing comprehensive profitability management (cf. in particular *Hofmann et al.* 2004). Recent studies looking at non-listed companies from the year 2006 confirm the trend towards greater use of the cost of sales method, despite the existing dominance of the total cost method. According to the surveys, 63 % of participants solely use the total cost method, while 37 % exclusively or additionally use the cost of sales method. The latter stated that they were also developing the cost of sales method into contribution costing (cf. *Kramer, Keilus* 2006).

The following summary can be derived from a comparison of the presented cost accounting systems. Standard costing, various systems of direct costing, and activity-based costing are firmly established in practice. However, changed production conditions and the increasing focus on services in many companies have resulted in high overheads and generated new needs for management intervention. Under these conditions, traditional standard costing on a full cost basis is becoming increasingly inadequate as a decision-making instrument, as it does not enable cost allocation on the basis of a cost causation principle. In contrast to this, systems of direct costing, in particular multi-level contribution margin costing as well as activity-based costing, create greater cost transparency whilst making the cost information more relevant for decision-making.

2.3.1.5 Target costing

Traditional methods of cost and profit accounting are aligned to companies' internal economic efficiency, and focus on the production of goods or services. The increasingly necessary focus on the market and customers requires radical reorientation in two respects:

- It is not internal costs incurred in the production process that should be used as a basis, but the costs accepted by the market. The focus is no longer the question, "What is the product cost?" Instead, it is: "What is a product allowed to cost?"
- Accordingly, cost planning and cost and profit accounting need to be used not only in the production phase, but as far back as the early phases of product creation. There is a direct link to strategy in this respect.

> **Target costing** is the approach that helps cost management to focus on the market and customer. The costs "accepted" by the market are derived from the achievable purchase price, by subtracting the defined profit based on planning. The "allowed" costs are compared with the forecast standard costs ("drifting costs") for the new product. The difference arising from this indicates the required cost reductions in the product development phase. The target costs are then derived thereafter (cf. **Fig. 4.52**).

 How is the upper cost limit for a product calculated in your company?

In this process, target costing is not restricted solely to setting cost objectives; it also includes the entire company and its relation to its environment (customers and suppliers).

In contrast to the target costing approach, cost-plus based price determination is often used in the company. This application differs from the target costing approach in that it calculates the offer price on an internal, company-driven rather than a market-driven basis. The procedure of cost-plus based offer price determination is described in **Fig. 2.23**.

The model for calculating the offer price using the cost-plus approach is as follows:

	Material costs
+	Manufacturing costs
=	**Production costs**

+   Administration and sales costs

=   **Own costs**

+   Mark-up (in % of own costs)

+   VAT (in % of own costs)

=   **Offer price**

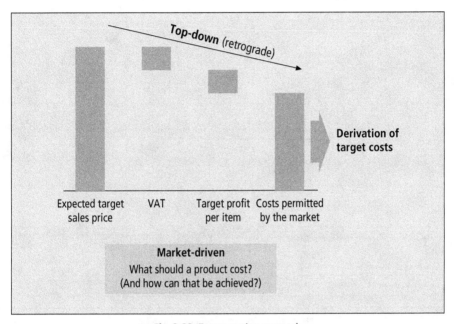

Fig. 2.22: Target costing approach

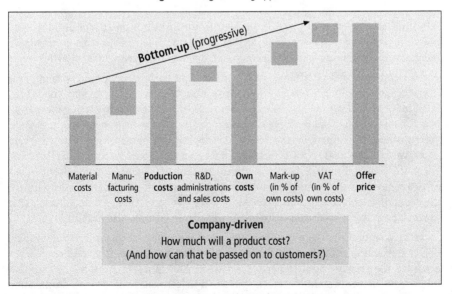

Fig. 2.23: Cost-plus based price determination

2.3.2 Investment appraisal

While cost and profit accounting anticipates 'given' capacities as a basis, at this point the question arises as to how changes to capacity impact profit. Steering financial resources

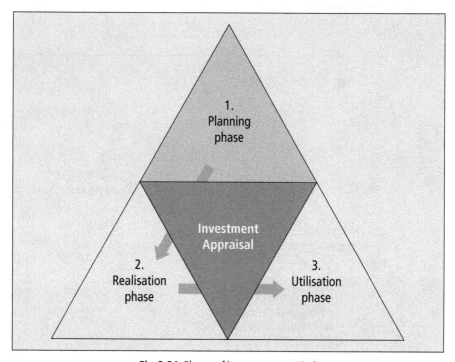

Fig. 2.24: Phases of investment appraisal

into profitable investment projects has significant influence on corporate value, and therefore requires investment planning that, based on strategic objectives, steers investment funds into projects that increase value (cf. *Bahlinghorst, Sasse* 2005, pp. 126 et seqq.).

A more comprehensive definition of this investment term is being used with growing frequency, and no longer relates only to investments in tangible, physical goods (e.g. facilities or buildings), but also includes intangible investments. This includes expenditure for staff or financial resources. Such expenditures may be understood to include, among others, investment in researching, developing, and purchasing existing technologies; various business services (leasing, shared services, outsourcing, etc.); basic and advanced staff training; or buying and using software (cf. *Götze* 2008, pp. 6 et seqq.). Effective investment appraisal handles this wide array of investment forms with the greatest possible degree of standardisation in respect of a structured decision-making process, as well as a uniform methodology in order to ensure comparability.

Investment appraisal does not end with the decision in favour of a specific investment object – even if in practice the planning and initiation phase of an investment is often accorded the greatest significance (*Meyer et al.* 2007, p. 634 et seq.). In the complete lifecycle of the investment object, the phases of investment realisation and utilisation follow the investment planning phase (cf. **Fig. 2.21**).

The planning phase covers the period leading to the decision to realise the investment object. This may not occur on schedule in special cases, but is generally included in the fixed planning and budgeting process for the company. Due to restricted financial capacities, various investment decisions are not made in isolation from one another; instead, a selection is made, the result of which is a recommendation for the best composition of the investment programme.

Once the investment decision for an object or a measure has been made, the realisation phase then follows. The goal is to make the object ready for use, or to complete the implementation of the measure. In this phase, investment appraisal mainly comprises project controlling tasks.

The project then finally enters the utilisation phase. Within investment appraisal, the utilisation phase requires investment control, i.e. the verification of compliance with previously set out assumptions and plans; where applicable, it also requires initiating corrective measures and furthermore obtaining and safeguarding findings (from planned/target/performance comparisons) for future investment decisions.

Objective, well-documented and forward-looking investment planning can make the later implementation and control phases easier, or even effectively enable them in the first place. Planning therefore represents the critical foundation of all investment appraisal. The instruments and methods that can be used to specifically organise and implement investment appraisal are presented in the following.

2.3.3 Investment appraisal methods

There are two distinguished investment appraisal groups.

Static investment appraisal methods do not consider the time factor for investments, or only do so to an insufficient extent. They relate to a single period; this is made possible by the use of average variables or the approach of a "representative year".

There are various criticisms of the informational value of static methods. For this reason, they are not addressed in detail here. However, **Fig. 2.25** provides an overview of static investment methods.

Task	Method	Criterion
Comparative cost method	Comparison of costs	The alternative with the lowest average costs is selected
Profit comparison method	Comparison of profits	The alternative with the highest annual net profit is selected
Profitability calculation	Establishing ROI	The alternative with the highest return is selected

Fig. 2.25: Static methods of investment appraisal

> **Dynamic investment appraisal methods** consider the entire lifecycle of the investment object. They assume changeable flows of payments in and out, which are made comparable through discounting.

According to an empirical study by Horváth & Partners on developments, trends, and the future need for action in the management of investments, dynamic methods clearly dominate in practice (cf. *Hofmann et al.* 2007, pp. 157 et seq.). For this reason, we will go on to explain the most important dynamic methods of investment appraisal in more detail.

 Do you use a dynamic investment appraisal method in your company?

Payback calculation:

Rather than applying to a monetary variable, this method applies to the payback period as the number of years needed to pay back the capital expenditure for an investment from the returns. In this respect, dynamic payback calculation considers the interest of the capital employed in the investment. The dynamic payback period represents the portion of the investment period during which the capital employed for an investment project plus the interest on this employed capital can be recovered from the financial returns of the investment project. An investment project is considered relatively advantageous if its payback period is shorter than that of every other investment available for selection. However, a short payback period must not be used as the sole criterion for an investment decision, as it does not provide any information on how financially advantageous the investment will be in reality. Rather, a limitation of the maximum payback period can be used as a filter to reduce risk.

Net present value method:

According to the study named above, the net present value method is the most frequently used method of investment assessment (cf. *Hofmann et al.* 2007, p. 198). The net present value, which is calculated by discounting cash flows on a reference date, is used to assess how advantageous an investment is. The assumption of an adequate rate of return is required for this; this states the investor's desired return. What are referred to as cash values are produced by discounting the financial returns using the discount factor. These express the value of future financial returns at the reference date (date of investment). The sum of all cash values represents the net present value (**Fig. 5.26**).

The calculated net present value should be interpreted as follows:

$C0 > 0$ ($C0$ = net present value at the current date)

The investor regains the invested capital through financial returns, and receives interest on the capital employed in the amount of the required rate of return. In addition, a cash-value surplus in the amount of the net present value is received. The investment is advantageous.

C0 = 0

If the net present value = 0, the invested capital is returned, and interest is added precisely at the required rate of return.

C0 < 0

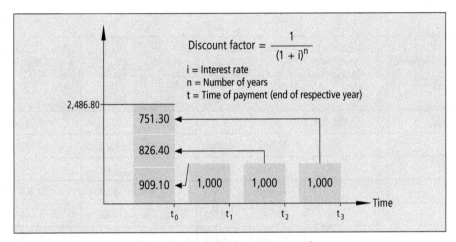

Fig. 2.26: Calculating the net present value

The investor would suffer a cash-value loss in the amount of the net present value if investment were made. This may firstly be due to the desired interest not being achieved, and/or because the capital return does not happen. The investment should therefore not be made.

With very little effort, the net present value method can be supplemented with a consideration of the effects on P&L and net income effects, in such a way that two significant financial performance indicators are considered (cf. *Grote et al.* 2003, pp. 61 et seqq.). This supports the increasing tendency to harmonise financial and management accounting.

A perfect capital market is used as a basis in the net present value method. This means that the debit interest rate is the same as the credit interest rate, and that this is constant throughout the planning period. Furthermore, capital is considered a homogeneous commodity, and the financial resources can be recorded or invested to an unrestricted extent. In particular, equating the debit and credit interest is unproblematic for investments concerning a source of financing that has already been used by another investment project. In this case, for example, accumulating investment surpluses could be used to repay loans that are also conditional upon other investments, and in this way reduce any other interest burdens. Furthermore, in many companies it is impossible, or almost impossible, to allocate specific financing to individual investments. Companies often draw on several investment sources with different conditions. Accordingly, a blended interest rate (as a target rate to cover costs of capital) is assumed for the individual investments (cf. *Sasse* 2003, pp. 120 et seqq.).

2 Management Accounting

Internal rate of return method

The internal rate of return represents the interest that is realisable through the temporary investment of financial capital in productive assets. Here the present value of the capital returns from the investment correspond precisely to the original capital expenditure (cf. *Männel* 2000, p. 331). The internal rate of return is calculated approximately, through graphical or interpolation (cf. **Fig. 2.27**).

Investment expenditure: € 100,000 in t0

Returns according to the table

Project lifecycle: five years

Date of payment t	Investment expenditure I_0 (present value)	Return R_t (present value)	Discount factors q^{-t} for $i_1 = 0.1$	Net payments (cash value)	Discount factors q^{-t} for $i_2 = 0.2$	Net payments (cash value)
0	100,000		1.0	-100,000	1.0	-100,000
1		30,000	0.9091	27,273	0.8333	24,999
2		40,000	0.8264	33,056	0.6944	27,776
3		30,000	0.7513	22,539	0.5787	17,361
4		20,000	0.6830	13,660	0.4823	9,646
5		20,000	0.6209	12,418	0.4019	8,038
Net present value				+ 8,946		− 12,180

$$i = 0.10 - 8,946 \frac{0.20 - 0.10}{-12,180 - 8,946} = 0.142$$

Graphical interpolation also provides the same result.

The internal interest rate is 14.2 %.

Due to reinvestment assumptions, the internal rate of return method is often incorrectly criticised. Although this hypothesis, which is unrealistic in practice, has frequently been applied owing to incorrect mathematical interpretations, it is fundamentally not a component of the method (cf. *Männel* 2000, pp. 333 et seq.).

Annuity method:

The annuity method is a special form of the net present value method. In it, the average annual pay-outs for an investment are compared with the average annual earnings. With the aid of compound computation of interest, both series of numbers are converted into equivalent uniform series, and the average cash in and out for the duration of the investment is calculated in this way. With the stated required rate of return, any investment is advantageous if it does not result in any negative differences between the average annual

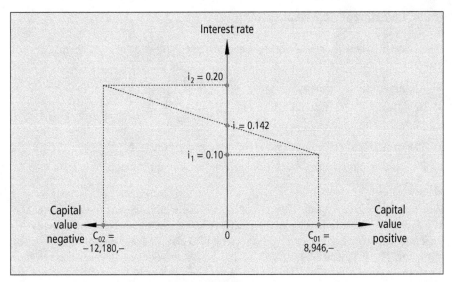

Fig. 2.27: Example of internal rate of return method

cash in and out (annuity). The annuity is a consistent amount that is available in each period alongside repayment and interest.

The annuity method has the same weak points as the net present value method; the only difference is that the differential investments required there are not necessary using this method.

Methods for the consideration of uncertainty:

In addition to static and dynamic investment appraisal methods, methods have been formed that consider the uncertainty of the data used. The following are available (cf. *Adam* 2000, pp. 353 et seqq.):

- The **correction method**, which considers uncertainty through the use of percentage-based risk surcharges or risk adjustments on the estimated cash in and out. Flat-rate surcharges or adjustments of course only capture the uncertainty here in an imprecise way.

- **Sensitivity analysis,** which examines the effects of assumed data changes on the calculation results – it only analyses the effects, and does not convert these into a decision-making criterion.

- **Risk analysis** that uses probability distributions in place of fixed numerical values. It is best suited to considering the uncertainty of expectations in investment planning.

- **Real options** enable different scenarios to be considered as part of investment appraisal. There are different types of real options (e. g. delay or growth options), which can be integrated into an investment appraisal in accordance with the net present value method, in order to portray uncertain events in the course of the investment (cf. e. g. *Briley et al.* 2008, pp. 283 et seqq.). However, this method is criticised due to its insufficiently well-founded transfer of financial options theory to the new context (cf. *Kruschwitz* 2009, pp. 393 et seqq.). This complex method is not yet at all well established in practice.

2 Management Accounting

2.3.4 Investment appraisal system

The following specific questions are relevant to the composition of investment appraisal, and must be considered:

- Alignment to the strategy,
- Investment appraisal standardisation,
- The use of threshold values for simplification,
- The combination of monetary and non-monetary valuation,
- Performing target/actual-performance comparisons and variance analysis.

Alignment to the strategy:

Any business activity should directly, or at least indirectly, support the achievement of the overall organisation's long-term objectives, which are anchored in the strategy. Accordingly, the strategy and strategic objectives also play a substantial role in investment planning. The Balanced Scorecard (BSC) has proven to be one of the most effective tools in strategy communication. The BSC enables the strategy to be described so specifically that, at a minimum, the contribution of individual investment projects towards achieving strategic objectives can be qualitatively represented – this can and should be demanded by applicants as standard.

Investment appraisal standardisation:

A certain level of standardisation is required in order to enable the comparison and review of the investment project. For this, it is firstly necessary to assess the investment project in all units in a company or group, and therefore make it comparable. Secondly, efforts must be made to ensure that a common valuation method is also guaranteed for different investment types (e.g. tangible and intangible investments). The standardisation of the investment appraisal must extend to the assumptions being taken into account (e.g. the inflation rate), to the calculation methods (e.g. the internal rate of return method on a standardised basis across the company), and to the organisation (decision-makers and process).

The use of threshold values for simplification:

Depending on the level of detail in their execution, investment appraisals can be very time-consuming. An important question is which permitted simplifications should be provided for in operational practice. One work effort gradation that has been tried and tested in practice concerns value limits: For relatively small investments, it is generally envisaged that only a file with basic information, such as how the submitted object links to the BSC objectives, needs to be completed. If the project exceeds the value limit, a detailed basic principles sheet must also be filled out, stating reasons for the submission, a representation of checked alternatives and similar. At the next stage, the applicant is also required to provide a project plan and a simple net present value calculation. For very large investments, cost-benefit analyses and specially generated, more extensive profitability assessments are also used. If the value limits are set skilfully on a company-specific basis, the project volume for the investment submission can be kept manageable, whilst ensuring however that the vast majority of the budget is approved due to extensive information and assessments. Analyses found that over 90 % of the submitted objects regularly do not reach the bottom limit for value limits that have been well set; however, these only make up 10 % of the overall budget volume in total. As a result, it is entirely justifiable to omit a very detailed evaluation for the majority of projects.

The combination of monetary and non-monetary valuation:

The combination of net present value and a cost-benefit consideration takes into account the fact that a purely monetary valuation results in the perception of certain investments as less advantageous compared to others, or as generally disadvantageous, although they are not in reality. The additional consideration of a non-monetary valuation that weighs the qualitative benefits of the investment yields meaningful results here.

Cost-benefit analysis is an appropriate method here, in which several qualitative target variables are taken into account and weighted according to their significance for the decision-maker. The method of cost-benefit analysis comprises five steps:

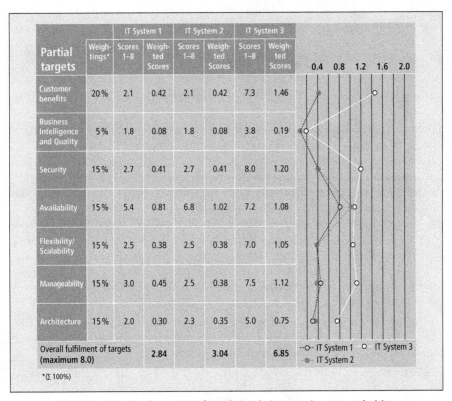

Partial targets	Weigh-tings*	IT System 1		IT System 2		IT System 3	
		Scores 1–8	Weigh-ted Scores	Scores 1–8	Weigh-ted Scores	Scores 1–8	Weigh-ted Scores
Customer benefits	20 %	2.1	0.42	2.1	0.42	7.3	1.46
Business Intelligence and Quality	5 %	1.8	0.08	1.8	0.08	3.8	0.19
Security	15 %	2.7	0.41	2.7	0.41	8.0	1.20
Availability	15 %	5.4	0.81	6.8	1.02	7.2	1.08
Flexibility/Scalability	15 %	2.5	0.38	2.5	0.38	7.0	1.05
Manageability	15 %	3.0	0.45	2.5	0.38	7.5	1.12
Architecture	15 %	2.0	0.30	2.3	0.35	5.0	0.75
Overall fulfilment of targets (maximum 8.0)		2.84		3.04		6.85	

*(Σ 100%)

⋯○⋯ IT System 1   ○ IT System 3   ● IT System 2

Fig. 2.28: Example of a cost-benefit analysis relating to an investment decision

2 Management Accounting

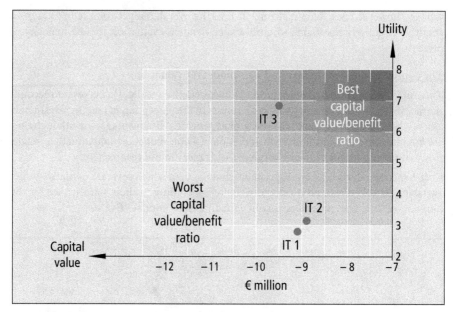

Fig. 2.29: Net present value – cost-benefit diagram for three investment alternatives

(1) In the first step, the relevant target criteria for the decision problem must be determined in stages. The result of this is a hierarchical tree of objectives.

(2) The second step of this method consists of weighting the objectives that have been formed. The weights awarded should reflect the decision-maker's preferences.

(3) Next, the benefits of the action alternatives with respect to the individual subobjectives are established using an assessment scale.

(4) The fourth step involves determining the overall cost-benefit of the individual alternatives through e. g. adding or multiplying the sub-objectives. The higher this figure is, the more advantageous the considered alternative is from a non-monetary perspective.

(5) By comparing the cost-benefits between each other, as well as with the decision makers' aspiration level, the advantageousness of the action alternatives can now be assessed in the fifth step (cf. **Fig. 2.28**).

Taking into account the findings from the net present value calculation, as well as from the cost-benefit analysis, i. e. in the event of a combined monetary and non-monetary valuation, the following picture emerges (cf. **Fig. 2.28**).

These findings can be used to very clearly illustrate the necessity of including qualitative factors in the investment decision. In a purely monetary consideration, IT system 2 would be selected in the example case, as this shows the lowest negative net present value.

However, the benefit consideration shows that the purpose of the investment would not be achieved. By contrast, a combined valuation shows IT system 3 as the most advantageous object. Although it has a more negative net present value, it also has a significantly greater benefit than alternatives 1 and 2.

Do you also use non-monetary ratios, variables, and indicators in the investment appraisal in your company?

Performing target/actual-performance comparisons and variance analyses:

In light of the uncertainty of the data pool, it would be expected that investment controls would be performed regularly in practice. However, that is not the case. Difficulties in capturing performance data, time-intensive calculation, and arguably also reservations with respect to possible high target/actual-performance deviations, often result in investment controls not being carried out. The study cited above, by *Hofmann et al.*, shows that planned-performance comparisons during the usage phase are not regularly performed ("only for major investments" in 30 % of companies, and "occasionally" in a further 48 %; cf. *Hofmann et al.* 2007, p. 158).

Investment controls are required in four directions:

- Financial controls determine the extent to which the target and actual cash out are in alignment within investment management.
- Profit and loss controls calculate the economic efficiency of the investment using the performance data.
- Strategy controls review the real contribution the investment makes towards achieving the objectives defined in the strategy.
- The deviations analysis must deal with the performance values stated in the plans that formed the basis of the investment, from both a computational and qualitative perspective.

If the main task of Controlling is to support management processes, investment appraisal also provides the information required for investment decisions. The controller continues to coordinate the actions taken by organisational units with respect to the shared corporate objective. In practice, it is observed that the controller is included in the decision-making process for the investment, due to his/her neutral position.

Investment and financing are considered to be two sides of the same coin, as each investment also needs to be financially offset. Financial accounting is examined in more detail in the following.

2.4 The configuration of effective financial accounting

Economic efficiency, which was the focus in the previous chapters on management accounting, is only one of the company's relevant target figures. Consistently maintaining liquidity is an important basic requirement for any enterprise. After all, the operational performance process can only run flawlessly if cash flows are coordinated in such a way that the company is always solvent. However, it is unprofitable if liquidity is too high, and this therefore should be avoided.

Static or dynamic instruments are used to monitor liquidity. Static instruments include liquidity status, liquidity scales, and various performance indicators for liquidity. These show liquidity at a certain point in time. By contrast, financial accounting systems comprise dynamic instruments and relate to a certain period of time. They are concerned with capturing and forecasting liquidity by contrasting cash in with cash out.

The most important forms of financial accounting are as follows:

- The "capital commitment plan": A mid-term financial forecast. This provides information as to whether the company is financially balanced in the long term.
- The "financial plan": Contrasting the cash in and cash out with a short- and long-term time horizon.
- Daily financial disposition planning: This is used for the smooth handling of daily payment transactions.
- Cash flow statement: As the third element in the annual financial statements, this completes the gaps in information in the balance sheet and P&L statement, and is therefore now also established as a mandatory component of the annual closing.

Contrasting cash in with cash out provides the cash surplus or shortfall. Where the cash flow statement documents accounting events that are relevant to liquidity, whilst also serving internal control and statutory reporting, the three first-mentioned forms of financial accounting can be assigned to internal liquidity planning.

Financial plan

Financial plans show the cash in and cash out for a future period. They may be restricted to a few months, or take in the entire subsequent business year. Annual budgeting generally includes the preparation of a planned cash flow statement, which – analogously to the (actual) cash flow statement – is structured into the areas of operating, investment, and financing activity. On the one hand, financial plans show the financing gap or financing surplus, and the planned measures for covering or using the lacking or surplus liquid assets.

Fig. 2.30 shows the annual financial plan, structured cash in and out from ordinary and extraordinary items. As well as monetary holdings, the estimated cash in and cash out from the ongoing corporate process are contrasted initially. In addition, there are the cash out and cash in due to capital transfers and investments.

2.4 The configuration of effective financial accounting

Annual financial plan (information in millions of €)	Planned figures	Performance figures
A. Initial monetary holdings		
1. Petty cash	62	62
2. Postal checking account credit balance	43	43
3. Cash at bank	677	677
Sum, 1 to 3	782	782
B. Cash in and out from ordinary items		
I. Cash in from the ongoing operations		
1. Based on estimated total sales, estimation of the proportion of "cash" sales	10,075	
2. Cash in from target sales from the prior period	4,259	
3. Interest in	83	
4. Cash in for services, sum of cash in, 1 to 4	212	
Total cash in, 1 to 4	14,629	
II. Cash out from ongoing operations		
1. Cash out for material which is bought and must be paid for in the planning period (estimation making allowance for the initial material stock, expected material consumption, and desired material stock)	5,274	
2. Cash out for material that was bought on credit in the prior period	607	
3. Cash out for staff	4,952	
4. Interest out	301	
5. Cash out for services	677	
6. Tax payments	815	
7. Dividend	209	
Total cash out, 1 to 7	12,835	
III. Cash in or cash out surplus from the ongoing corporate process (I-II)	1,794	
C. Cash in and out from extraordinary items		
I. Capital transfers		
1. Cash in from debtors to repay loans	668	
2. Cash out to creditors to repay loans	810	
Positive or negative balance from capital transfers	− 142	
II. Investments/divestments		
1. Cash in from the sale of property	−	
2. Cash out for buildings constructed by the company itself	639	
3. Cash out for machinery	731	
Positive or negative balance from investments/divestments	− 1,370	
III. Cash in or cash out surplus from I and II	− 1,512	
D. Monetary holdings	− 1,064	

Fig. 2.30: Example of an annual financial plan

2 Management Accounting

The breakdown of the cash in/out statements requires scheduling using cash-based accounting. Due-date information can be used to determine when credited income and expenditure become cash in and cash out.

Liquidity assurance tasks are generally not undertaken by the controller, but by the treasurer. The controller is responsible for "profitability", while the treasurer is responsible for "financial management".

In controlling practice, the linking of financial management and profitability is often referred to as financial controlling. With the aid of statements of changes in financial position, cash flow statements, or other financial statements, the financial controller is able to analyse and record correlations between the areas of finance and operating profit. In so doing, he/she first and foremost provides support in the detection and handling of structural correlations, and is less focused on controlling day-to-day operations.

Cash flow statement

The cash flow statement provides a breakdown of the liquidity trend, cash flow, investment processes, and financing measures for the most recent period. In current practice, it is often structured by cash flow from operating activity, cash flow from investment activity, and cash flow from financing activity. This shows an enterprise's ability to finance its investments, and therefore to open up future sources of income, repay financial debt, and distribute profits. The liquid funds generated from business activity minus the required net investments and profit distributions are referred to as free cash flow. The cash flow and the free cash flow are important parameters for both internal and external recipients of information (cf. **Fig. 2.31**).

The cash flow statement has become a fixed component of statutory financial reporting for most enterprises over recent years. This is, on the one hand, due to the increasing proliferation of international accounting standards (IFRS, US-GAAP), in which it is mandatory, in principle, to record a cash flow statement in the consolidated financial statements. On the other hand, this requirement has also been anchored in the German Commercial Code (HGB) for listed companies since 1997, and for all groups since 2002.

Cash flow statement	
Payments from customers	
./. Payments to suppliers	4,060
./. Payments to staff	−1,830
./. Payments for interest	−910
./. Payments for other operating expenses	−110
Cash flow	**910**
Investment area	
Investments	
./. Purchase of machinery	−240
./. Purchase of holdings	−350

./. Purchase of real estate	−400
Disinvestments	
Sale of land	300
Sale of movable assets	50
Disposal of securities	40
Free cash flow, gross	
Financial area	
External financing	
Mortgages	240
Disinvestment	
./. Repayment of leasing obligations	−100
./. Repaying investment credit	−280
./. Distribution of profits	−100
Free cash flow, net	**70**

Fig. 2.31: Example of a cash flow statement

2.5 Practical example[1]

2.5.1 The Fischer corporate group

Among the general public, the Fischer brand is primarily associated with fixing systems, kinematic components for vehicle interiors, and construction models for children. The Fischer corporate group is structured into the corporate areas of "Befestigungssysteme" (fixing systems), "Fischer Automotive Systems", "fischertechnik" (Fischer Technology) and "Fischer Consulting". The largest corporate area, which also represents the core of the corporate group, is the fixing systems division. In this area, Fischer offers a diverse range of fixing solutions comprising 14,000 items, and is the market leader in major areas of the fixings industry. One important success factor for Fischer continues to be the company's power to innovate, which is reflected in the disproportionately high number of patents the corporate group holds. In this way, this family-owned company, founded in 1948, with its registered office in Waldachtal-Tumlingen, has been on a path of constant growth from a workshop company to an international medium-sized business with 43 national subsidiaries and production sites in Argentina, Brazil, China, Germany, Italy, Czech Republic and the USA. In 2014, the entire corporate group, with 4,160 employees worldwide, achieved consolidated sales of € 661 million.

---

[1] We would like to thank Anja Schäfer, Head of Controlling at Fischer, for her kind support.

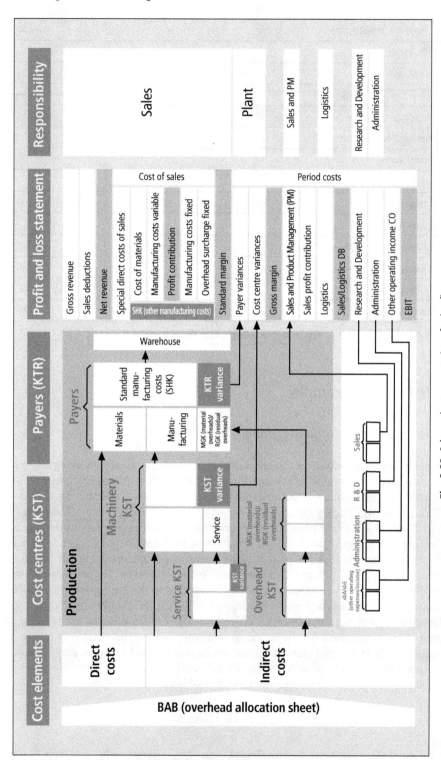

Fig. 2.32: Schematic representation of value flows

2.5.2 Project: Reconfiguring cost and profit accounting and financial reporting

In order to enable the targeted management control of further corporate growth, an integrated system for holistic, functional corporate management control has been developed at Fischer, with a focus on operational production and sales management. The integration of the different management control approaches requires a fundamental reconfiguration of cost and profit accounting. In addition to defining a harmonised cost allocation sheet, this also comprises redesigning cost centre accounting, standardising price determination, and defining value flows that are standardised group-wide, as well as reconfiguring cost object accounting.

The objectives here are to provide management-relevant information that is appropriate for the recipient, reduce complexity in cost and profit accounting whilst simultaneously increasing quality and transparency, and ensuring that the management control information is relevant to decision-making.

As part of redesigning cost and profit accounting, the system of flexible standard costing based on standard product costs and deviations is used, and includes the application of target costs. In order to implement flexible standard costing, it is necessary to initially formulate and implement cost accounting principles. As a result, for flexible standard costing to be used in a uniform way across the company, it is important that a harmonised cost allocation sheet (CAS) exist, in the framework of which the same items can be treated in the same way, and summarised at the same CAS hierarchy level, across the company. It is recommended that the CAS hierarchy levels be sorted by their cost volume in this process. Furthermore, in order to enable meaningful information in cost and profit accounting, it must be ensured that all cost elements and therefore all postings are considered in the CAS.

A further fundamental component of an efficient Controlling system is how cost centre accounting is configured. Here, the cost centres must be defined in such a way that supports the cost causation principle; that is relevant for management decisions; that clearly allocates costs to functional areas; and that unambiguously reflects management responsibilities. Furthermore, at Fischer all cost accounting instruments including cost centres and cost objects such as internal orders, projects, and production orders are being used solely for their original purpose, in order to ensure smooth technical implementation.

Building on the basic cost accounting framework, value flows and allocations principles that are consistent group-wide are defined at Fischer, for example for purchasing and production. Here, direct cost allocation replaces cost allocation via allocation key where possible. At Fischer, surcharges are used in product calculation for cost components for which neither direct cost allocation nor causation-based cost allocation is possible. This means that, e. g. material and residual overhead costs is allocated to the individual material or production costs via dedicated surcharge rates. Provided that it is possible with reasonable expense, causation-based cost allocation is also applied when allocating general overhead costs. Examples of this include defined costs for IT and buildings.

In order to perform the described cost allocation from cost centres to other cost accounting objects within flexible standard costing, a planned price or cost centre rate is required in addition to the actual level of utilisation. As part of establishing the cost

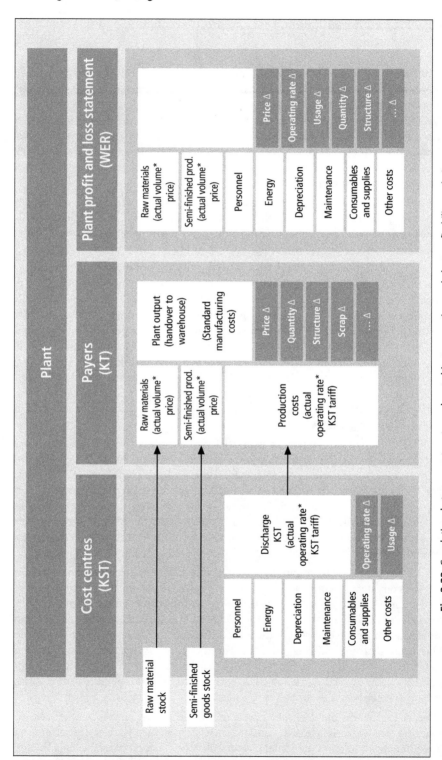

Fig. 2.33: Correlations between cost centre and cost object accounting, and plant profitability analysis

centre rates, a distinction is made at Fischer between the variable and fixed rate. When establishing the variable cost centre rate, the planned variable costs for the relevant cost centre are applied with respect to the planned activity of the cost centre. In contrast to this, when calculating the fixed cost centre rate, the fixed planned costs for the cost centre are based on the technically real capacity of the cost centre. Here, the technically real capacity is the available cost centre capacity, reduced by the structural and operational periods of downtime, such as shift operation or maintenance. The use of the technically real capacity, together with the approach of cost accounting depreciation, guarantees consistent cost centre prices throughout the year, without influencing monthly fluctuations in capacity utilisation and depreciation. On this basis, the Fischer corporate group is able to establish consumption and utilisation level deviations in the cost centres, analyse their root-causes, and derive counter-measures on a monthly basis.

In addition to cost element and cost centre accounting, cost object accounting, and in particular establishing standard product costs, is an important component in operational management control. In this respect, Fischer applies a clear definition of standard product costs, which is consistent across the company. Standard product costs are updated on an annual basis using planned purchase prices and planned costs, and are the valuation basis for inventory, determining deviations, and for defining consistent indicators such as the standard margin for sales control. Further significant management control information is derived based on standard product costs. In this way, all standard product costs, for example all medium-term and variable standard product costs, represent the short-term price floor. The standard margin is the basis for assessing product and customer profitability, and therefore the basis for portfolio decisions. In contrast from establishing standard product costs on an annual basis, recalculation of standard product costs during the fiscal year is recommended if highly volatile components are considered in the product cost calculation. In addition to valid information for pricing, this means that a consistently current basis for portfolio decisions is always guaranteed.

On the input side, the cost object variances established with the aid of standard product cost calculation can be split into five categories: input price, input quantity, scrap, structure and remaining input deviations. On the output side, Fischer makes a distinction between the mixed price, lot size, transfer price, and remaining variances, therefore enabling the company to analyse the causes of variances at cost object level and derive concrete counter-measures. Together with the cost centre variances, the cost object variances represent a significant foundation for a "plant profitability analysis", which summarises these for the operational management control of production.

The main performance indicators for operational production control are efficiency and productivity. Efficiency measures the development of standard product costs over time at the level of the end products and product cost components, such as material or manufacturing costs. Productivity measures whether the plant deviates from the specifications in the standard product cost calculation, and at Fischer is available at team and therefore profit centre level. In order to safeguard a responsibility-based and complete plant management control, it must be ensured that the plant profitability analysis contains only elements for which the respective plant manager is responsible; these may also go beyond the two main financial performance indicators mentioned above. Additional performance indicators such as capacity utilisation, quality, and the degree of fulfilment, are therefore added to plant management control at Fischer.

2 Management Accounting

In addition to operational management control of the production function, a system of operational sales planning is introduced at Fischer based on cost and profit accounting information; this in itself is based on the principles of management relevancy, controllability, and orientation on decisions. The key performance indicator here is the calculated group contribution margin with which sales are assessed at group product costs, i. e. without inter-company margins. This enables Fischer to increase the transparency of earnings in the local subsidiaries, as well as eliminating tax-related transfer pricing effects that are not relevant for management control.

2.5.3 Lessons learned

Given the volatile nature of business environments, management control systems must be regularly reviewed and, if necessary, adapted to altered and new requirements. These changes to cost and profit accounting systems and their components, both initial and recurring, require a great deal of work not only within Controlling, but also in adjacent business functions.

The reconfiguration of cost and profit accounting always offers a company the opportunity for change, within and beyond Controlling. The following aspects have proven particularly important at Fischer:

- Only through engaging deeply with multiple involved stakeholders and business functions with existing information structures, and the management's information-related needs, was it possible to open up, comprehensively assess, and optimise existing structures.

- The inclusion of many contributing employees increased acceptance of the new control approaches in the company, particularly in an international environment.

- Strong support from management in reconfiguring cost and profit accounting was one of the central success factors for the successful implementation of the developed concepts.

In addition to the close integration of design work and implementation, another important success factor for implementation and acceptance of the changes was the formulation of a consistent group-wide policy that was integrated for the various management control approaches, and which established the methodology of cost and profit accounting. Setting up an effective Controlling function, managing the internal change process, and the expansion of internal components, will ideally also be supported by external momentum. The integrated management control system created in this way offers an information data pool that is harmonised on an international basis, for targeted management control.

2.6 Configurations checklist for managers and controllers

 Ensure all aspects are allocated by cause.

 Clarify roles and responsibilities.

 Enable plan(target)-actual comparisons and carry out variance analyses.

 Secure your quantity and time/price structures as the basis for calculating values.

 Ensure the consistency of internal and external accounting for all areas and divisions.

 Work as precisely and detailed as necessary to make decisions.

 Document the terms, ratios, variables, indicators and calculation methods used clearly and uniformly.

Further reading

If you would like to find out more about the overall area of management accounting:

Coenenberg, A. G., Fischer, M., Günther, T. (2016), Kostenrechnung und Kostenanalyse, 9th ed., Munich, 2016.

If you would like to find out more about cost and profit accounting:

Friedl, G., Hofmann, C., Pedell, B., (2013), Kostenrechnung, 2nd ed., Munich, 2013.

If you would like to find out more about investment appraisal:

Grob, H. L. (2006), Einführung in die Investitionsrechnung, 5th ed., Munich, 2006.

3 Strategic Planning

3.1 Chapter objectives

In this chapter, the key steps and most important instruments of strategic planning are discussed. By the end of the chapter, the reader should understand and be able to apply the process and instruments of strategy development.

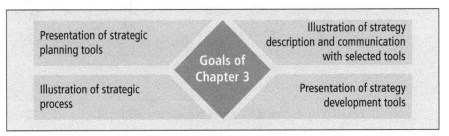

Fig. 3.1: Chapter objectives

3.2 Introduction

This chapter primarily deals with Controlling tasks and instruments, which are considered within the context of information acquisition. However, if we claim that the purpose of Controlling must be to comprehensively improve companies' management capabilities, then strategic aspects cannot be dismissed.

The success of a company is the result of exploiting the potential for success. If a company wants to not just react but consciously shape its development, the entire company must be focused on the potential for success. For this purpose, the company uses strategic planning to develop ideas of its overarching goals for the coming years. Strategic planning is also used to decide on the ways in which these goals will be met.

There is a close feedback process between the various stages of planning. Strategic planning gives an indication of whether management can also approve mid-term or annual planning. It also becomes clear during annual planning (operational planning) whether the strategies are actually feasible and not just wishful thinking. Therefore, operational planning may result in the necessity to revise strategic planning. Targets may have to be scaled down or pursued indirectly with new strategies.

A reasonable and feasible operational plan (see chapter 4.3 on operational planning) can also only be produced on the basis of strategic planning. This is because the direction the company actually wants to take is not clear otherwise.

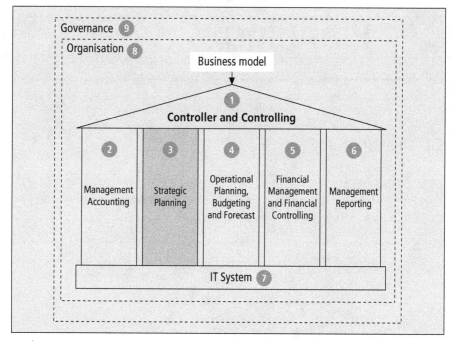

Fig. 3.2: Classification of the chapter in the "House of Controlling"

3.3 Creating an effective strategic plan

The definition of the company's mission forms the basis of strategic planning.

> The company's **mission statement** defines the company's identity and lays down the basic guidelines for company members' conduct. For example, if a company's mission is to be a supplier of high-quality branded products, activities involving distributing mass-produced goods must be almost completely excluded during operational planning.

Strategic goals are what the company wants to work towards in its operating activities. For example, if the goal is to achieve a market share of 10 % in the USA within the next five years, this could result in a strategy to establish a subsidiary in the USA. Strategies are the ways in which goals will be met. They lay down the path of development to be shaped in mid-term and operational planning with specific individual steps. Mid-term planning converts strategic targets into key operating indicators that, when achieved, lead step-by-step to the achievement of the strategic goals. Development towards the strategic goals is realised in mid-term planning, which thus enables strategic planning to be monitored too.

The purpose of strategic planning is to define the framework in which the company wants to be active in the future. Strategic planning is also intended to identify and develop new potential for success as well as secure existing potential. It already influ-

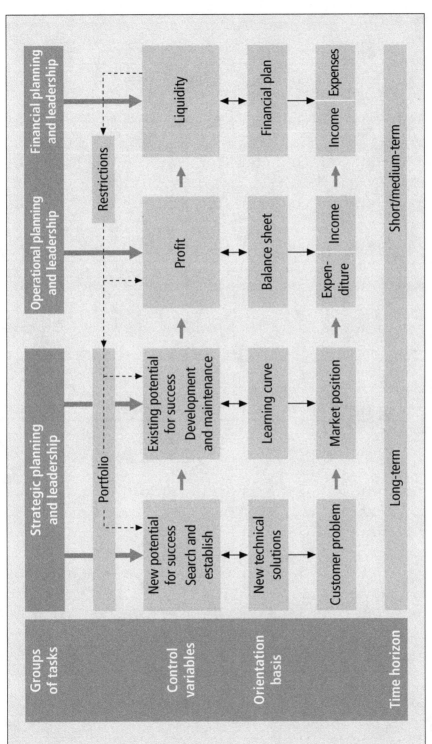

Fig. 3.3: Strategic corporate planning

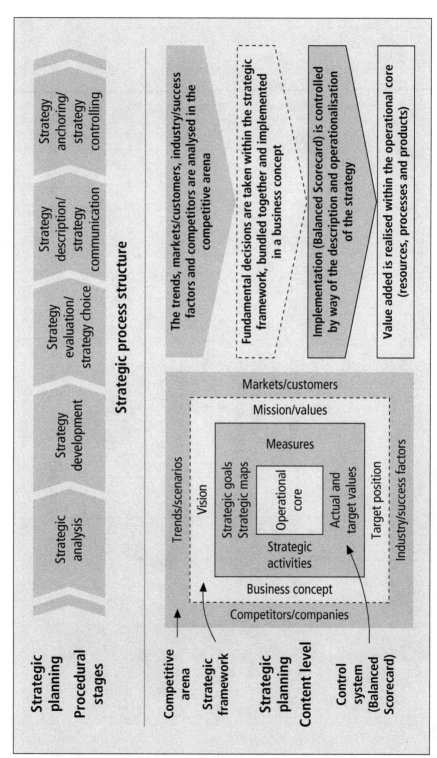

Fig. 3.4: Strategic management: Approach and content of procedure

ences future success and liquidity at a point in time when the company still has various means of action at its disposal (cf. **Fig. 3.3**). Therefore, it forms the cornerstones of the intended corporate development that will be shaped and laid down in concrete terms in subsequent planning stages.

Strategic planning also includes defining the premises on which the plan will be based. It is considered very important because the entire structure of the plan and, therefore, the company's activities are ultimately based on it.

3.3.1 Strategy process

Strategic management handles the development and implementation of the corporate strategy. It does so as part of a clearly defined process with typical approaches for every step (see **Fig. 3.4**).

In the strategic analysis phase, the competitive arena that the company is active in is examined first. Trends and future business scenarios are examined. It must be clarified in which markets and with which customers business will be conducted, and which factors of success are relevant to the industry. It is on this basis that the company competes with other companies; the company's own competitive position in relation to these companies is determined.

> During **strategy development**, a fundamental strategy is derived from the appraisal and the subjective ideas of the company's future role. This is reflected in the vision, the mission and the values of a company, and influences its subsequent steps during strategy development.

The mission statement clarifies which role the company wants to play and which duties it performs in this regard. In doing so, it gives details of the company's purpose (Who are we? Why are we here? Who do we benefit?) and touches on the company's goals, which can be derived from this. The mission statement also provides information on key values and can be supplemented to include principles of conduct.

A vision can be described as a company's guiding notion of its future development. It defines the fundamental character of the organisation and, in contrast to the mission statement, has a time limit. The vision results from the management's subjective ideas of the company's future role and is characterised by its meaningful, motivational and influential qualities (cf. *Müller-Stewens, Lechner* 2005, p. 235).

The target position – in contrast to the current competitive position, which was determined in the strategic analysis – describes which competitive position the company will reach in the future by realising its vision and strategy (Where do we want to go? Where do we stand in relation to our competitors at the end of our strategic planning horizon?)

The fundamental strategic orientation leads to a characteristic business concept with which a company clearly distinguishes itself from the competition and which is "recognisable" for customers. Good examples of this are Aldi, IKEA or Ryanair – we associate them with unique characteristics. This is important because it enables the company's value proposition to be brought in line with customers' expectations and disappointments to be generally avoided.

Once this strategic framework has been defined, the strategy has to be laid down in concrete terms. Usually, there is no "one-size-fits-all solution" but various conceivable strategic alternatives. Consequently, a strategy evaluation and strategy selection phase must follow. In a profit-oriented company, quantitative and qualitative factors are used for evaluation. Very often, the quantitative evaluation is based on the methods used by the managers who focus on the value of the company. This is illustrated in detail in the following sections.

However, the selection of the corporate strategy does not result in any change in the company's conduct, which is why the following step of strategy realisation is of great importance. Suitable instruments for strategy description and strategy communication must be established so that all relevant persons in the company understand where they are heading and how they can contribute to this. In practice, the Balanced Scorecard prevails as an important control system for strategy realisation (cf. *Horváth & Partners*, eds., 2005c). This concept is also illustrated in detail below.

Ultimately, the goal is to convert strategic thinking into strategy-compliant action by all employees. The strategy anchoring and strategy controlling phase serves this purpose. It involves ongoing performance evaluation at the operational heart of the business. The conclusions drawn from deviation analyses and a strategy review then lead to the execution of the strategy process again, usually in the following fiscal year.

Strategy Controlling also performs other important roles here related to the coordination of the strategy process and the supply of information that is relevant to decisions. The strategy process must first be organised as such, if it is not already, and the possible instruments for the individual phases that are relevant to company must be chosen from the multitude available (so-called "system-building coordination"). These tasks actually begin during strategic analysis – e.g. with instruments such as technology trend analysis, portfolio techniques and SWOT (strengths, weaknesses, opportunities and threats) analyses. Strategy development is a creative process, which can, however, be supported instrumentally by way of structured work on strategy options (e.g. using the morphological box method). Strategy evaluation is supported using value management instruments, description and communication using the Balanced Scorecard.

Using the instruments of information acquisition, analysis and interpretation is ultimately the role of Controlling during the "system-linking coordination" part of strategic management (cf. *Horváth* 2009, pp. 295 et seqq.).

Fig. 3.5 compares the key features of strategic and operational controlling.

Controlling-type features	Strategic controlling	Operational controlling
Orientation	Environment and company: Adaptation	Company: Efficiency of operating processes
Planning stage	Strategic planning	Tactical and operational planning, budgeting
Dimensions	Opportunities/risks, strengths/weaknesses	Expenses/income, cost/output
Targets	Ensuring continued company existence, potential for success	Efficiency, profit, profitability

Fig. 3.5: Strategic and operational controlling (cf. *Horváth* 2009, p. 222)

3.3.2 Selected strategic analysis instruments

Controlling assists with strategic planning by providing suitable planning instruments, among other things. These help with the as-is analysis of the company and with the subsequent development of strategies. In principle, there is a variety of strategic controlling instruments, of which a few are illustrated by way of example below.

> Do you know the strengths, weaknesses, opportunities and threats of your company?

One important instrument is the SWOT analysis.

> The **SWOT appraisal** examines a company's current strengths and weaknesses as well as its future opportunities and threats as part of strategic planning.

Analysing strengths and weaknesses is helpful when evaluating a company's current position. Criteria checklists are often used to ensure that the company's current position is evaluated from a broad enough perspective. The evaluation of whether a criterion should be considered a strength or weakness of the company is often made in consideration of the major competitors. By contrast, the opportunities/threats analysis focuses on future prospects. It asks: What are the future opportunities and threats that might arise from possible environmental development for the company if it does not change its current strategies and those that it has already planned? Therefore, alternative scenarios of how the environment may develop and which opportunities and threats may arise for the company are considered.

The significance of the SWOT analysis primarily depends on the planning team's creativity and ability to perform an assessment. It is now undisputed in theory and in practice that the controller belongs to the planning team. On the one hand, it is his/her duty to make the planning process more effective by preparing for planning meetings (e.g. solid and well-founded evaluation of the as-is situation, preparing recommendations). On the other hand, however, he/she may not influence the direction of the creative processes too strongly.

> Does your company reach its long-term targets?

Another classic analysis instrument for strategic planning is the gap analysis. It is based on the idea that there is a constantly growing difference (gap = "target gap") between the goals set during planning and the forecast for the actual achievement of goals. While forecasting the actual achievement of goals, it is assumed that current measures will be maintained and changes in strengths and weaknesses and/or opportunities and threats will arise from them, which ultimately creates the target gap. The target gap must then be filled using suitable strategies. **Fig. 3.7** illustrates this link.

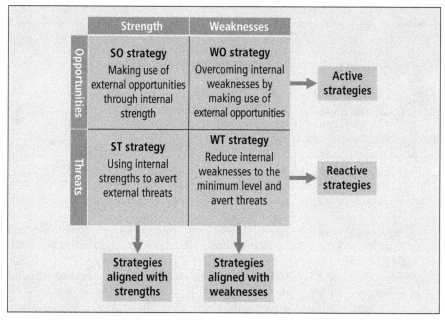

Fig. 3.6: SWOT analysis as a basis for various strategies

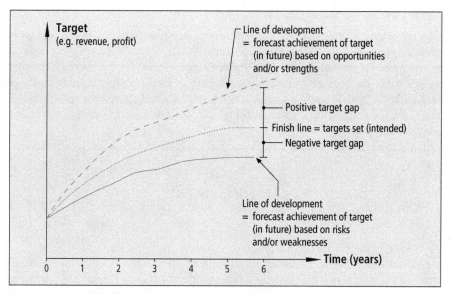

Fig. 3.7: Concept of the gap analysis

Finally, we present the instrument of portfolio analysis, which is very widespread in practice. In portfolio analysis, individual important company segments are strategically evaluated with the aim of directing resources to those segments in which market prospects appear to be favourable and the company can exploit relative competitive advantages.

Portfolio analysis starts by defining the strategically relevant segments of the company – also known as strategic business areas. They may result from the company's profit centres, for example, and are usually product/market combinations. These are classified in a portfolio matrix, which most commonly has the axes "relative market share" and "market growth" (cf. **Fig. 3.8**).

Which of your company's business fields will also be profitable in the future?

So-called standard strategies, which are recommended strategies for the fields, are proposed for each segment depending on their positions. These strategies are intended to guide the company from its actual portfolio to a target portfolio.

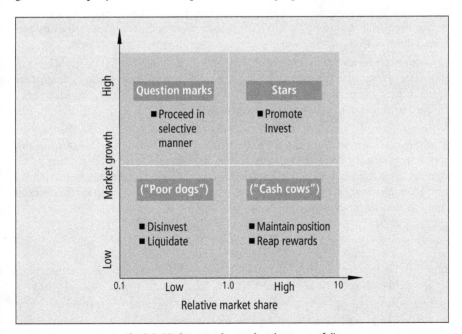

Fig. 3.8: Market growth – market share – portfolio

The bottom right quadrant contains items of least importance. Such products have a weak competitive position due to their low market share and simultaneous low market growth. They could only be brought into better positions at a great financial cost and should, therefore, be dropped.

Business areas that do, admittedly, have low market growth but a high relative market share, so-called "cash cows", should be considered much more advantageous. The cost advantages of the high relative market share can be exploited. No major investments are required for this purpose; in fact, they would be economically pointless in the long term. Instead, such products should be "milked". The remaining surplus can be used to support other business areas.

It is predominantly the "stars" but also the "question marks" that should be supported financially. The former should be supported because the high relative market share will also be retained in the future in the event of changing low market growth. With regard to business areas in the "question mark" quadrant, the company faces the decision of whether to improve the "relative market share" by way of high investment or leave this sector due to lack of opportunities.

One big advantage of the portfolio approaches lies in their simple illustration and, therefore, easy communicability. One disadvantage is the reduction of the multiple strategic contributing factors to just two dimensions. This gives the impression that a strategy can be selected using one clear diagram. The portfolio approach can only help with selecting a strategy; it cannot determine the selection according to a mathematical formula.

3.3.3 Selected strategy development instruments

Fundamentally, strategy development is – as already explained – a creative process. With regard to content, it must be driven by the management of the company or the business area. However, the controller can also provide instrumental assistance here.

A business model features a number of parameters which may be characterised by various strategy options (cf. chapter 1.6). For a structured comparison of such options, there is the method of the "morphological box", in which the actual and target positions can be compared. **Fig. 3.9** gives this instrument as an example.

With regard to the characteristics of individual fields of activity within the business models of well-known companies, we would like to point out, by way of example, how strategy options are handled. **Fig. 3.10** contains decisions made as part of strategy development by companies such as McDonalds, Disneyland Paris, Intel or Microsoft. It must also be emphasised here that the instruments are merely a structuring aid for decision making, but can never anticipate the decision itself.

One fundamental decision to be made during strategy development is whether a company

- is striving for greater market penetration in its core business, or
- would like to expand into new markets (e.g. Southeast Asia) with existing products, or
- would like to expand into existing markets with new products (e.g. a key manufacturer expanding into chip cards or biometric access control systems).

The classic product/market matrix by Ansoff can be used as a structuring aid for this question (cf. **Fig. 3.11**). The highest growth strategy path – and, at the same time, the most difficult – is diversification, i.e. targeting new markets with a wider product range.

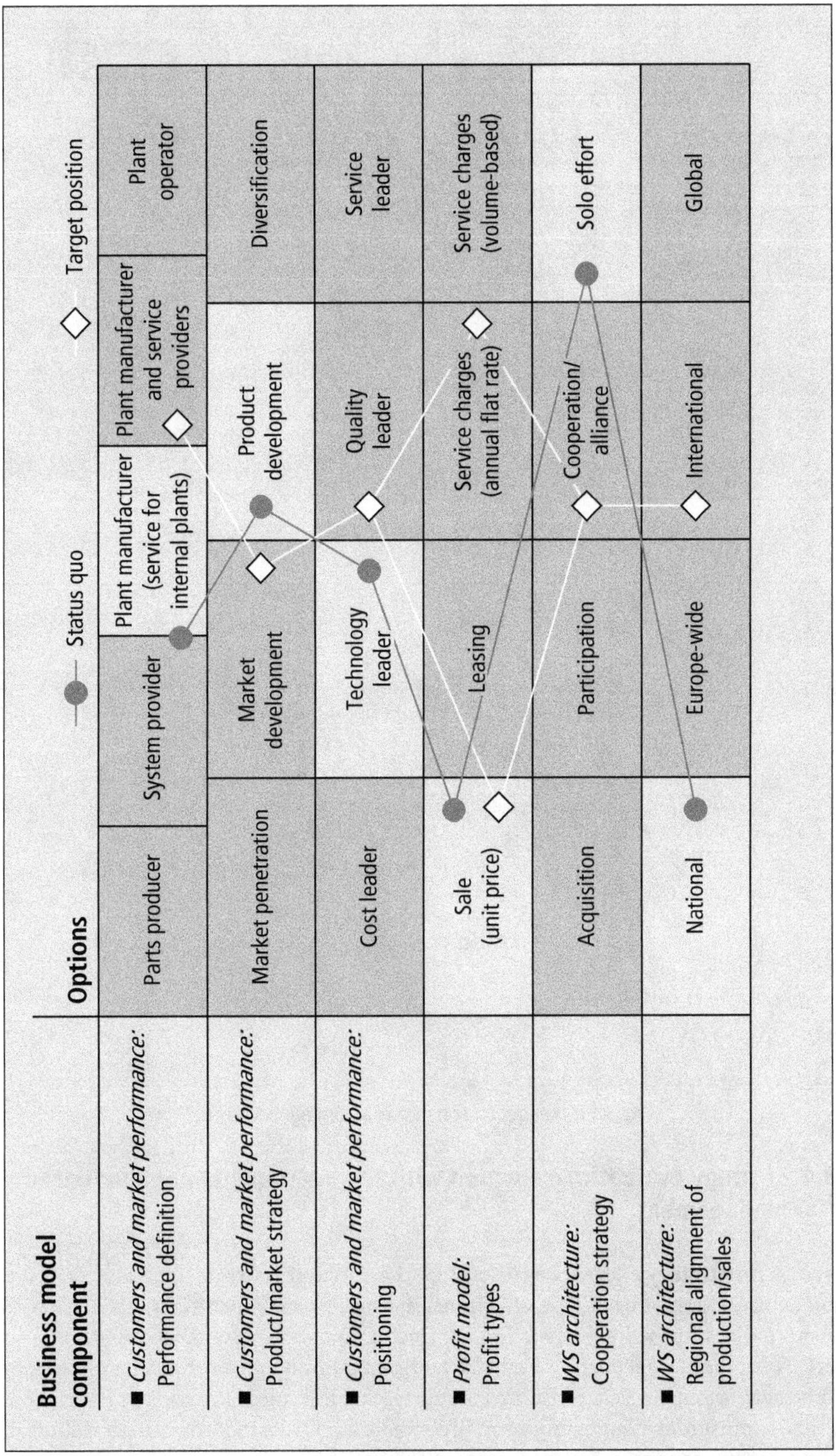

Business model component	Options					
■ *Customers and market performance:* Performance definition	Parts producer	System provider	Plant manufacturer (service for internal plants)	Plant manufacturer and service providers	Plant operator	
■ *Customers and market performance:* Product/market strategy	Market penetration	Market development	Product development	Diversification		
■ *Customers and market performance:* Positioning	Cost leader	Technology leader	Quality leader	Service leader		
■ *Profit model:* Profit types	Sale (unit price)	Leasing	Service charges (annual flat rate)	Service charges (volume-based)		
■ *WS architecture:* Cooperation strategy	Acquisition	Participation	Cooperation/alliance	Solo effort		
■ *WS architecture:* Regional alignment of production/sales	National	Europe-wide	International	Global		

— Status quo ◇ Target position

Fig. 3.9: Selecting strategy options

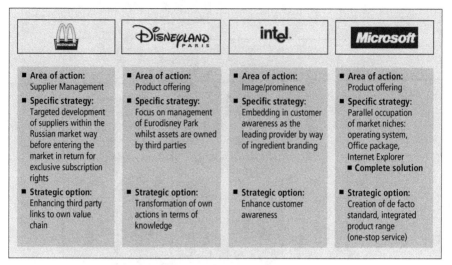

Fig. 3.10: Examples of well-known companies' strategy options

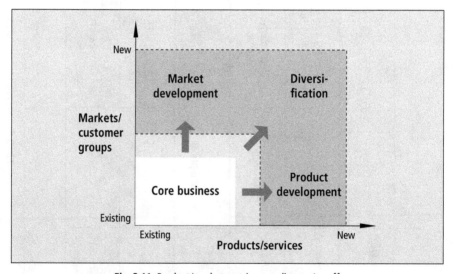

Fig. 3.11: Product/market matrix according to Ansoff

3.3.4 Strategy evaluation/selection with the instruments of value-based management

Based on the strategy alternatives discussed, the question arises during strategy evaluation and selection of what type of commercial success a company could achieve with the alternatives in the long term. Today's frequent target of profit maximisation falls short. This is because reporting a profit by no means always guarantees that a company will be able to remain successful in the future. Small to medium-sized enterprises in particular must make more long-term investments, but this requires a high volume of investment in advance, which may exceed the profit for the period many times over.

Small to medium-sized enterprises have recognised the inadequacy of focusing solely on profits and are increasingly turning to value-based corporate performance management. In this context, a value focus means that a company must, based on operating profit in consideration of investments to be made in research and development, production and organisational structure, for example, be able to meet expectations of returns from equity owners and external investors, too. Only under these conditions can crucial support from capital lenders be guaranteed in the long term. The primary goal of value-based corporate performance management when making these considerations is not achieving profit maximisation but rather an adequate increase in company value that is sustainable in the long term.

Often, the internal financing options available within a company – primarily those arising from the sales process – are not sufficient to cover investments and growth to the necessary extent. External financing using borrowed capital from banks or other capital market institutions and external financing using equity (issuing additional company shares or stocks to shareholders) are gaining importance. The increased importance of bank ratings when granting loans guarantees medium-sized businesses, for example, secure, favourable financing with negligible risk for the lender. Plausible, sustainable value-generating strategies enable the acceptability of risk to be justified in the best way.

Equity lenders take a significantly higher risk than the banks. While the banks have a contractually guaranteed – and, in the event of insolvency, preferential – claim to interest and capital repayment because of their position as a creditor, this is not true of shareholders or equity holders. In the worst case, they lose their entire investment and only receive interest or a dividend in the event of a profit. Consequently, due to the higher risk, their expectation of a return is also higher – equity capital is more expensive than borrowed capital. One particular argument against the use of the key performance indicator "profit", which is frequently used in many companies, is the disregard of the costs of the equity capital employed in the necessary amount. This weakness is also found accordingly in indicators that build on profit, such as return on investment (ROI). This does not take into account a "minimum profit" from the equity lenders' perspective. The full balance sheet is taken into account when calculating the return. The fact that some liabilities on the balance sheet are not subject to interest, e. g. short-term reserves or trade liabilities, is disregarded.

How do you evaluate different strategy alternatives?

It is clear that Controlling needs another instrument to evaluate strategies from the perspective of the lenders who ultimately finance them. Initially, it must be clarified how high the average expectation of return is for the capital employed. To this end, the expected return for the relevant form of financing (equity and borrowed capital) must be calculated and weighted in proportion to use. The result is the applicable "minimum return" – the average expectation of return. An increase in company value only arises when strategies are evaluated and selected during strategic planning in such a way that

3 Strategic Planning

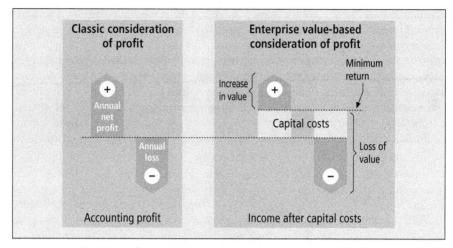

Fig. 3.12: Profit-orientated vs. company value-orientated consideration

they lead to a return greater than the required minimum return. **Fig. 3.12** clarifies the difference between the traditional profit-orientated and company value-orientated perspectives.

When evaluating a strategy at company level, the existing business areas and business area strategies must first be examined. In the case of value-based corporate performance management, the company must build on or expand a portfolio of value-generating business areas and, logically, sell business areas that cannot be developed into value-creating units. This comes down to a long-term consideration: In the short term, a business area that is currently in an investment phase will often not be able to generate the return desired by equity and external lenders. In the long term, however, the potential for success will be expanded for the future. This is why importance is placed on the anticipated change in the future (delta analysis) in addition to the current return, which may be greater or lesser than the minimum return. In line with classification in the value-generating portfolio, a distinction is primarily made between value creators and value destroyers, but also between value retainers and value reducers (cf. **Fig. 3.13**).

In value-based corporate performance management, a distinction is made between two fundamental management and evaluation procedures, which we discuss below (cf. *Currle* 2001). On the one hand, there is the quantitative evaluation of business units, investments, product ranges, etc. in a full consideration over the entire life cycle using dynamic multi-period investment calculation procedures. As a rule, the so-called discounted cash flow (DCF) is used here. On the other hand, there is the periodical performance evaluation of organisational units using value added methods. The most prominent example of such methods is the "Economic Value Added" concept (EVA®)[2].

---

[2] EVA® is a registered trademark of Stern Stewart & Co.

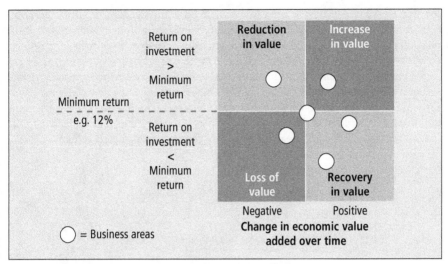

Fig. 3.13: Value-increasing portfolio for business areas

3.3.4.1 Discounted cash flow method (DCF)

> The **DCF method** is a procedure focusing on the streams of payments received and made. The investment associated with a strategic decision is evaluated based on which payments (total investment and current expenses) are and will be incurred today and in the future, and which payments (usually arising from sales, license revenues and similar) are, by contrast, received. The method takes the time value of money into account.

This is based on the fact that a payment of € 1,000 that only accrues in three years, for example, is worth less than this on today's date. If the amount was already available today, it could be subject to interest over the next three years and would then – with an interest rate of 5 % p.a., for example – be worth € 1.157 in three years. The minimum return stated above is applied as the interest rate. Future payment flows are "discounted" to the current date using this minimum return.

The minimum return is calculated using the equity and borrowed capital costs, which are weighted based on their proportion of total capital. The simplified formula is as follows:

Minimum return = Equity share × equity cost rate + borrowed capital share × borrowed capital cost rate

Current market conditions apply to the cost rate of borrowed capital. For example, they result from loan agreements, lease terms or the legally defined return for pension provisions, which is set regularly by the German Federal Bank. It is clear from this that pension provisions should be considered interest-bearing borrowed capital.

There are various models available for calculating the costs of equity capital. Generally accepted – even if it is not without its critics methodologically – is the Capital Asset

3 Strategic Planning

Pricing Model (CAPM). It is used to calculate an equity lender's required return in consideration of systematic risk. In the Capital Asset Pricing Model, the excepted return on equity corresponds to the amount of return from a risk-free investment (e. g. returns on long-term fixed-rate securities from issuers with a first-class credit rating) and a so-called market risk premium, which is applied to compensate for the systematic risk of an equity investment in a certain industry. This is expressed as a so-called beta factor (β), which indicates how much the value of an investment fluctuates relative to the value of the market portfolio and can be interpreted as the risk of the security relative to the market portfolio. In detail, the required equity cost rate is calculated as follows:

r^A	$= i + [\mu\,(r^M) - i] \times \beta\,A$
r^A	= excepted return on investment A
i	= risk-free rate
$\mu\,(r^M)$	= expected return on market portfolio
$\beta\,A$	= β factor of investment A

Normally, the discounted cash flows can only be estimated, i. e. planned, over a limited period of time in the future. As companies and often investment projects too have a longer life span, an assumption regarding the "final value" must be made for the period after the planning horizon. There are also different approaches to this, such as estimating a liquidation (sale) value or calculating a perpetual annuity based on the last forecast cash flow. These approaches will not be discussed here. The final value must also be discounted.

The calculation of the capital value and discounted cash flow is illustrated again below in **Fig. 3.14**. The enterprise value or total value of an investment is calculated using the following formula:

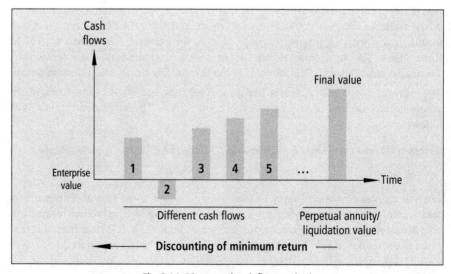

Fig. 3.14: Discounted cash flow method

Enterprise value = Cash flow in 1st period + cash values of the cash flows in the planning periods + cash value of the final value

The shareholder value, which is often cited in this context, is the enterprise value less the shares to which external lenders are entitled:

Shareholder value = Enterprise value − market value of borrowed capital

3.3.4.2 Economic Value Added method (EVA®)

The term "value added" has already been used in the illustration of the value-enhancing portfolio in **Fig. 3.15**. The Economic Value Added method is the most well-known method of calculating this value added. The ongoing implementation of a strategy poses the question: How much value would be added by the operational realisation of the strategy or, for example, by a business area in the current period?

> The aim of **Economic Value Added** is to express, from an economic perspective, the results of operating activities per period in consideration of the assets employed operationally and equity and external lenders' minimum return expectations. In doing so, the profit and loss statement, among other things, is adjusted to allow for accounting- and tax-related effects and the operating assets adjusted to allow for the interest-free capital to which we have already referred and assets that are not reported on the balance sheet.

In companies with high expenditure on research and development, this can be classed as investment spending. In addition to accounting in accordance with the Commercial Code, it is also capitalised and amortised per period based on the life span of the products. These adjustments are reflected in the adjusted result and the operating assets. Therefore, it should be noted that the calculation of the Economic Value Added has to be adjusted for each company individually. When applying international financial reporting standards such as IFRS or US-GAAP in companies, adjustments almost do not play a role anymore. The reason for this is that the international standards are based very strongly on market values and not on the principle of prudence found in German commercial law. Therefore, the "effects" discussed above barely feature in the actual market perspective, even in the original balance sheet and profit and loss account statements. By way of example, the calculation of the Economic Value Added is explained below.

The Economic Value Added is an absolute financial indicator and is reported as an operating surplus (value added) on a yearly basis. **Fig. 3.15** illustrates the calculation procedure that is referred to as a "value lever tree". The main components are the profit figure and the capital costs, with the Economic Value Added calculated based on the difference between them:

Economic Value Added (EVA®) = Profit figure − capital costs

= NOPAT − (NOA × minimum return)

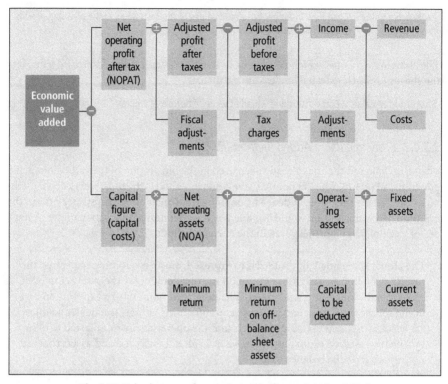

Fig. 3.15: Value lever tree for calculating the Economic Value Added

The profit figure (NOPAT = Net Operating Profit After Taxes) is calculated based on the result, adjusted by financial items from non-operating activities, i. e. only on the basis of the "operating result". The figure is calculated before interest (which is already included in the minimum return requirement) but after tax. The capital figure (capital costs) is the product of the net operating assets (NOA = Net Operating Assets) and the minimum return.

The calculation procedure stated allows the value added for a company or a business area to be reported by period. This mean that it can be determined whether a company is increasing or reducing its enterprise value per period, as **Fig. 3.16** illustrates. If the Economic Value Added is positive, the company was able to generate more from operating activities than necessary to cover equity and external capital costs. The company has ultimately created added value during this period. In contrast, a negative Economic Value Added indicates the loss of enterprise value, as total capital costs cannot be covered and the lender would have attained a higher return with an alternative investment with the same risk profile.

Using the methods illustrated, strategy alternatives can be evaluated from the perspective of value-orientated management following strategy development. The financial result is supplemented by qualitative aspects such as fundamental decisions for penetration in the core business or diversification (cf. **Fig. 3.11** above in this regard). The strategy is selected based on the overall evaluation. Periodical performance assessment using value added also allows the ongoing success of implementing all strategies in a business area or company to be tracked.

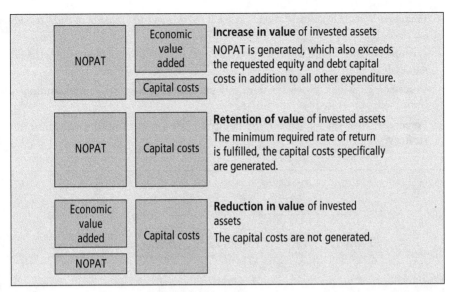

Fig. 3.16: Connection between capital costs, NOPAT and value added

3.3.5 Strategy description and communication with strategy maps and the Balanced Scorecard

When undertaking value-orientated management, the key value levers are the increase in profitability and profitable growth. These levers are put into use by identifying so-called value drivers (cf. **Fig. 3.17**).

Value drivers are all those factors that have a significant positive effect on the increase in company value. These may be of a monetary and non-monetary nature. The latter occur before monetary value drivers and, when actively managed, predominantly ensure the sustainability of the increase in value. To identify, capitalise and track value drivers, i. e. consistently implement a value-orientated strategy with the aim of attaining a long-term sustainable increase in company value down to operating level, the strategy must be described in a well-balanced way and clearly communicated to the managers and employees.

What are the value drivers in your company?

The Balanced Scorecard (BSC) has established itself as an important instrument for this. Repeated empirical studies since 2000 have shown that the instrument is increasingly becoming a standard procedure for strategy implementation and that users are having outstanding success with it (cf. *Horváth & Partners*, eds. 2005c). The Balanced Scorecard lays down the strategy in concrete terms by taking various perspectives into account and avoiding a purely financial focus. In general, these perspectives answer the following questions:

3 Strategic Planning

- **Finances:** Which financial targets do we have to meet to implement our strategy successfully?

- **Customers:** How should we be perceived by our customers to implement our strategy successfully?

- **Processes:** In which processes does our performance have to be outstanding to implement our strategy successfully?

- **Potentials:** How do we achieve the ability to change and improve to realise our strategy?

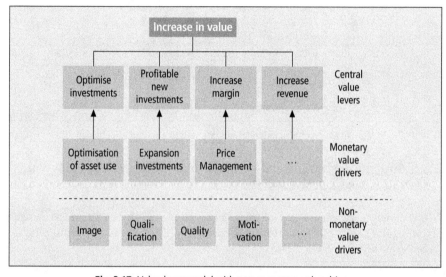

Fig. 3.17: Value lever model with non-monetary value drivers

The balanced view takes into account that financial success can only be achieved if outstanding products and services – i.e. ones that can differentiate us from the competition – are produced for customers. Our processes must perform at the highest level in order to produce such products or services both economically and ensure that they are high-quality. For functional processes, it is ultimately necessary for the optimum resources and potential to be available. For example, this may be employee qualifications and satisfaction, innovative strength, rights and patents, or perhaps the management of company networks and IT resources.

A complete – and thus promising – Balanced Scorecard concept contains a limited number of clearly focused strategic goals for the four perspectives. These are provided for performance assessment with key figures, actual and target figures, and measures for ensuring strategy implementation (cf. **Fig. 3.18**).

The easily communicable graphical representation of the target system with prioritised connections between content is called a "strategy map". The strategy map is an integral part of a complete BSC concept (cf. *Gaiser, Wunder* 2004). The targets on the strategy map feature traffic lights according to the level of implementation of the strategy determined using key figures to enable transparent reporting of the current status (cf. **Fig. 3.19**).

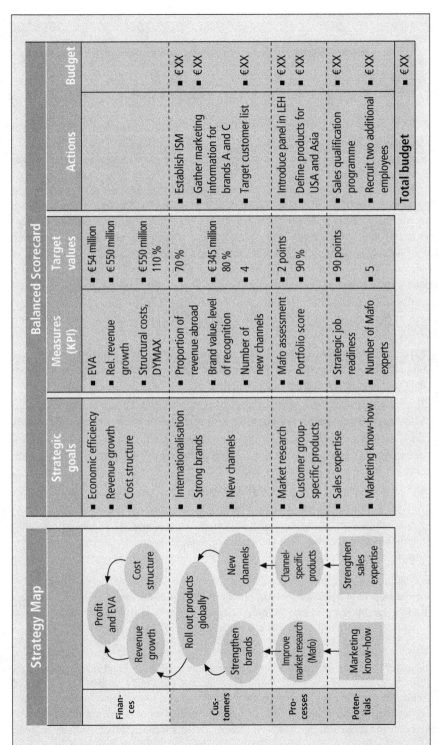

Fig. 3.18: Complete Balanced Scorecard concept (based on *Kaplan, Norton* 2004, p. 47)

Which cause-effect relationships exist between the strategic objectives of your company?

The scope of the Balanced Scorecard is based on vision and strategy. At its centre is the strategic orientation of all corporate goals and activities, down to employee level. Linking the goals with corporate strategy ensures that every employee contributes to achievement of these goals. This enables managers to evaluate their company's performance quickly and comprehensively. Key financial indicators that reflect the results of previous activities are also taken into account. However, these are supplemented by operating figures relating to customer satisfaction, internal processes and possible ways of improving performance and promoting innovation. It is important, however, that strategic goals are not isolated when featuring next to each other on a Balanced Scorecard, but that – as shown in the figure – they are connected to each other and with the company's vision.

The following **phase model** illustrates the process of implementation and the key activities to be performed when structuring a Balanced Scorecard (cf. *Horváth & Partners* 2007, pp. 74 et seqq.):

> First, the organisational framework must be created so that successful implementation can be guaranteed. This includes, among other things, defining areas of application and structuring the organisation and progress of the project.
>
> The strategic fundamentals must be clarified, i. e. top management must at least have a consistent understanding of the strategic direction and anchor the BSC in strategy development.
>
> Only now does the actual development of the Balanced Scorecard begin by deriving strategic goals and a strategy map that builds on them, as well as defining performance indicators, target figures and actions.
>
> The roll-out of the BSC begins with the definition of a structure that breaks down into subordinate units and coordinates the units that are next to each other in the BSC.
>
> Finally, the continuous application of the BSC must be guaranteed. This is done by integrating it into the existing management and control systems, planning and reporting, among other things.

Management cooperation with the development of the BSC is a key part of the concept. It is often helpful to consult experienced external consultants too, as they are often met with more openness and clarity in interviews and workshops and their important practical experience from other Balanced Scorecard projects can be put to use.

Meanwhile, many successful practical examples have shown that linking value-orientated management with the Balanced Scorecard enables a consistently value-orientated process of strategy identification, formulation and implementation to be realised. The Balanced Scorecard makes the company's strategy tangible and real for everyone, while the value-orientated approach makes the effect of strategic decisions on the company's value clear and underpins them with facts. The value-orientated approach thus forms the strategic basis that the Balanced Scorecard adopts, lays down in concrete terms, communicates

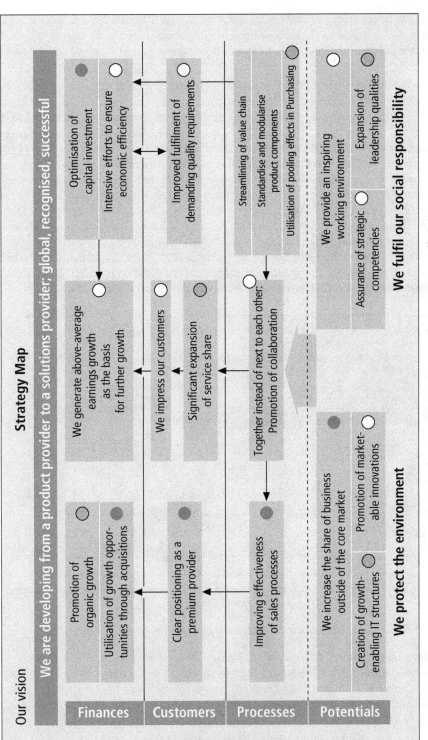

Fig. 3.19: Example of a strategy map with status information using traffic lights

within the company and implements operationally. It is in this way that value-generating potential is exploited throughout the entire organisation, with the strongly finance-focused company value-orientated approach being completed by a consistent, balanced concept.

During the value-based orientation of the Balanced Scorecard, the fiscal value drivers with the greatest influence on the increase in company value are first identified based on the value lever model and sensitivity analyses presented. These are directly incorporated into the financial perspective of the Balanced Scorecard. A prerequisite for the development of further value drivers is the value-based strategic direction of the company. Based on this direction, the strategic goals are clearly formulated in concrete terms. These are analysed and prioritised in terms of their relevance as value drivers. When doing so, every concrete strategic goal is evaluated in terms of relevance to the company value (What influence does the goal have on the increase in company value?) and its necessity for action (Are changes required to achieve relevant, value-orientated goals and does the status quo absolutely have to be maintained?). If the strategic goal is of high priority, it is a value driver relevant to the BSC. There should not be more than 15 of these to ensure that business management can focus on the essentials. **Fig. 3.20** illustrates the process of developing the most important strategic value drivers.

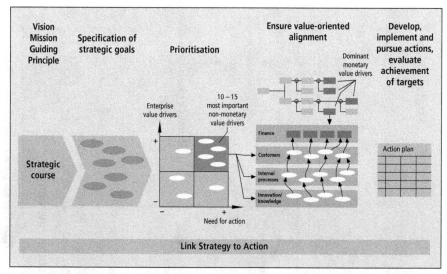

Fig. 3.20: Process of value-orientated management with the Balanced Scorecard (cf. *Voggenreiter, Jochen* 2002, p. 619)

3.3.6 Strategy anchoring and strategy controlling

Developing Balanced Scorecards and linking them with value driver management, as well as defining plans of action, are the first key steps towards strategy anchoring. However, these instruments should not only be used once during the development phase, but must be integrated into the company's management systems and into an ongoing process. Controlling has a particularly important role in this regard.

This means that both value management and the Balanced Scorecard become parts of "value-orientated controlling". This creates a conflict between the priorities of the corporate environment (e. g. customers, employee representation, the tax authority, the general public) on the one hand and the capital lenders (particularly the shareholders) on the other hand (cf. **Fig. 3.21**). Goals for increasing the shareholder value and potential for success arise from the strategy and must be integrated into the process of strategic and operational planning (cf. *Greiner* 2004 and *Gaiser, Greiner* 2003). Financial planning for equity and borrowed capital has – as described – a considerable influence on the expected minimum return. Strategy implementation is systematically monitored via the process of reporting and control. This also includes revising targets during Balanced Scorecard reviews.

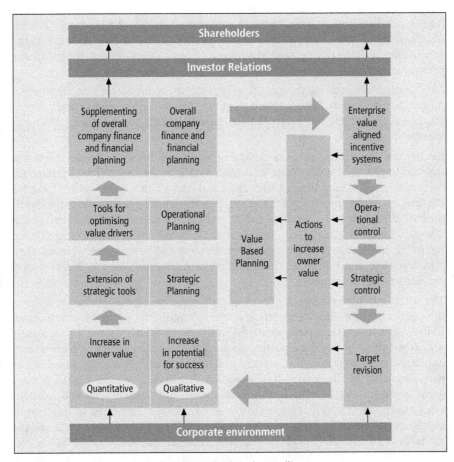

Fig. 3.21: Value-based controlling

A process has often already been defined for strategic planning. This must be modified when using the Balanced Scorecard. The strategic goals are defined by developing or revising the BSC and are quantified with target figures.

In mid-term planning, the strategic goals are implemented in concrete programmes and tasks in the form of key figures.

One statement made by mid-term planning would be, for example, that by year N+3, a special product line would be introduced for the USA. To this end, the development would have to be completed by year N+1, and by year N+2, the necessary production capacities would have to be ready.

A mid-term plan is usually structured as a rolling plan. This means that every year, the plan is reviewed and the planning horizon is moved forward by one year into the future. This revolving plan system means that plan figures are updated yearly and ensures that the plan corresponds to the latest information.

In the next stage of planning, the detailed annual plan is derived from year 1 of the mid-term plan. The mid-term plan thus assumes an intermediary role between strategic planning and annual planning. Their task is to convert strategic projects and medium-term key figures into concrete measures for the next financial year. By deriving the annual plan from the strategic and longer-term considerations, the operating activities performed in a fiscal year are aimed at achieving the strategic goals.

Clear operational goals for the next fiscal year are set in the annual plan for all those responsible. The annual plan is a planning calculation, i.e. the plans for the higher stages are converted into concrete figures. Expected results for the financial year are specified in detail.

Usually, the resources available for budgeting have largely been determined in terms of their use by personnel costs, amortisation, etc. So that the strategy can be implemented, parts of the budget (e.g. 10 to 15 %) must be reserved for strategic measures from the BSC and necessary investments. Therefore, it is also important that when developing the BSC, the necessary expenditure and investments are actually estimated and noted. The parameters of value-based management, i.e. value added, capital commitment, etc. in the current assets and minimum return must also be taken into account when planning. Here, controlling has the task of attending to these issues for mathematical plausibility and completeness.

The successful implementation of strategy and value management must be ensured throughout the year. Regular reporting on the key figures for operating activities and analysis of deviation from plans are useful for this (operational control). This is usually performed monthly. Regular reporting on progress in relation to targets, performance indicators and actions from the Balanced Scorecard is usually executed quarterly or, in part, also monthly, if necessary. It is in this way that strategy implementation is monitored (strategic control). The development of key value-based figures and financial value drivers is also largely subjected to a quarterly check. When doing so, it is a major restraint that balance sheet figures – that is, data related to the operating assets and the capital costs – are ideally provided in quarterly financial statements, but can hardly ever be provided monthly. With regard to reporting and control, Controlling has the task of acquiring and preparing information, and often interpreting it for management too. Increasingly, the controller is also needed as a creative sparring partner and provider of ideas during the development of countermeasures. The importance of management-orientated presentation of information – i.e. supported by graphics, and compact – should not be underestimated either. This usually results in a significant increase in acceptance of the controlling function within the company. In many companies, the controller – together with the IT department – initially has a "system-building" role. The requirements of an IT solution, e.g. for BSC reporting, must be established and suitable tools must be selected (cf. *Bange et al.* 2004) (cf. chapter 2.7.7 on the process of selecting standard software). Meeting all of the needs of the Balanced Scorecard concept using software solutions is completely different. This issue also inspired Horváth & Partners, together with MIS AG, to provide an application that fully did the concept justice.

The contents of the Balanced Scorecard are – once created – not applicable forever. During BSC reviews, it should – as a starting point – be reviewed whether changing conditions, new strategic priorities or the handling of goals that are temporarily being focused on require different content (target revision). In this process, the controller must, on the one hand, ensure that a BSC review is held in the first place. On the other hand, he/she provides the necessary information and occasionally acts as a moderator for the BSC review too.

 How do you supervise strategy implementation?

"Make strategy a daily task for everyone!" was a key statement made by the BSC inventors *Kaplan* and *Norton*. Should this be the case, it is not enough for a few managers (executive board or management, company development, Controlling) to understand what is meant. Middle-level management down to the heads of departments and groups, technicians and foremen, and, ultimately, all employees must be taken along on the "path to the goal". To this end, two fundamental components apply:

- Communicating and providing training on the purpose, benefits, method and employees' own contributions in relation to the concepts of Balanced Scorecard and value-orientated management.
- Connecting strategic company or department goals with employees' individual targets using incentive systems and target agreements (cf. *Horváth & Partners,* eds., 2005b and *Currle, Witzemann* 2004).

The HR department is usually consulted as a coordinator with regard to these issues. However, due to his/her profound knowledge of methods and content, the controller should also make a significant contribution. The order of the components is not accidental. "Develop" first, then "challenge", as the saying goes.

The first step must be to create understanding and acceptance. This is primarily achieved through direct communication between management and employees, e. g. during corporate events/roadshows. Ultimately, it is the executive board or management who are responsible for the strategy and must advocate it credibly. A number of other means of communication have proven to be successful in practice: articles in employee newsletters, posters in the company restaurant, the strategy map as a mousepad, and many more. Take the time to choose clear measures that are specific to the target group. After all, the "first impression" made when conveying business concepts that are perceived as being difficult to understand is one of the critical factors of success.

It makes sense and is necessary to integrate the goals of organisation into the incentive system as a second step, i. e. after conveying the "why" and "how". The incentive system includes the target agreement as well as monetary and non-monetary compensation. Target agreements and non-monetary remuneration are usually also possible where sanctioning through collective labour agreements or the personnel law in the public services sector is difficult. Individual target agreements contain strategic goals and measures for the employee's area of responsibility – usually from the perspective of finances, customers and processes. Targets from the perspective of potential are easily connected with the employee's individual targets related to qualifications and career development. Finally, operational goals and tasks, such as those from the job description or the budget, also play a role. Connecting these targets with monetary and non-monetary remuneration creates an entirely personal incentive to behave in compliance with the strategy. As a result, strategy anchoring can thus be ensured or at least greatly supported.

3.4 Practical example

3.4.1 Prints GmbH[3]

"Prints GmbH" is a strategic business unit of High Tech Group Electronics AG. It deals with the development, manufacturing and distribution of copiers.

The parent company, High Tech Group Electronics AG, primarily operates in Europe and America from the head office in Hamburg and employs over 45,000 employees worldwide. The range of products and services includes, in particular, the development, production and marketing of audiovisual hardware, lighting technology, installation and automobile technology, communications and security technology, telecommunications and a range of other related business areas. Due to a cumbersome organisational structure, the company was fundamentally reorganised in 2011. Prints GmbH emerged from this as an independent company.

Prints GmbH, based in Munich, combines all copier development, manufacturing and marketing activities and has 2,300 members of staff. The Prints GmbH product range is broadly diversified and ranges from copiers in the mass market segment (e. g. desktop copiers for offices) to demanding industrial applications. Turnover has now increased to approximately 700 million euros.

Since the reorganisation, the management of Prints GmbH has set itself ambitious goals. Due to unsatisfactory results in previous years, the management decided to use the Balanced Scorecard concept to consistently achieve a strategic position.

3.4.2 Project: Development of a Balanced Scorecard

Prints GmbH followed a systematic procedure to develop the Balanced Scorecard. In order to do so, the strategic direction of Prints GmbH was determined before the strategic goals were deduced. Starting with the relevant strategic goals, they were combined in a strategy map, and the cause and effect relationships were determined. For operationalisation and anchoring in the company, measurement parameters were selected, target figures for the measurement parameters were set and strategic activities were defined:

---

[3] This practical example reflects practical experience gained from numerous consulting projects for the implementation of Balanced Scorecards. All company and industry information given here is deliberately fictitious.

Due to the significant change at Prints GmbH during the restructuring, it was very important to clarify its strategic direction. The management decided to hold a workshop and personal interviews for strategic clarification.

The findings discussed demonstrate the strategic direction of Prints GmbH:

- Clear commitment to a **dual strategy** on the customer side. Prints GmbH aims to successfully supply copiers not just in the mass market segment but also in the high-price segment.

- Development will be towards the higher priced segments. In the dual strategy areas, a higher **price level** will be justified by strictly aligning the products with customer requirements and **improving image** related to the functional reliability of the copiers.

- Prints GmbH intends to become the **cost leader** in the **mass market segment**.

- The process orientation of Prints GmbH should be of a **model nature**.

- Prints GmbH will grow **sustainably** with its employees.

Following the strategic clarification workshops, the management of Prints met to derive a strategic target system for the Balanced Scorecard. They began by gathering together their ideas for strategic goals, based on brainstorming with the managers. A total of 135 target proposals were compiled. To reduce the targets to a manageable number of about 20 targets, the proposals were discussed intensively. The subsequent categorisation of the targets enabled the targets to be selected and thus the important targets to be focused on. Four categories were formed for this purpose:

- **"Fundamental goals"** (if the target proposal was too general for the Balanced Scorecard)

- **"Strategic goals"** (for the goals that would be included in the Balanced Scorecard)

- **"Possible strategic action"** (for target proposals that seemed to be too specific) and

- **"Operational goals"** (for goals that facilitated the maintenance of current operations instead).

Categorisation helps to increase the effectiveness and quality of the Balanced Scorecard, as only targets that are appropriate to the strategy are carried forward. After the targets compiled during brainstorming have been categorised, they are grouped into the four dimensions (finances, customers, processes and potential) of a Balanced Scorecard. 16 targets were defined.

Based on the strategic goals, the management of Prints developed its strategy's cause and effect chain. The resulting cause and effect chains should reflect the causality of the strategic considerations.

For the discussion, the project team prepared documents in which the targets are arranged in the dimensions to facilitate discussion in the workshop.

The specific interrelationships between the individual goals were discussed intensively. The result of the workshop is the strategy map, in which the goals and their interrelationships are illustrated visually (see arrows). This was then compared with the strategic directions of Prints GmbH and amended. Employees' suggestions and concerns were recorded and discussed at all times to illustrate the goals and their interrelationships as precisely as possible. The final strategy map, which the workshop participants approved, is provided in **Fig. 3.22**.

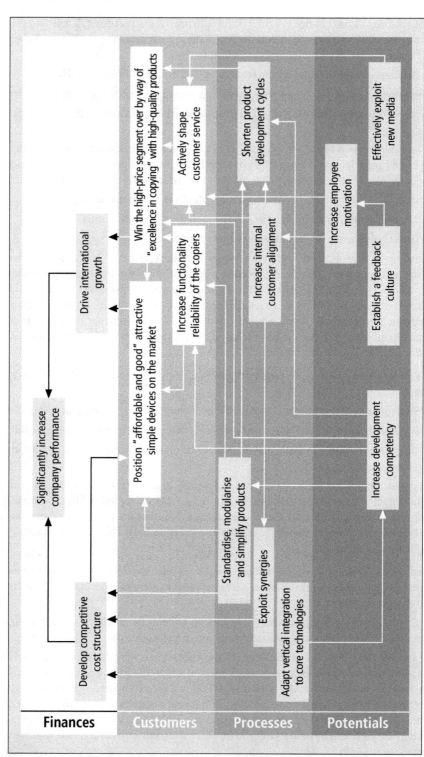

Fig. 3.22: Prints GmbH strategy map

The cause/effect relationships illustrated in the strategy map were promptly recorded in a "Story of the Strategy". For example, target connections within Prints GmbH's goal "Create a competitive cost structure" are explained:

A competitive cost structure is created as an initial strategic lever by way of three fundamental elements:

- Standardise, modularise and simplify products
- Exploit synergies
- Adapt vertical integration to core technologies

Standardising, modularising and refining means significantly reducing the parts used as well as more intensive use of common parts. Additionally, stronger modules will be defined and used in all devices in the future. Refining primarily means reviewing the functionalities and product features of devices in the mass-market segment to identify and reverse over-engineering in the past.

The conversion of the company offers good opportunities to exploit synergies by avoiding the duplication of work. However, cooperation between the departments must meet the requirements of a process-orientated company. This should be ensured by way of stricter internal process orientation.

Adapting production to core technologies allows alternative suppliers' cost advantages to be exploited. These core technologies have not yet been defined precisely. Building on this, it is important to check whether individual production stages can be outsourced abroad.

Concentrating on core technologies will not just lead to positive effects in production but also in development. This would make it possible to focus on fewer developmental core areas than before.

Regardless of the emphasis on these three fundamental levers for adapting Prints GmbH's cost structure, however, it is still necessary to continuously explore and take opportunities for reducing costs in all departments.

Based on the target system developed, the management of Prints GmbH laid down performance indicators for the Balanced Scorecard. This is the only way of ensuring that the strategic goals are clear and unmistakable. By setting a performance indicator and a target figure, the strategic goal is described completely. For example, the dimension "customer perspective" is illustrated at this point:

Customer perspective				
Strategic goal	Performance indicator	Unit	Actual value	Target value (3-year horizon)
"Affordable but good": Position attractive simple devices on the market	Market share in the mass market segment (core markets)	%	9	15
	Retailer rating (points scale from 0 to 120)		69	110
	% copiers whose functions can be learned in half a day	%	30	80

Customer perspective				
"Excellence in copying": Win the high-price segment over with high-quality products	Market share in the high-price segment (core markets)	%	9	17
	Customers image value	Index points	45	80
	Level of recognition	%	28	60
Increase functionality reliability of the copiers	Average number of failures per copier per month	#	18	5
Actively shape customer service	Repeated sales rate in the high-price segment	%	55	75
	Visits/target customer		1.3	2.5

Fig. 3.23: Target values of the dimension "customer perspective" of Prints GmbH

The management of Prints GmbH developed the strategic actions it considered necessary to implement the strategic goals. After performing a resource estimation and prioritisation, the management presented a plan of action. **Fig. 3.24** gives this as an example for the customer's dimension.

Customer perspective					
Strategic goal	Strategic activities	Start date	End date	Responsible	Status
"Affordable but good": Position attractive simple devices on the market	Marketing campaign "The copier that can't be copied" (including new information materials for retailers)	01/2015	05/2000 (Drafts) 12/2015 (Campaign)	Mr Krug	Approved
	Hold retailer forum	03/2015	05/2015	Mr Kriger	Approved
	Revive rebate system	01/2015	06/2015	Mr Kriger	Approved
"Excellence in copying": Win the high-price segment over with high-quality products	Design offensive	06/2015	06/2016	Mr Mayer	Approved
	New marketing material "The Mercedes of copiers"	03/2015	06/2015	Mr Krug	In alignment
	Direct mailing to target customers Advertising offensive in business magazines	06/2015	07/2015	Ms Silblinger	In alignment
Increase functionality reliability of the copiers	Set up "No Excuses" project group	03/2015	03/2016	Dipl. Ing. Hoffmann	Approved
	RCP technical conversion	01/2015	06/2016	Dipl. Ing. Huber	In alignment

Customer perspective					
Strategic goal	Strategic activities	Start date	End date	Responsi-ble	Status
Actively shape customer service	Set up Key Account Management	06/2015	12/2016	Ms Brommel	Approved
	Put yearly sales meeting under the motto "After sales – our lost opportu-nities"	01/2015	05/2015	Mr Sale	Approved
	Training offensive 2015	05/2015	06/2016	Mr Sale	Approved
	Unburdening of sales from back office activities (see "Prints 2018" project)	07/2014	08/2015	Mr Sale	Approved (ongoing project)

Fig. 3.24: Strategic actions of Prints GmbH from the customer's perspective

3.4.3 Lessons learned

The following lessons learned can be derived from similar projects on the development of a Balanced Scorecard:

- To guarantee the high quality and effectiveness of the Balanced Scorecard it is very important to perform review and amendments during Balanced Scorecard develop-ment. Accordingly, deriving strategic goals is of high importance.
- As the cause/effect relationships are an important means of communication, they must be clear and well-founded. The company should focus on a small number of relevant cause/effect relationships.
- Ideally, the Balanced Scorecard will include innovative performance indicators, even though the cost of implementation can be high. However, these indicators often have the advantage or recording the target to be measured better.
- The targets should indeed encourage employees but not overwhelm them. Therefore, targets are ideally formed by including employees.
- No strategic activities may be determined without assigning responsibilities. Only in this way can behaviour be influenced and the effectiveness of strategic activities be guaranteed.

3.5 Organisational checklist for managers and controllers

Create clarity about the strategy alternatives your company has.

Connect your strategic corporate objectives using a Strategy Map and a Balanced Scorecard.

Connect your strategic planning with operative planning using multi-year planning.

Further reading

If you would like to know more about the field of strategic planning, read:

Coenenberg, A., Salfeld, R. (2007), Wertorientierte Unternehmensführung [Value-Orientated Management], 2nd ed., Stuttgart 2007.

If you would like to know more about strategy description using Balanced Scorecards, read

Horváth & Partners (eds., 2007), Balanced Scorecard umsetzen [Implement a Balanced Scorecard], 4th ed., Stuttgart 2007.

4 Operative Planning, Budgeting and Forecasting

4.1 Chapter objectives

This chapter aims to present the reader with instructions on how to design effective operative planning, budgeting and forecasting. After studying the chapter, readers should understand and be able to apply the functions and tasks of these three tools.

Fig. 4.1: Chapter objectives – Operative planning, budgeting and forecasting

4.2 Introduction

While companies may perceive economic profit as a key objective, on closer examination corporate planning in many companies often lacks consistent, systematic profit planning. Instead, the focus is on planning actions (for example investment measures). Frequently, individual departments are given no requirements which could highlight their key contribution to profit. This prevents both profit-focused monitoring and variation analysis, nor can the consequences of decisions on profit be measured. And this happens in spite of the fact that ensuring a company's success and increasing its efficiency are the main roles of operative planning, alongside risk identification and reduction, as well as increasing flexibility and reducing complexity. A profit planning system (budgeting), which has been coordinated to clearly match action planning, must therefore form the heart of an effective controlling system.

Find out below how to effectively design operative planning, budgeting and forecasting.

4 Operative Planning, Budgeting and Forecasting

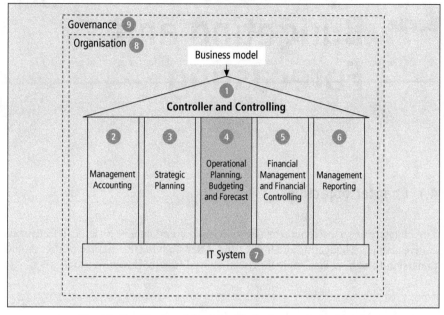

Fig. 4.2: Classification of the chapter in the "House of Controlling"

4.3 Designing effective operative planning

During **operative planning**, the targets for the planning period are defined and different alternative ways to achieve them are developed.

Developing the detailed measures needed to achieve the targets, as well as their quantification, are at the heart of operative planning. Each corporate unit requires a plan, which must clearly and quantitatively set out the targets that the unit must achieve as output, costs, income etc.

All individual plans are combined to make up the planning result for the upcoming financial year.

Do you derive your operative planning from strategic planning?

Do you link your operative planning with finance planning?

Do you take forecast values into account when planning?

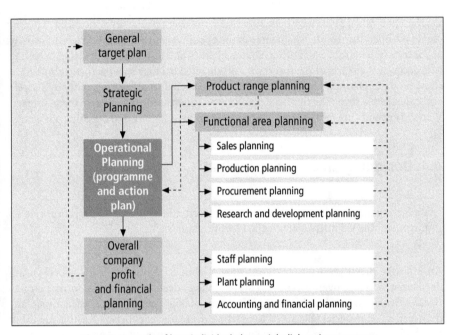

Fig. 4.3: Example of how individual plans might link up in a company

State-of-the-art operative planning should start by stating objectives or at least by choosing benchmarks ("frontloading"). These targets are then used to compile sales and revenue plans. The Sales department must then specify the number of items it predicts will be sold in the coming year for each product type. In addition to operative planning of sales volumes, the planned prices for the individual products must also be determined. The sales plan is the main input source for the production plan. The number of items to be produced is calculated by comparing the planned volume required and the current volume produced and then either increasing or reducing production to achieve the planned inventory.

This production programme must then be broken down into bills of material and work schedules based on capacity. The bills of material are then broken down to determine the raw materials needed and the components that must be purchased to fulfil the planned production programme. This information forms the main input source for deducing the procurement plan. Again, planning must take into account the planned inventories of production materials.

When broken down into work schedules, the production programme can be used to calculate direct wage hours and equipment time. Employee and equipment capacities available for each workspace are compared with staff planning to determine capacity excess and shortfalls. Excess/shortfalls can impact staff and investment planning. If any bottlenecks identified in the short term cannot be removed, the production programme might need to be changed.

The production plan is used as a starting point for cost planning. A distinction is made between unit costs and overheads. Overheads are normally planned by cost element and cost centre. A first step consists of determining the primary cost centre costs, followed by charging secondary cost centre costs using internal cost allocation.

Once all individual plans have been submitted, the result plans can be deduced. This includes the operating result, which sets out the operative expenditure and income, usually as contribution margin accounting. Financial profit and loss is then calculated by taking into account the planned neutral result. A budgeted balance sheet is then compiled to show how the planned business activities are expected to affect the company's assets and capital structure. The financial plan is used to assess the budget's financial impact. Planned expenditure and income are converted into incoming and outgoing payments.

4.4 Designing an effective budget

> **Budgeting** means focusing all of a company's activities on value-adding corporate targets. In the US, this is often called "profit planning".

An effective profit plan sets out consistent contributions to profit for all corporate departments. In the overall planning system, the budget focuses on the formal targets which can be expressed as the company's financial objectives. By contrast, action planning focuses on material objectives. In practice, the boundaries between action planning and budgeting are blurred, as value-adding targets can only reasonably be planned alongside the required actions.

Literature offers different definitions of budgeting. In this context, budgeting describes the entire budgeting process, i.e. in particular compiling, issuing, and monitoring budgets as well as variation analysis. The budgeting system is thus the subsystem of the planning and monitoring system to which any planning and monitoring related to formal targets can be allocated.

4.4.1 Budget system

> A **budget** is a plan formulated in value-adding parameters, which a decision-making unit is bound to apply for a defined period of time with a specific degree of commitment.

Based on this definition, we can distinguish between the following features:

- Feature **Decision-making unit**:
  - horizontal differentiation based on functions, products, regions or projects
  - vertical differentiation based on corporate hierarchy levels

- Feature **Validity period**, for example:
  - monthly budget
  - quarterly budget
  - annual budget
  - multi-year budget
- Feature **Value dimension**, for example:
  - spending budget
  - cost budget
  - contribution margin budget
  - revenue budget

We also distinguish between fixed and flexible budgets. Fixed budgets assume a specific utilisation level, whereas flexible budgets differentiate between requirements based on utilisation. Flexible budgets are used particularly by manufacturing cost centres. Traditional budget types, for example, include the annual budget of an advertising department or the monthly budget of a manufacturing cost centre.

Taken together, the coordinated individual budgets make up the budget system.

The budget system also includes condensed individual budgets.

Budgets can be condensed in three ways:

- budgeted P&L statement,
- financial resources budget (financial plan),
- budgeted balance sheet.

When designing the budget system, the relationship between the individual budgets and between the different budget components must be determined. The budget structure should be chosen based on the principle of budget responsibility. Each budget component must be clearly marked as the responsibility of a specific person. To ensure that the budget system is accepted and consistent, it should cover all company departments and roles. This is also a prerequisite for creating individual budgets which can be consolidated to make up the budgeted P&L, balance sheet and cash flow statement. This is called integrated financial planning, i.e. the integration of the budgeted balance sheet, budgeted P&L and budgeted cash flow statement. These three must be components of the budget system to ensure that the effects on the overarching profit and liquidity targets become apparent. In practice, the budget system structure is often based on the organisational structure. For instance, the budgeted P&L is usually compiled by Controlling, whereas the budgeted balance sheet and budgeted cash flow statement are normally the responsibility of Financial Accounting.

To determine the budget structure, the budget must also provide the right level of detail and be sufficiently differentiated regarding timing. There is no one-size-fits-all solution. Instead, the budget must match the company's individual characteristics. For instance, a high production proportion often means that production budgets must be split into production level budgets for manufacturing, sub-assembly and final assembly. Where company revenue is subject to strong seasonal fluctuations throughout the budget year, real monthly budgets might be required, whereas for constant revenue, it might be sufficient to divide annual revenue by 12.

Fig. 4.4 summarises the main design features of a budget system.

Which design characteristics do you consider in your budgeting system?

	Elements of budgeting	Description	
Core budgeting (narrow)	Budgeted timetable	Written guidelines regarding standardisation of the budgeting process: Standardised terms and contexts, responsibility (personnel-related), general and current schedule, cost element and cost centre plan (including cost element groups), instructions on how to determine the functional plans (e.g. standardisation of staff planning, costing time calculation), tools (e.g. forms, files), requirements, previous year's results & extrapolations etc.	**Extended budgeting (broad)**
	Functional plans	Plans for the individual functional areas/departments to achieve the internally/top down defined targets on a quantity basis.	
	Performance budget	Profit plan based on the P&L/contribution margin accounting for each expense type/cost element and cost centre.	
	Financial plan	Planned asset and capital position from the performance budget and financial plan.	
	Budget negotiations	One or more rounds of negotiations to consult on and/or coordinate the subplans/budgets and achieve the desired overall objectives/budgets.	
	Classic variance analysis	Analysis of planned/actual variances (total variance) and/or target/actual variances (price, sales, consumption, operating rate and/or special consumption variances (e.g. bills of material, intensity, procedural variance).	
	Future-oriented variance analysis (Forecasting)	Extrapolation of cumulative actual values (e.g. January to May) within a year over the expected final value for the year (date). Indicates expected developments and reinforces existing variance and, thus, pressure to act. Also referred to as preview or calculation; procedures are backward-looking, according to forecasts or plan-oriented.	
	Rolling Forecast	Current plan-oriented determination of forecast over a fixed period instead of up to a fixed date (e.g. always one year or six quarters into the future); often on a quarterly basis, whereby imminent quarters are planned more specifically. May (partially) replace traditional planning/budgeting.	

Fig. 4.4: Elements of budgeting (see *Gleich et al.* 2009, p. 62)

Fig. 4.5 below shows a company's budget system (also see the numerical example in **Fig. 4.6** to **4.10**)

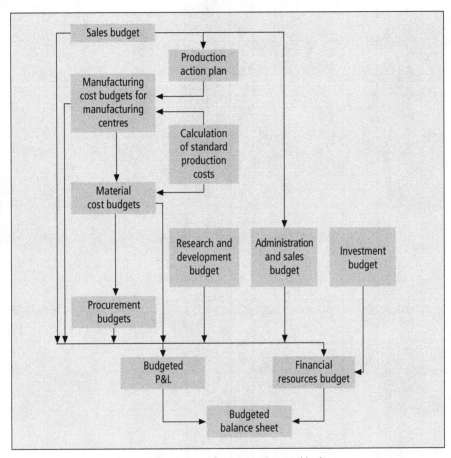

Fig. 4.5: Example structure of a company's annual budget system

Sales budget

Product	Sales volume	Price	Sales revenue
A*	7,000	80	560,000
B*	5,000	120	600,000
C*	4,000	110	440,000
			1,600,000

Production action plan

Product	Sales volume	Budgeted final inventory	Initial inventory	Quantity to be produced
A*	7,000	700	900	6,800
B*	5,000	500	200	5,300
C*	4,000	400	400	4,000

Manufacturing cost budgets for manufacturing centres

| | Manufacturing centre 1 | | | | Manufacturing centre 2 | | | | Manufacturing centre 3 | | | |
| | Standard hours | | Standard costs | | Standard hours | | Standard costs | | Standard hours | | Standard costs | |
	per hour	total	fixed	variable	per hour	total	fixed	variable	per hour	total	fixed	variable
1		11,000	66,000	44,000		14,000	56,000	56,000		13,000	260,000	65,000
2			6.00	4.00			4.00	4.00			20.00	5.00
3	1.00	6,800	40,800	27,200	1.2	8,160	32,640	32,640	0.1	680	13,600	3,400
4	0.6	3,180	19,080	12,720	0.8	4,240	16,960	16,960	1.2	6,360	127,200	31,800
5	0.2	800	4,800	3,200	0.2	800	3,200	3,200	0.5	2,000	40,000	10,000
6		10,780	64,680	43,120		13,200	52,800	52,800		9,040	180,800	45,200
7		220	1,320			800	3,200			3,960	179,200	

Row	Manufacturing centre 4				Manufacturing centre 5				Total manufacturing costs budget		
	Standard hours		Standard costs		Standard hours		Standard costs				
	per item	total	fixed	variable	per item	total	fixed	variable	fixed	variable	Total
1		8,000	80,000	80,000		12,000	48,000	144,000	510,000	389,000	899,000
2			10.00	10.00			4.00		121,040		
3	0.3	2,040	20,400	20,400	0.5	3,400	13,600	121,040	207,760	124,040	245,480
4	0.8	4,240	42,400	42,400	0.1	530	2,120	207,760		110,240	318,000
5	0.2	800	8,000	8,000	2.0	8,000	32,000	88,000	88,000	120,400	208,400
6		7,080	70,800	70,800		11,930	47,720	416,800	416,800	355,080	771,880
7		920	9,200			70	280	93,200	93,200		93,200

Fig. 4.6: Example of a budget system I (*Ulrich et al.* 1994, pp. 87 ff.)

Row 1 = Standard costs of normal capacity

Row 2 = Per hour

Row 3 = Standard time and costs of manufacturing 6800 A*

Row 4 = Standard time and costs of manufacturing 5300B*

Row 5 = Standard time and costs of manufacturing 4000C*

Row 6 = Total standard hours and standard manufacturing costs*

Row 7 = Capacity usage variance for fixed costs

Cost of materials budget

Material quantities and values

	Number of items to be produced	Type I — per item	Type I — Total	Type I — Standard value (1.00 per kg)	Type II — per item	Type II — Total	Type II — Standard value (2.00 per kg)	Type III — per item	Type III — Total	Type III — Standard value (3.00 per kg)	Type IV — per item	Type IV — Total	Type IV — Standard value (4.00 per kg)	Total cost of materials
		Standard volume in kg			Standard volume in kg			Standard volume in kg			Standard volume in kg			
A *	6,800	4	27,200	27,200	1	6,800	13,600	1	6,800	20,400	0	0	0	61,200
B *	5,300	0	0	0	2	10,600	21,200	3	15,900	47,700	1	5,300	21,200	90,100
C *	4,000	2	8,000	8,000	0	0	0	0	0	0	4	16,000	64,000	72,000
Material consumption during production				35,200			34,800			68,100			85,200	223,300

Procurement budget

Material quantities and values

	Type I		Type II		Type III		Type IV		Total procurement budget
	Standard volume in kg Total	Standard value (1.00 per kg)	Standard volume in kg Total	Standard value (2.00 per kg)	Standard volume in kg Total	Standard value (3.00 per kg)	Standard volume in kg Total	Standard value (4.00 per kg)	
Material consumption by production	35,200	35,200	17,400	34,800	22,700	68,100	21,300	85,200	223,300
+ budgeted final inventory monthly consumption x2	5,866	5,866	2,900	5,800	3,783	11,349	3,550	14,200	37,215
− initial inventory	12,000	12,000	1,000	2,000	8,000	24,000	10,000	40,000	78,000
	29,066	29,066	19,300	38,600	18,483	55,449	14,850	59,400	182,515

Fig. 4.7: Example of a budget system II (*Ulrich et al.* 1994, pp. 87 ff.)

4 Operative Planning, Budgeting and Forecasting

Calculation of standard production costs

Cost of materials

Product		A*		B*		C*	
Material type	Standard price per kg	Standard volume per kg	Standard value	Standard volume per kg	Standard value	Standard volume per kg	Standard value
I	1.00	4	4.00	–	–	2	2.00
II	2.00	1	2.00	2	4.00	–	–
III	3.00	1	3.00	3	9.00	–	–
IV	4.00	–	–	1	4.00	4	16.00
Total			9.00		17.00		18.00

Manufacturing costs

Manu-facturing centre	Standard cost rate per hour		Standard time (hour)	Standard costs A*			Standard time (hour)	Standard costs B*			Standard time (hour)	Standard costs C*		
	fixed	vari-able		f	v	t		f	v	t		f	v	t
F¹	6.00	4.00	1.0	6.00	4.00	10.00	0.6	3.6	2.4	6.00	0.2	1.2	0.8	2.00
F²	4.00	4.00	1.2	4.8	4.8	9.6	0.8	3.2	3.2	6.4	0.2	0.8	0.8	1.6
F³	20.00	5.00	0.1	2.00	0.5	2.5	1.2	24.00	6.00	30.00	0.5	10.00	2.5	12.5
F⁴	10.00	10.00	0.3	3.00	3.00	6.00	0.8	0.8	8.00	16.00	0.2	2.00	2.00	4.00
F⁵	4.00	12.00	0.5	2.00	6.00	8.00	0.1	0.4	1.2	1.6	2.0	8.00	24.00	32.00
Total		–		17.8	18.3	36.1	–	39.2	20.8	60.00		22.00	30.1	52.1
Standard manufacturing costs per unit						45.1				77.00				70.1

Fig. 4.8: Example of a budget system III (*Ulrich et al.* 1994, pp. 87 ff.)

Research and development budget

Total (fixed) costs	. . . .	180,000
attributed to:	Product A*.	25,000
	B*.	10,000
	C*.	35,000
not attributable:	Project D*.	40,000
	E*.	70,000

Administration and sales budget

Total (fixed) costs	. . . .	140,000
attributed to:	Product A*.	10,000
	Product B*.	30,000
	Product C*.	20,000
not attributable:	. . . .	80,000
variable costs (commission, freight, various)		10 % of sales revenue

Budgeted P&L

	Total	A*	B*	C*
Sales volume		7,000	5,000	4,000
Sales price		80.00	120.00	110.00
Sales revenue	1,600,000	560,000	600,000	440,000
Volume produced		6,800	5,300	4,000
Standard production costs per unit		45.10	77.00	70.10
Standard production costs per production cycle	995,680	306,680	408,100	280,400
Change in inventory (quantity)		– 200	+ 300	0
Standard production costs of change in inventory	– 14,080	+ 9,020	– 23,100	0
Standard production costs of products sold	981,100	315,700	385,000	280,400
Attributable research costs	70,000	25,000	10,000	35,000
Attributable administration and sales costs (fixed)	60,000	10,000	30,000	20,000
Attributable variable administration and sales costs (10 % of revenue)	160,000	56,000	60,000	44,000
Total attributable costs	127,100	406,700	485,000	379,400
Gross profit (GP)	328,900	153,300	115,000	60,600

Fig. 4.9: Example of a budget system IV (*Ulrich et al.* 1994, pp. 87 ff.)

Non-attributable research costs	./. 110,000
Non-attributable administration and sales costs	./. 80,000
Capacity usage variance for manufacturing costs	./. 93,200
Net profits	./. 45,700

Investment budget

Property	50,000
Machinery and equipment	160,000
Total	210,000

4 Operative Planning, Budgeting and Forecasting

Financial resources budget

Opening balance	Cash, postal orders, bank balances		120,000
+ receipts	Sales revenue	1,600,000	
	+ Receivables opening balance	200,000	
	− Receivables closing balance		
	(= $^1/_6$ of sales revenue)	267,000	1,533,000
− Expenditure:	Materials purchased		182,515
	+ Total manufacturing costs	771,880	
	+ Capacity usage variance	93,200	
	+ R&D	180,000	
	+ Fixed administration and sales costs	140,000	
	+ Var. administration and distribution costs	160,000	
		1,345,080	
	− Depreciation on machinery	90,000	
	Property	60,000	1,195,080
	+ Investment spending		210,000
	+ Reduction in payables		10,200
	Total expenditure		1,597,795
Closing balance			55,205

Budgeted balance sheet

Assets	Opening balance	±	Closing balance
Liquid funds (cash, postal orders, bank balances)	120,000	− 64,795	55,205
Receivables	200,000	+ 67,000	267,000
Materials	78,000	− 40,785	37,215
Finished products	84,030	+ 14,080	98,110
Equipment, machinery	540,000	+ 70,000	610,000
Property	600,000	− 10,000	590,000
	1,622,030	+ 35,500	1,657,530
Liabilities	Opening balance	±	Closing balance
Payables	170,000	− 10,200	159,800
Loans	450,000	−.−	450,000
Equity including reserves	1,002,000		1,002,030
Profit	600,000	+ 45,700	45,700
	1,622,030	+ 35,500	1,657,530

Fig. 4.10: Example of a budget system V (*Ulrich et al.* 1994, pp. 87 ff.)

Again, planning starts with a sales budget. Three different products are produced and sold. If inventories are taken into account, an action plan for production can be drawn up, which in turn forms the basis of the manufacturing cost budget and of the cost of materials budget applying the standard material consumption per product unit. The procurement budget is based on the opening and closing balances of the cost of materials budget. Flexible budgeted costs are used to calculate the machine hourly rates for the manufacturing sites. The costs of materials and the manufacturing costs per unit are added together to determine standard production costs. A flat rate is used for fixed research and development costs, as well as for administration and sales costs, some of which are attributed to the products and some to the company as a whole. Taking all planned costs into account, these calculations can now be summarised in the budgeted P&L. This now allows for an investment plan to be drawn up, and the budget focus can now shift from mere imputed to cash-based accounting. Cash-based accounting comprises a financial resources budget and a budgeted balance sheet.

4.4.2 Budgeting process

Budgets can generally be derived in one of three processes: top-down, bottom-up or mixed (top-down/bottom-up) planning. Top-down (or "retrograde") planning looks at higher-level budgets in the budgeting process to derive lower-level budgets. By contrast, bottom-up (or "progressive") planning compiles higher-level budgets by summarising lower-level budgets starting with the lowest possible level. The first method offers the benefit of ensuring that the budget definitively incorporates a company's targets. The second method, on the other hand, encompasses greater awareness of details and higher motivation at lower ranks of the hierarchy. The mixed process attempts to combine the benefits of both methods.

The most commonly used method is the mixed process based on an initial top-down approach. In this method, company management sets the targets of the budgeting process, for example, benchmarks or planning assumptions, and the different departments then compile their budgets based on these requirements. This process is depicted schematically in **Fig. 4.11**.

Benchmarks are set in line with strategic planning and the resulting key parameters of multi-year planning. Benchmarks can also be influenced by specific targets which management has set for the year. Normally, values are extrapolated from the figures for the current year in order to take the current business situation into account.

Benchmarks basically translate the strategic objectives of management into specific targets for the upcoming financial year. This makes strategic planning an essential prerequisite for well-founded planning benchmarks. In practice, a Balanced Scorecard (BSC) can often be implemented as a highly effective way of linking strategic corporate objectives and operative planning. This defines strategic corporate objectives which subsequently form the basis of operative KPIs and ensure that operative planning is integrated into strategic planning.

The divisions and departments can use this to draw up their individual budgets. Their planning targets are based on the benchmarks set by management. Volumes must be used for planning wherever possible and where this makes sense. These volumes are then converted into values at a later stage. Since the individual budgets are often linked and mutually dependent, they can be coordinated closely during budget creation. Controlling offers budgeting advice to the different departments, provides budgeting information and tools, coordinates the individual budgets and works towards achieving the budget targets. An appropriate budgeting software is also essential, as many companies would struggle to handle the great complexity of planning and budgeting (for more on this topic, see, in particular, *Meier et al.* 2002).

4 Operative Planning, Budgeting and Forecasting

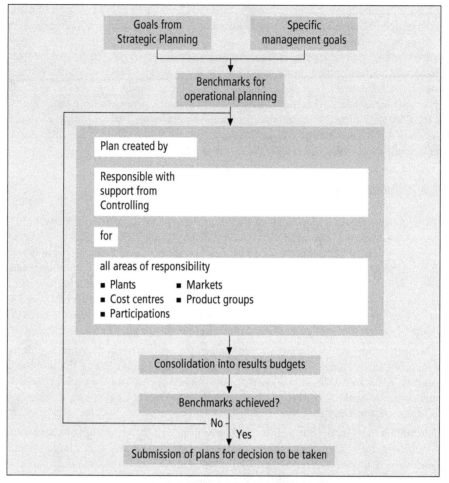

Fig. 4.11: Development of operational planning

Once the individual budgets are finalised, Controlling combines them to create a results budget. This instantly shows the extent to which the benchmarks are reached based on the current planning status. If the benchmarks are not reached, the budget must be adjusted to ensure that all possible opportunities are utilised. This means that Controlling must work with the different departmental budget officers to closely investigate the individual budgets with the goal of further increasing revenue or lowering costs using additional measures.

If the benchmarks have been achieved, or if it turns out to be impossible to achieve them in spite of all reasonable efforts, Controlling must prepare the budget for management. Management then decides whether to approve the budget in its current form. Especially where the benchmarks cannot be reached, management must decide whether the values chosen had been too high and must be corrected, or whether there is still room for improvement.

Traditional planning and budgeting is based on the premise that a company's environment tends to be predictable and foreseeable; as well as on the assumption that planners have sufficient information for precise budgeting. Nowadays, this is often not the case given shorter and shorter product life cycles and growing competition. Many external factors influence corporate decisions and hence planning and budgeting. The most important external factors in this context are complexity and dynamics:

- Environment complexity: The number of external factors that must be taken into account in a decision and how these differ from each other.

- Environment dynamics: How often, how regularly and how much these factors change.

- If an environment is both highly complex and highly dynamic, this is called turbulent. The opposite is a simple and stable environment.

The degree of turbulence is material in influencing the level of detail and the time horizon of the budget. The level of detail might thus vary, especially in diversified companies. It is necessary to regularly assess the business areas' environment (static, dynamic, turbulent) to find a reasonable level of detail. Detailed planning makes little sense in stable markets with a low degree of complexity and dynamic because this provides no additional information. In such instances, actual to actual comparisons with previous years suffice. By contrast, detailed planning over a period of 12 months plus an average additional planning period of four months is desirable in more turbulent markets, i. e. a total planning period of 16 months, but this is not really feasible as the planning would be out of date too quickly.

When a budget is approved, it becomes a valid basis for action for the upcoming fiscal year. If management only approves the budget subject to certain conditions, Controlling must incorporate these into the existing budget. Where the budget is rejected altogether, the planning cycle must recommence.

For decentralised budgeting to work, the basic information required to compile the budget must be available on time. Since interdependencies result in information from some budget components influencing others, and vice versa, simultaneous budgeting must be implemented. However, in practice, the complexity involved often turns budgeting into a successive process. The budgeting calendar is the most important tool for timely coordination. This sets out the exact times and responsibilities for the individual budgeting steps. The budgeting process will only run smoothly if all individual deliveries are on time, even though these budget areas interlink. Checkpoints might need to be incorporated where many items are codependent, to make it easier to coordinate the budgets later on.

Numerous budget planning tools are available to draw up budgets. Forecast methods are particularly important, given that budgets attempt to predict the future. These can, for example, be used to determine revenue in the period under review.

The different accounting instruments provide most of the information and are used as the main tools for most budgets.

- Investment budgets often also use investment methods.
- Manufacturing cost centres normally use standard costing for their budgets.
- R&D departments tend to rely on project planning methods (for example Earned Value analysis).
- Marketing budgets are frequently generated using product profit and market segment profitability statements.

4 Operative Planning, Budgeting and Forecasting

- These different short-term profit calculation methods can be used to deduce the budgeted profit and loss statement.

Budget Control is responsible for monitoring compliance with the budget. Target/actual comparisons are used to identify any deviations from the budget and to find the employees responsible for the relevant budget. However, the work of Budget Control must not end with identifying deviations. Its main task consists of revealing the causes. The different variance analysis methods mentioned above are the main budget monitoring tools, as countermeasures can only be devised after identifying what caused the deviations. This also closes the cycle consisting of planning, monitoring and correction.

The cost and profit accounting systems used determine which analysis tools are best suited to this task. For instance, if costs are calculated using flexible standard costing, then production in particular has a highly differentiated analysis system at its disposal. First, partial deviations are identified, and then their causes can be investigated in more detail, for example, using cause keys recorded in checklists.

But not only what caused the deviations matters: it is also essential to determine their significance. Special attention should be paid to any deviations which might sustainably affect the result or liquidity. Individual deviations can, for example, be weighted based on their impact on the result. Budget Control also uses various statistical methods. For instance, these can be used to evaluate the significance of deviations. Statistical methods also provide findings about future developments, for example, using trend analyses.

The planning process can also incorporate elements of "Better Budgeting", "Beyond Budgeting" and "Advanced Budgeting" to limit the cost of planning and budgeting and increase benefits (see **Fig. 4.12**).

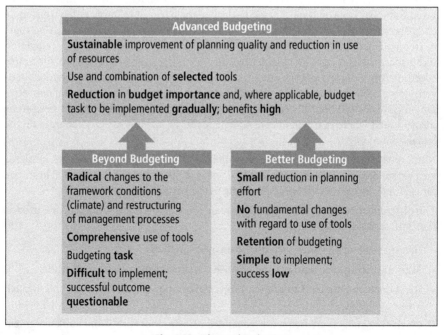

Fig. 4.12: Advanced Budgeting

Proponents of Better Budgeting do not tend to disagree with using traditional budgeting as a tool. Instead, this approach pursues the core aims of increasing efficiency and simplifying planning and budgeting. This evolutionary approach is characterised by small steps of incremental, permanent changes to planning and budgeting.

The proponents of Beyond Budgeting take a rather different approach. In 1998, the "Consortium for Advanced Manufacturing International (CAM-I)" tasked itself with developing a new management model for the transition from the industrial to the information age, as part of its "Beyond Budgeting Round Table Projects" (see *Bunce et al.* 2002, pp. 5 ff.). Its aim is to improve corporate management without using a budget. This is replaced with the following tools: Balanced Scorecard, Process-Oriented Performance Measurement, Benchmarking and Rolling Planning. However, Beyond Budgeting focuses on changing the mental attitude of managers. This corporate culture is characterised by adaptive management processes and subsidiarity in decision-making.

While traditional planning and budgeting may be criticised by some, they have generally been proven to be a successful tool. It therefore seems unlikely at least for the time being that they would disappear altogether, particularly in light of the fact that corporate culture tends to change rather more gradually.

Advanced Budgeting thus aims to reduce the importance of budgets in the medium-term, while raising budget quality and lowering budget costs in the short-term.

Modern budgeting uses six main recommendations, developed by the Modern Budgeting Expert Group of the International Association of Controllers (see *Gleich et al.* 2009). These recommendations are split into Processes and Structures, on the one hand, and Planning Contents, on the other hand (see **Fig. 4.13**).

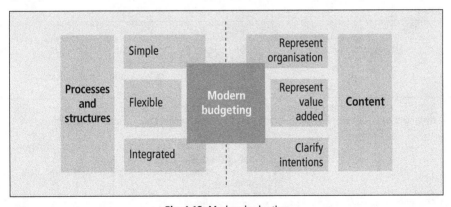

Fig. 4.13: Modern budgeting

The recommendations relating to Processes and Structures comprise suggestions on how to design planning processes and levels and on how to select planning tools. The key features are:

- **Simplicity:** Companies should disregard any content not relevant to control, use efficient processes and only implement effective IT tools and methods. More specifically, planning should be based on a limited number of input variables, such as utilisation rate in service business, which can then be used to deduce further variables.

- **Flexibility:** Companies should establish a corporate and leadership culture based on openness, realism and the willingness to implement changes during the year and to learn from mistakes. This can, for example, be achieved by using scenarios, setting relative targets or through rolling forecasts. During the year, it should also be possible to adapt budgets to changing circumstances without the need for long-winded, complicated coordination processes.

- **Integration:** Central planning systems, levels and deadlines in companies should be considered together and coordinated. This can, for example, be achieved by selecting only a limited number of highly specific, mutually dependent requirements.

For planning contents, modern budgeting recommendations include:

- **Mapping value creation:** Corporate planning should take into account the different steps of the value chain. This should be based on the targets, and on any bottlenecks and restrictions that are identified in relation to the company's profit and growth.

- **Mapping the organisation:** Companies should map the structural and process organisation in planning and budgeting. Specific clear targets and plans should be developed for each organisational unit. The targets and plans for each area should be based not on optimal departmental performance, but on the company's overall targets.

- **Highlighting intentions:** Companies should specify their targets such that all those affected clearly understand the intentions pursued. The employees should be responsible for implementing these targets; in other words, only top-down targets and premises should be planned, but not individual steps or measures.

Modern budgeting must be implemented as part of a wider budgeting system and budgeting processes to provide answers to the challenges faced by many companies (see **Fig. 4.14**).

Challenges	The responses of modern budgeting
"Balance benefits and costs"	• Reduce complexity: "make it simpler" in terms of IT tools, methods, and processes • Limit yourself to key planning contents relevant to management control
"Provide a flexible framework for dynamics and constant changes"	• Introduce new tools: "make it flexible", for example using scenarios, rolling budgets and forecasts or relative targets • Make it rough: Annual targets as a framework; specify specific short-term targets • Tailored: Set the rhythm and scope to suit the individual companies
"Balance out behaviour control and decision-making support"	• Budgeting should focus on offering decision-making support • Set variable remuneration based on a balanced mixtures of short-term and long-term, personal, departmental and corporate targets. Also take into account that motivation is more likely influenced by non-monetary instruments.
"Incorporate planning and budgeting into the overall leadership system"	• Consider the context (for example the industry, organisation, value creation, market situation) when designing the plan and budget • Increase the strategic focus of short- and medium-term planning; integrate action planning: "make it integrated"

Fig. 4.14: The responses of modern budgeting

4.4.3 Budgeting bodies

When arranging the budgeting organisation, a decision must be reached as to who will take on what tasks during the budgeting process.

A distinction must be made between tasks related to drawing up the budget, and budget management tasks related to maintaining and developing further the budgeting system.

Line managers must compile the budgets, with the same persons normally responsible for action plans and budgets. Generally speaking, employees lower down the corporate hierarchy must develop budget suggestions and submit these to their supervisors for approval. Line managers must especially be involved in budgeting tasks during the planning period. Normally, a special body must be set up to deal with the many budget management tasks. The Controller plays a key role in this context. His or her key responsibilities primarily consist of setting up and monitoring the budget system and providing information to the budgeting units. In practice, this separation of tasks as outlined above is not observed consistently. Special budgeting bodies often also take on material tasks, and in turn line managers take on formal tasks in some companies. However, the larger a company, the more likely it is to separate these tasks as described.

4.5 Designing an effective forecast

Forecasts are a good planning basis for turbulent markets. A "rolling forecast" is a dynamic alternative to the traditional forecast. Both methods are presented below.

4.5.1 Traditional forecast

Usually, corporate objectives or targets are only set once a year, on the budget date, taking into account the planning premises valid and assumed at the time. Therefore, if the general conditions change during the year, this causes target deviations. Companies normally respond to such changes during the year by drawing up a forecast.

> A **traditional forecast** is a budget report which predicts the expected actual values at the end of the period based on currently available knowledge.

Such forward-looking information makes it possible to deduce more substantiated control measures than can be gathered from a mere budget/actual comparison (see *Horváth, Reichmann* 2003, p. 98). As a result, the purpose of a forecast is to make regular predictions – normally every quarter or every six months (start of medium-term planning and start of operative planning) – about the results which at the time of making the prediction can be expected to be achieved during the remaining budget year.

Forecasting aims to answer the following question: Will we be able to reach our budget objectives under the current conditions?

In practice, it is often difficult to implement this sensible purpose of a traditional forecast – i.e. predicting business development – effectively.

- This is largely because of the difficulty inherent in making predictions. Forecasts are often treated as a budget reworking or revision and take the format of a new budget.
- Given their level of detail, original forecasts frequently require cooperative input. This in turn means that they require significant resources and often take too long to compile to be of any use in decision-making.
- Traditional forecasts only cover the budget year so that the period under review gets shorter during the course of the year. This treats the company as if it is likely to stop operations and shut down when the year ends.

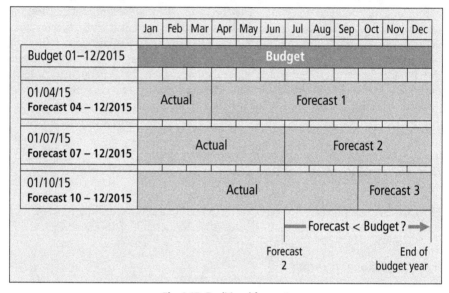

Fig. 4.15: Traditional forecast

4.5.2 Rolling forecast

A **rolling forecast** can be defined as a system which is adapted regularly as new information becomes available while offering increasing levels of detail (see *Horváth, Reichmann* 2003, p. 547) (see **Fig. 4.16**).

The idea of "rolling reporting" is far from new. In practice, departmental budgets have for a long time used various rolling methods (see *Hahn* 2003, p. 98). Liquidity planning is the most immediate example; this is carried out either monthly or quarterly. Medium-term planning also tends to be a rolling plan. Sadly, with the exception of operative budgeting, rolling methods are rare in practice.

Below are shown the key features of a rolling forecast which distinguish it from a traditional forecast:

- The period under review remains the same (independently of the financial year).
- Frequency: normally compiled every quarter.

- If applicable, the level of detail combines features of detailed and rough reporting, important monetary and non-monetary content.

The number of quarters forecast can vary depending on how dynamic or complex the environment happens to be (see *Buchner et al.* 2000, pp. 130 ff.). Forecasts normally cover at least five quarters and no more than eight quarters. This is because the quality of the forecast cannot be guaranteed for any longer periods.

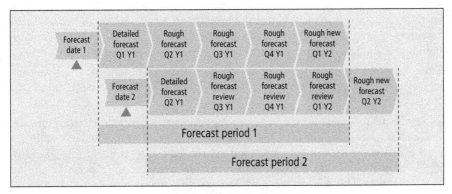

Fig. 4.16: Rolling forecast

The lower limit of 5 quarters is chosen to ensure that, when the fourth quarter of a calendar year is reached, budget and forecast values are available for the entire upcoming calendar year, to match traditional annual budgeting. In addition, forecasts over at least 5 quarters allow equivalent quarters to be compared across different years, for example Q1 2005 and Q1 2006. This can provide important corporate management support particularly in a strongly seasonal business.

Rolling revisions ensure that the period for which predictions are made remains constant as different forecasts are created over time, and that new information is integrated into the relevant forecasts. In this context, the level of detail can be scaled. Each upcoming quarter (Q1 in the January 2009 forecast) is presented in greater detail than later quarters (Q2 2009, Q3 2009, Q4 2009 and Q1 2010).

How often do you carry out a forecast in your company?

Each quarter, the planning system presented provides a forecast for subsequent quarters. At Forecast Time 1, only Q1 of Year 1 is examined in detail. The forecast for the remaining 4 quarters is rougher, i.e. aggregated. At Forecast Time 2, Q2 of Year 1, which had previously been presented roughly, is examined in greater detail, whereas the remaining three quarters (Q3 Y1, Q4 Y1, Q1 Y2) are still aggregated, and the forecast for Q2 Y2 is added for the first time.

The rolling forecast offers significantly more control information compared to the budget (budgeting is performed once) and the traditional forecast. This is particularly true in relation to departmental budgets for sales but also for production planning and control. Rolling forecasts are updated to match the most recent information available, with the result that they are as up-to-date as possible. This can have a significant impact especially for companies listed on the stock market, because share prices are, for example, derived from expectations of future development. At Forecast Time 2, therefore, predictions are made as far ahead as the first two quarters of the next financial year. Expectations are managed accordingly. Rolling forecasts also do not require many resources, so long as the level of detail is set appropriately. It is also possible to combine liquidity planning and detailed quarterly forecasts to avoid duplicate work.

The rolling forecast presented here is an idealised version. The following company and audience-specific design features must be taken into account when designing such a system:

- The frequency and forecast periods are key issues when designing a rolling forecast. There is no one-size-fits-all solution for this as different companies and audiences within companies will have different control requirements. Generally speaking: The more dynamic and complex the company environment, the shorter the forecast periods should be, and the more often forecasts should be drawn up. If the forecast period is too long, forecasts are at risk of becoming rolling medium-term plans, and requiring too much maintenance. The same applies to choosing the right period for a detailed forecast; this can also be longer than one quarter.

- The level of detail of a rolling forecast is another aspect which must be matched to the forecast audience. Forecasts need only contain the key performance indicators. They must not end up causing the same planning effort as the annual budget four times a year. Forecasters must keep asking themselves whether the level of detail chosen is appropriate for the control objectives.

A rolling forecast is an important modern planning tool and a fixed component of integrated planning. This combines strategic planning with operative planning ("vertical planning integration"). The Balanced Scorecard (BSC) is the best strategic and operative planning tool for meeting the following criteria:

- using specific action programmes to ensure that the strategy is implemented,
- including non-financial performance indicators, and
- considering all performance levels.

Balanced Scorecard processes include choosing appropriate measures, known as strategic actions, to achieve the strategic objectives. The measures are combined responsibilities to ensure that they are implemented, and they are constantly monitoring as part of a rolling forecast.

Process and financial targets are used as clear objectives (top-down approach) for operative planning. Whereas the widespread bottom-up approach offers an answer to the question: "What can be achieved?", this approach provides a stronger focus for operative planning by answering the question: "What should be achieved?" The strategic objectives are supported by benchmarking, or "learning from the best". This need not be external benchmarking. Internal benchmarking, i. e. a comparison with other organisational units within the same company, is another alternative. For example, where a company runs a number of retail branches, this offers great opportunities for comparing the performance of the individual branches. Top-down, aggregated budgets can be sufficient. It is not always necessary to add further detail. Budgets need only be broken down into many different cost elements, cost centres, market segment profitability characteristics, etc. where this is essential and makes sense from a business management perspective. The degree of turbulence of the environment must be taken into account.

If we want to make sure that a strategy is implemented, it is not enough to formulate it only for the company as a whole. A BSC must be broken down into individual target contributions for all departments. The target agreements used to choose the measures and responsibilities as part of the BSC processes ensure that individual actions are based on the strategy and not on the operative budget.

Where performance of units with close links to the market is evaluated according to fixed budget requirements, this is unlikely to yield a result as developments of the market environment (market development, key competitor development) are not taken into account. In this context, overly positive plan presentation can result in wrong or premature conclusions, especially where the relevant environmental factors are disregarded. For instance, actual revenue which is 10 % higher than budgeted revenue might trigger a bonus payment. But if we consider a simultaneous increase in market volume by 25 %, and the fact that one major competitor grew by 32 % during the same period, then the sales employee's performance will appear in a very different light. If we want to avoid absolute budget values, it makes sense to use relative values which change automatically by being coupled to the development of relevant environmental factors (see *Gleich, Kopp* 2001, p. 431).

Finally, it is worth noting that the planning and budgeting process can be sustainably improved by using suitable software solutions. In particular, benefits can be derived from working without the widespread spreadsheet applications. Familiarity with spreadsheet software cannot make up for the high maintenance effort, lack of multi-user capabilities, low processing speed and inconsistent data structures etc.

Again, the planning environment must be considered when choosing the right planning tool. Nowadays, spreadsheet software only makes sense in very simple business areas (low complexity). More complex markets require standard planning software. These offer an integrated approach summarising all steps from planned data input to report output in a single package (see *Dahnken, Banges* 2002, pp. 20 f.). The costs and work involved in setting up such a software remain reasonable. Software solutions are ideally suited to business areas which are subject to frequently changing external factors (dynamic, turbulent environment) and which therefore depend on simulations. They offer greater flexibility in budget design but also involve significantly higher costs.

Advanced Budgeting is based around IT-supported, rolling and integrated strategic and operative planning, which focuses on objectives and takes account of the corporate environment. The approach of Horváth & Partners adds automatically adjusting targets, process orientation and benchmarking.

 Do you also use non-monetary content in your forecast?

4.6 Practical example

4.6.1 Safety Ltd

The company "Safety Ltd" is an international provider of fire protection and gas detection systems for private and business customers. Last financial year, the company generated revenue in the region of EUR 1.5 billion. 70 per cent of these came from fire protection systems, and the remaining 30 per cent from gas detection systems.

The devices are manufactured at three sites, one in Germany, one in the Czech Republic and one in South America. The revenue is generated primarily from products manufactured in discrete standard production, whereas a small proportion of revenue comes from individual projects for specific customers. The products are sold globally from more than 40 branches in Europe, America and Asia.

The company was founded 40 years ago as a specialist in fire extinguishing agents, expanding over the years, including through various company acquisitions. A new business area was added 20 years ago when companies producing gas detection systems were acquired, and this was run largely independently based on a divisional management system. Last year, the company changed this divisional management system to a functional management system to make better use of synergies and economies of scale.

The management of Safety Ltd, and even some members of the Controlling department, found planning and forecasting too resource-intensive and saw little or no benefit in relation to management control. Before the company underwent the reorganisation, neither positive nor negative deviations were reported in advance. The forecast had been largely a political exercise, and was not used to redefine countermeasures, such that it made no noticeable contribution to company performance management. The forecast (or "year-end obligation") period was designed to end at the end of a year and always forecast the year-end value. It was not split into individual quarters nor did it attempt to predict performance during the next year. Using the same structures as the budget and actual reporting meant that the forecast was strongly based on the budget.

A decision to change the forecast required major changes to the environment such that Safety Ltd would be subject to great uncertainty and dynamics. A consistent control of measures and more dynamic planning thus gained importance.

4.6.2 Project: Developing a new forecasting process

The first step towards developing a new forecasting process required a vision to be prepared summarising the main features of the new approach:

- Clear target focus based on the strategy
- Short, lean, low-cost planning process
- A rolling forecast continuously updated with information relating to the future
- Consistent focus on management control measures by integrating the key measures in planning and forecasting

This approach aims to both reduce the costs of forecasts and increase the effect of management controls. Forecasts needed to be redesigned in order to overcome the strong budget focus of previous forecasts. The role and purpose of forecasts needed to be redefined.

Therefore, communication measures ("change management") needed to be implemented to change people's behaviour, so that forecasts would no longer be seen as "budget confirmation tools" and instead as honest predictions of the expected, foreseeable development. Behaviour changed as a response to top management (Board of Directors and second-level management) reactions to the reported forecast results. Now, the focus has shifted away from deviations from the budget objectives, and management instead looks at the quality of the forecast: It now takes a critical view not of differences between the forecast and the budget but of foreseeable developments which are reported too late. This is an attempt to encourage the (decentralised) forecasters to highlight and report foreseeable deviations from plan assumptions. This greatly increased the quality of the forecast, and therefore also its benefits and importance. **Fig. 4.17** summarises the main changes compared to previous forecasts.

It was decided that the forecast should incorporate a rolling component and not, as previously, be focused solely on the end of a year, in order to match the increasingly dynamic environment. To achieve this, a "traditional" rolling forecast covering 6 quarters was to be used as a starting point. This was to provide a medium-term perspective, as required to determine the effect of any measures taken. However, discussions also revealed the disadvantages of such an approach. In particular, this posed the question whether there was any point in forecasting a year ahead while still in the first half of a year. Where there is no need for information relating to these quarters, these can be dropped from the forecast.

A decision was therefore reached to apply a partial rolling approach. This does not add an additional quarter each time, but instead looks at the whole of the subsequent year. Since capacities are limited at the start of the year, and there is an overlap with year-end closing, Forecast 1 is based only on the data available from Forecast 4 of the previous year and on medium-term planning (referred to as "Business Planning"). Forecast 2 then updates the three remaining quarters of the current year and gives a total for the subsequent year.

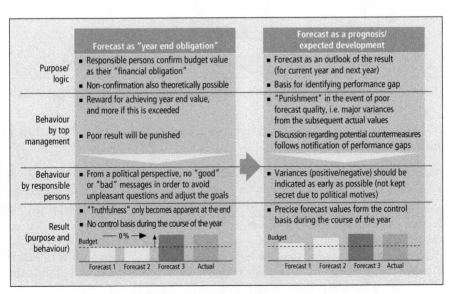

Fig. 4.17: Rolling forecast repositioning in the organisation

Forecast 3 splits the subsequent year into two quarters plus one remaining half year. The subsequent year is only fully split into four separate quarters in Forecast 4. Each forecast tends to use each previous forecast's (or medium-term planning) figures as suggestions.

While production and sales previously used a parallel forecasting process, a sequential process should now be used which includes two sequential process steps enabling sales and production units to coordinate centrally (see **Fig. 4.18**). As a first step, the sales and service units must forecast revenue, standard product costs and their functional costs. After undergoing a brief review by the relevant sales region manager, this forecast information is made available to the production areas as a report, and these in turn can now forecast their internal revenue and production costs. Additional units (especially R&D and central functions) can draw up their forecasts at the same time, as this is not on a critical path. Finally, the different forecasts are combined into one company forecast in a simple management consolidation. This forecasting process takes approximately three weeks. It does not end when the forecast information has been compiled, and instead triggers what is known as a forecast review during which the results are discussed and countermeasures are agreed.

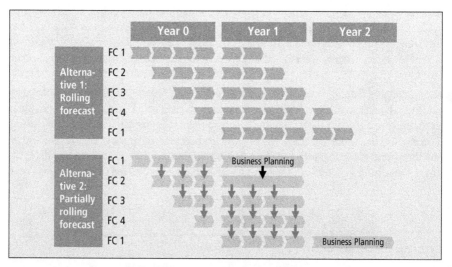

Fig. 4.18: Rolling forecast period vs. partial rolling forecast period

Budgets are no longer drawn up in their previous format of a "negotiated" annual plan. Instead, they are replaced with:

- annual targets deduced from general objectives ("What are we trying to achieve?"),
- as well as forecast values based on the partial rolling forecast ("What can we expect to achieve?").

Instead of using just one tool to present both ambition/motivation and prediction/realism, these two budget functions are now split into two tools. This leaves the medium-term plan called the "Business Plan", which is compiled once a year in October alongside the last forecast for the year, which covers the years following the partial rolling forecast period, i.e. years 2–4.

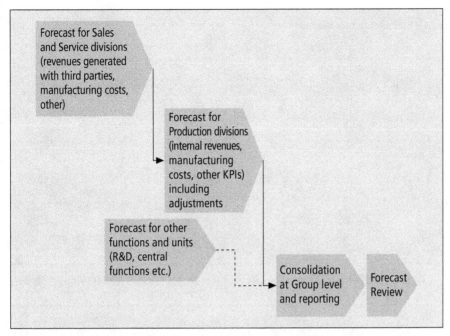

Fig. 4.19: New sequential forecasting process (simplified view)

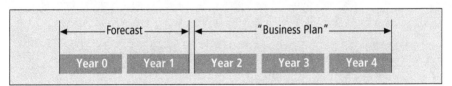

Fig. 4.20: "Business Plan" period defined by forecast period

The medium-term plan is aimed at, on the one hand, presenting the (medium-term) financial effects of the key measures that have been defined, and on the other hand, showing up any remaining gaps in relation to the (deduced) targets. This makes it possible to integrate measures (see below) and continuously forecast business development at minimal cost.

Measures are now not only defined and implemented at specific points in time (such as when the planning process starts), but at any time. This ensures that the company can implement improvement potential at any time. In addition, it now becomes possible to respond to changes in the economic situation short term by altering the priorities of the previously defined portfolio of measures.

This portfolio of measures must always be kept reasonably small to ensure that measures are always managed efficiently and that the organisation and management are not overtaxed. Measures which fall below a specific materiality threshold must be combined into bundles or managed separately (i. e. outside the planning and forecasting process).

In addition, all measures must be planned using standardised templates to allow for comparisons between them. The measures can be defined according to one of the fol-

4 Operative Planning, Budgeting and Forecasting

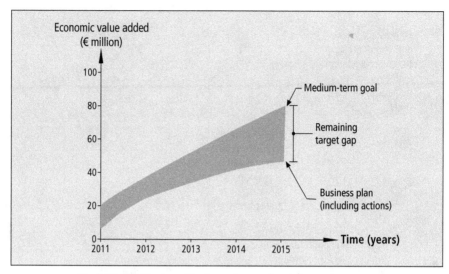

Fig. 4.21: The "Business Plan" reveals a gap in relation to the targets

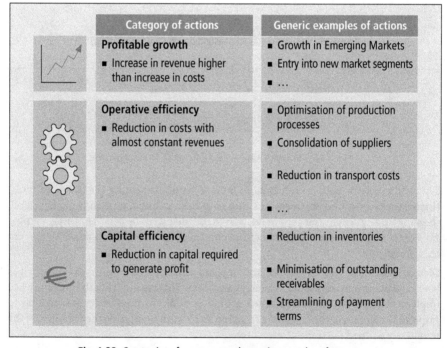

Fig. 4.22: Categories of measures and generic examples of measures

lowing categories: profitable growth, operative efficiency and capital efficiency. Each category must highlight decision-making processes and criteria to enable measures to be prioritised (see **Fig. 4.22**).

The effects of this portfolio of measures must be updated continuously as part of the forecasting process. To this end, the employees responsible for the measures must report the implementation status. Management is thus kept up-to-date on re-prioritisations or any other need for action in relation to the portfolio of measures. Status reporting also offers a further psychological effect: The employees responsible are more likely to submit a realistic plan for measures for which they know they will have to submit regular implementation reports later on. Consistent tools and templates must be used to make it possible to compare measures. This includes, for example, clearly defining key ratios which must be planned.

4.6.3 Lessons learned

Planning and forecast redesign greatly increased management and Controlling satisfaction. Both planning and forecasting have become valuable management tools. Planning is used to set ambitious but realistic objectives, and to define measures to close possible gaps in relation to the targets. By contrast, forecasting is a prediction tool used to continuously and objectively evaluate short-term economic development. It was also possible to significantly reduce planning costs, because the values used are no longer determined in detail using complicated, coordinated, bottom-up processes. Instead, they are systematically deduced from a 5-year target value.

The redesign was defined and implemented over a period of 12 months and required a significant investment. The key success factors for the implementation were

- a structured change management, and
- the use of a new system to implement the IT requirements.

These made it possible to meet the ambitious project deadlines, and also to ensure that the changes to the planning and forecasting system are not just communicated but also sustainably integrated into the company's organisation.

After the system was implemented, only minor changes were made to the original design. The encouraging fact that the ambitious 5-year value was almost reached as early as the second year has triggered further design-related discussions. These are currently focused on when the multi-year target value can or should be adjusted.

4.7 Organisational checklist for managers and controllers

Derive operative planning from strategic planning.

Link operative planning (e. g. sales planning) with finance planning (P&L, balance sheet and cash flow statement).

Pay attention to the design characteristics of your budgeting system (differentiation and completeness, bindingness, budget level, budget slack, budgets and strategic plans).

Design your budgeting process in line with the required characteristics (vertical co-ordination of budget planning, chronological coordination of budget planning, level, frequency and method of control, tolerance limits, flexibility).

Use a rolling forecast which always has the same horizon.

Also use non-monetary content in your forecast.

Consider forecast values in your planning.

Further reading

If you would like to find out more about planning in general, the following might be helpful:

Hahn, D., Hungenberg, H. (2001), PuK – Wertorientierte Controllingkonzepte, 6th ed., Wiesbaden 2001.

Anthony, R. N., Govindarajan, V. (2006), Management Control Systems, 12th ed., Boston 2006.

If you would like to find out more about modern planning, read:

Gleich, R., Kopp, J., Leyk, J. (2003), Advanced Budgeting: better and beyond, in: Horváth, P., Gleich, R. (Hrsg.), Neugestaltung der Unternehmensplanung, Stuttgart 2003, pp. 315–329.

5 Financial Management and Financial Controlling

5.1 Chapter objectives

Fig. 5.1: Chapter objectives

This chapter aims to introduce the reader to the Financial Management/Financial Controlling component. It starts by setting out the tasks of Financial Management/Financial Controlling, followed by a presentation of the Financial Controlling tools and their application.

5.2 Introduction

A company can only function as a going concern if it is financially solvent. Sufficient financial resources are an essential prerequisite for establishing, building, growing and operating the company. A company's success is also primarily dependent on financial resources, as its aim must be to increase initial investment.

As a result, planning, management and control of financial resources are eminently important corporate management tasks which require specific support from Controlling. Financial Management is responsible for securing liquidity in the short term and in the long term, and as such for handling the mentioned tasks. Financial Controlling plays an important role by providing both tools and information to support Financial Management in performing its tasks. It is of key importance for Financial Management and Financial Controlling to cooperate efficiently. This begs the question of how to organise interaction between Financial Management and Financial Controlling effectively.

5 Financial Management and Financial Controlling

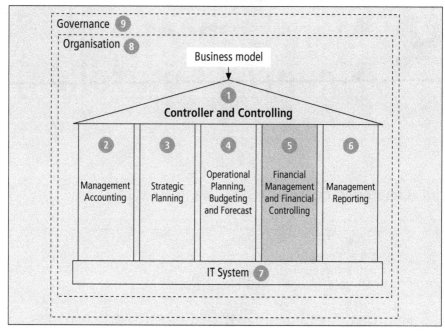

Fig. 5.2: Classification of the chapter in the "House of Controlling"

Therefore, this chapter describes which tasks Financial Management has and how Financial Controlling supports Financial Management in performing these tasks. It also introduces Financial Controlling tools and how to use them.

5.3 Designing effective Financial Management and Financial Controlling

Financial Management is responsible for ensuring the company's liquidity both in the short term and in the long term. Financial Controlling provides both tools and information to support Financial Management. **Fig. 5.3** illustrates the interaction between Financial Management and Financial Controlling.

Fig. 5.3: Interaction between Financial Management and Financial Controlling

How Financial Management and Financial Controlling should be designed strongly depends on a company's size and industry. Nevertheless, tasks can be split based on some general principles. The section below describes the tasks of Financial Management and Financial Controlling in more detail. In particular, it explains how Financial Controlling can support Financial Management in securing liquidity. It also gives a detailed overview of the most important tools used by Financial Controlling in practice and how they are applied.

5.3.1 Financial Management

> **Liquidity** is essential for ensuring a company's continued existence. Corporate Financial Management must focus on maintaining the company as a going concern. As a result, the core task of Financial Management is to ensure liquidity in the long term.

This core task can be broken down into the following three sub-tasks:

- **Situational safeguarding of liquidity:** This deals with safeguarding liquidity on a day-to-day basis by coordinating payments.
- **Short- to medium-term financing:** This is focused on calculating the capital requirement in consideration of risks and obtaining financing from free internal funds, external equity and third-party financing.
- **Structural safeguarding of liquidity:** Ensuring that a financial structure in line with the strategy is in place.

Financial Management is responsible for managing the Finance division itself and for financially coordinating all processes within the company. A company's processes must be coordinated financially in order to record, coordinate and control the impact of operational business processes on payments, capital retention and financial success.

Three development levels of financial management can be identified based on these core tasks (cf. **Fig. 5.4**).

From a **short-term operations perspective**, the main objective must be to continuously safeguard liquidity. Financial Management is focused entirely on liquidity.

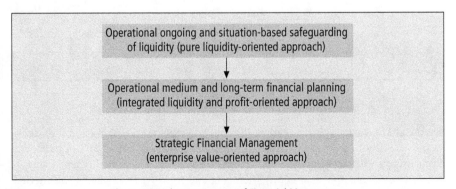

Fig. 5.4: Development stages of Financial Management

How do you ensure long-term liquidity in your company?

From a **medium- to long-term operations perspective,** liquidity must be viewed as a consequence of decisions resulting in payment. Financial Management approaches can be found in all company business functions. Accordingly, Financial Planning must be integrated with the other corporate planning components, such as by using integrated financial and results planning. Financial Management is focused not merely on liquidity but has an integrated focus on liquidity and results.

The **strategic stage** of Financial Management is dominated by the aim of sustainably increasing company value. This includes the capital structure, obtaining equity and third-party financing, and designing the corporate strategy taking financial aspects into account. This stage no longer has an internal focus but instead also considers the external (capital) market. Financial Management is focused on increasing enterprise value.

In corporate practice, Financial Management tasks are closely linked to operational management tasks (cf. **Fig. 5.6**).

Investment Management comprises real and financial investments and investigates how best to invest. Real investments involve acquiring material assets (property, machinery, etc.), whereas financial investments are investments in financial assets. Financial assets include so-called participation rights (e.g. shares) and creditor rights (e.g. bonds).

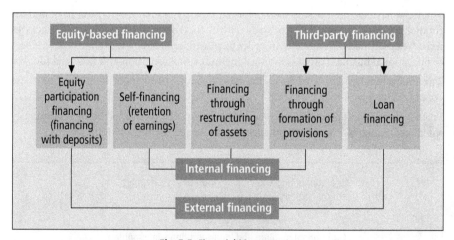

Fig. 5.5: Financial Management

Financial Management is made up of internal and external financing and thus determines how and by what means financing can be obtained (cf. **Fig. 5.5**). It is important to distinguish between internal and external financing. These two types of financing can be further split into equity financing and third-party financing. In internal, equity-based financing, the company provides the financing itself. Existing equity is used for the financing. By contrast, internal third-party financing involves raising third-party balance sheet capital by reversing existing provisions, for example. External, equity-based financing takes the form of equity participations financing. For instance, a capital increase can be used to obtain the necessary funds. External, third-party financing takes the form of loan financing. For example, a loan may be taken out to finance an acquisition.

Financial Risk Management is used to identify, analyse and evaluate a company's financial risks. To be precise, this involves defining criteria based on which risks can be evaluated, as well as methods to identify risks. In addition, responsibilities must be assigned, resources made available to avert risks, communication channels defined and staff trained (cf. Section 9.3.1 on Risk Management).

Cash management is concerned with how to organise payment transactions and how to invest and obtain liquid funds. It therefore concerns all corporate tasks aimed at safeguarding liquidity in order to maintain the company as a going concern.

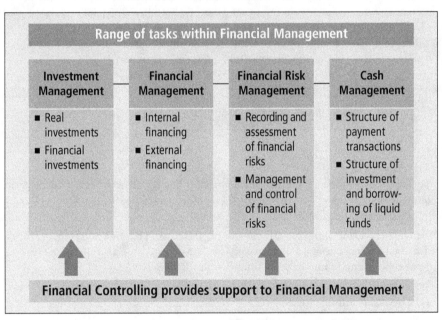

Fig. 5.6: Financial Controlling supporting Financial Management

The tasks depicted in **Fig. 5.6** must be specifically adapted to a company's size and structure, its industry and the geographical scope of its operations.

Financial Controlling provides specific tools to assist with individual Financial Management tasks. These are determined based on the Financial Controlling process set out below.

Are all fields of activity covered by your finance management?

5.3.2 Financial Controlling

5.3.2.1 Tasks of Financial Controlling

> **Financial Controlling** is tasked with supporting the management of the company and, in particular, Financial Management with performing their task of safeguarding liquidity while meeting the requirements of the different business functions in relation to profits.

In particular, this includes the following tasks:

- **Coordinated support for financial planning and control:** This task comprises both periodic and case-by-case assistance (e. g. during investment projects). It relates both to operative and to strategic planning.
- **Ensuring financial information supply:** Comprises all information for financial and company management relating to safeguarding liquidity, financially evaluating all company processes and coordinating the liquidity target with the target result.
- **Setting up and developing the Financial Controlling system:** Comprises all topics related to tasks, processes, organisation, tools and IT support.

How are finance management and finance Controlling organised in your company? Which tasks do both functions carry out?

Like Financial Management, Financial Controlling has a dual focus. As a result, its tasks comprise departmental support for Financial Management, as well as support during the external coordination of liquidity and result targets.

The Financial Controlling process must be organised as a planning and control process with organisational design being strongly context-dependent. This consists of creating, implementing and monitoring the financial plan (cf. **Fig. 5.7**).

The hierarchy levels of the Financial Controlling planning process are the same as those of the overall planning process:

- long-term/strategic financial planning
- medium-term operative financial planning
- short-term operative financial planning

These planning stages are supplemented by day-to-day liquidity management and control.

The relevant financial planning deadlines are based on the product cycle and production process (e. g. companies following current fashions will have a shorter planning horizon than investment business).

The Financial Controlling process must be coordinated with the general planning and reporting process. Alignment across different business functions poses a particular coordination challenge.

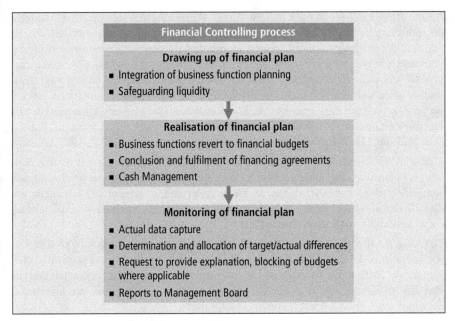

Fig. 5.7: The annual Financial Controlling process

Small- to medium-sized enterprises often combine the roles of Financial Management and Financial Controlling in one person. However, it is important to remain aware of the distinctions between these two areas.

5.3.2.2 Financial Controlling tools

The Financial Controlling process is supported by several tools. The main tools include:

- Short- and long-term Financial Planning
- Working Capital Controlling
- Financial Disposition Controlling
- Liquidity Controlling
- Financial Risk Controlling

Short-term Financial Planning should involve the integration of the different operational budgets. Integrated results, balance sheet and financial planning must take a holistic view and fully link up the operational budgets taking into account the company's liquidity and results targets. Cash flows for short-term financial planning can then be deduced either directly from operational budgets (e.g. sales, procurement, production and investment plans) or indirectly from the balance sheet and profit and loss statement. If the company deduces them directly, operational budgets should primarily contain information relating to payments. This ensures accurate planning.

What information do you use to create your short-term financial plans?

5 Financial Management and Financial Controlling

Financial Controlling can use long-term financial planning to review whether long-term decisions can be implemented financially and to identify areas where action may be required. Depending on the company and industry, the planning horizon for financial planning is between 1 and 5 years. Balance sheet movements and cash flow statements provide the basis to determine expected incoming and outgoing future payments, mainly based indirectly on planned balance sheets and planned income statements (cf. section 2.4 on Cash Flow Statements). Long-term financial planning thus consists of a number of consecutive cash flow statements with a forward-looking focus (cf. *Franke, Hax* 2009, pp. 124 et seq.).

Financial and investment planning can be either simultaneous or successive. In simultaneous planning, decisions on how to use capital at the operational level are made alongside decisions on how to generate capital. As a result, investments and financing are coordinated and it is clear which investments are selected taking into account financing costs, availability and maturity structure.

Planning is called successive if the first step involves a decision on how to invest at the operational level and the second step deals with planning capital acquisition (cf. *Eilenberger* 2003, p. 69). Investment and financial plans should be coordinated and the cash effectiveness of investments should be evaluated when looking to reach investment decisions (cf. Section 2.3.2 on Investment appraisal).

How do you coordinate the long-term planning of investments and finance in your company?

Financial Disposition Controlling is a tool to help determine cash availability, one of the main tasks of financial management. To organise short-term financing and financial investments, the use of available funds for internal and external financing must be coordinated.

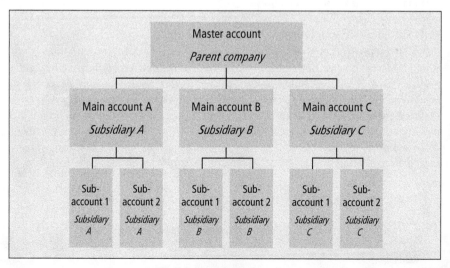

Fig. 5.8: Example: Cash pooling

5.3 Designing effective Financial Management and Financial Controlling

Financial Disposition Controlling benefits from the centralised processing of payment transactions for the company as a whole. Centralisation simplifies the coordination of payment transactions and payment reporting. Besides centralised processing, payment transactions are subject to two other conditions: cash pooling and netting (cf. *Perridon, Steiner, Rathgeber* 2009, pp. 145 et seq.).

- Cash pooling automatically consolidates the balances of several payment transaction accounts with one target account (cf. **Fig. 5.8**)
- During netting , internal group receivables and liabilities are netted, reducing effective payment transactions in the company (cf. **Fig. 5.9**)

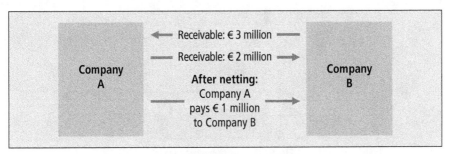

Fig. 5.9: Example: Cash netting

Financial disposition control should be carried out daily, or at least weekly, in order to ensure optimum disposition of financial resources (cf. *Mensch* 2008, pp. 34 et seq.). For example, through balance reporting, Financial Controlling can combine all accounts, including the details of accounts transactions, in one presentation.

Working Capital Controlling is another Financial Controlling tool aimed, on one hand, at improving the balance sheet structure, or, more precisely, working capital. On the other hand, in internal financing, Working Capital Controlling can be used to reduce capital retention by improving cash conversion cycles.

How often do you carry out financial disposition control in your company?

Working capital is the difference between current assets and current trade liabilities. Current assets are made up of liquid funds, inventories and receivables. Working capital is calculated based on monetary fair value. A cash-to-cash cycle time is used as a KPI in order to manage working capital (cf. **Fig. 5.10**).

The cash-to-cash cycle time is the time period between payment to suppliers and settlement of claims by customers for the deliveries and services rendered. These are measured based on the values of "Days Sales Outstanding", "Days Inventory Outstanding" and "Days Payables Outstanding" (cf. **Fig. 5.11**). Reducing the cash-to-cash time period can lead to negative working capital so that parts of the assets are offset by current liabilities. At the same time, this increases the significance of liquidity and financing risks.

5 Financial Management and Financial Controlling

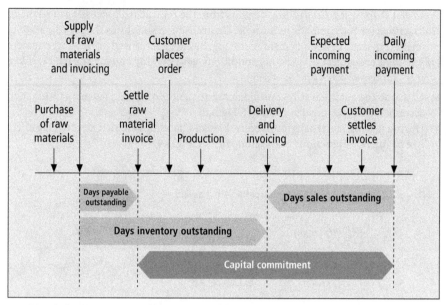

Fig. 5.10: Cash Conversion Cycle

KPI	Calculation	Interpretation
Days Sales Outstanding	$\dfrac{\text{Trade liabilities}}{\text{Turnover}} \times 365$	Indicates how long it takes for customers to pay their invoices; should be lower than Days Payables Outstanding.
Working Capital	Current assets – current liabilities	Indicates which part of current assets is not used to pay for current liabilities
Days Payables Outstanding	$\dfrac{\text{Liabilities}}{\text{Turnover}} \times 365$	A low Days Payables Outstanding value indicates that the company makes use of discounts and does not have liquidity problems
Days Inventories Outstanding	$\dfrac{\text{Inventories}}{\text{Turnover}} \times 365$	Indicates how long inventories are able to cover demand for
Cash Conversion Cycle	DSO (Days Sales Outstanding) + DIO (Days Inventories Outstanding) – DPO (Days Payables Outstanding)	The time period between the inventories purchasing date and the day on which payment from the customer is received; indicates how long liquid funds are retained in inventories; the shorter this time period, the better.

Fig. 5.11: KPIs in Working Capital Controlling

The general consensus is that active Working Capital Controlling can improve the result and thus increase profitability by up to 20 %. An analysis of the top 1,000 companies in the European manufacturing and services industry showed that approximately € 600 billion was tied up due to inefficient working capital planning. A study by the International Association of Controllers shows that from the perspective of finance professionals, Working Capital Controlling is one of the most important topics for companies.

Which working capital performance indicators do you use and why?

Liquidity-related KPIs can help to analyse the current and forecast the future financial situation (cf. *Mensch* 2008, p. 175). They keep interested parties inside and outside the company abreast of the company's condition. The following **Fig. 5.12** provides an overview of the most important liquidity KPIs and shows how they are calculated.

KPI	Calculation	Interpretation
1st degree liquidity	$\dfrac{\text{Liquid funds}}{\text{current liabilities}} \times 100$	Indicates what proportion of current liabilities a company can settle using its liquid funds
2nd degree liquidity	$\dfrac{\text{Liquid funds} + \text{current receivables}}{\text{current liabilities}} \times 100$	Indicates what proportion of current liabilities a company can settle using liquid funds and incoming payments from current receivables; ideally, this should be greater than 100 %
3rd degree liquidity	$\dfrac{\text{Liquid funds} + \text{current receivables} + \text{inventories}}{\text{current liabilities}} \times 100$	If 3rd degree liquidity is less than 100 %, a proportion of assets has been financed by short-term funds, which should be avoided at all costs; ideally, this should be greater than 120 %
Interest cover ratio	$\dfrac{\text{EBIT}}{\text{interest expenditure}} \times 100$	Indicates how well a company can pay its interest through operating activities; this must be greater than 1
Cash flow ratio	$\dfrac{\text{Cash flow}}{\text{revenues}} \times 100$	Indicates the proportion of sales which the company received as cash flows

Fig. 5.12: Liquidity-related KPIs

KPIs should be focused towards the future and incorporated into internal target setting in order to ensure that they are fully integrated into the internal performance management system. KPIs are used both for internal reporting and for external reporting and planning.

Which of the liquidity performance indicators listed do you use and why?

Financial risk controlling is another Financial Controlling tool. Planning, analysing and reporting financial risks are used to identify any developments that might put the company's continued existence or profitability at risk early on (cf. *Mensch* 2008, pp. 297 et seqq.). Financial risks include market price risks (e. g. raw material prices), credit risks (from trade receivables and other assets), liquidity risks (from payment fluctuations), currency risks and interest rate risks.

Financial Risk Controlling uses, amongst other things, "traditional" business administration methods such as scenario analyses, sensitivity analyses and a risk portfolio (see Section 9.3.1 on Risk Management). However, modern approaches such as Cash Flow at Risk, scoring models, Risk Adjusted Return on Capital, Corporate Value on Discounted Risk Value and Monte Carlo simulations are gaining importance (cf. *Gladen* 2011; *Gleich, Horváth, Michel* 2011; *Glaser* 2015). A company's own financial risk is lowered by including financial risks when planning new business relationships and supporting business partners with their risk management.

 Which methods do you use for early recognition of financial risks in your company?

5.4 Practical example

5.4.1 Media AG

Media AG has achieved constant growth since it was founded in 1990. Just two years after its foundation, it started expanding by opening branches across Europe. This was accelerated by further international acquisitions, and the media company now has more than 100 companies in around 20 countries. Media AG has 900 employees and generates sales of approximately EUR 500 million, making it one of the biggest players in the media industry. Its business areas include, in particular, the production of films and series, DVD sales and the marketing of film rights. The company is also active in other niche segments in the film industry.

The company is currently in a strong growth phase, driven by increasing internationalisation and the expansion of new business areas, resulting in constant and, at the same time, strongly fluctuating liquidity requirements. Combined with the lack of a liquidity planning concept, this is resulting in low planning precision. Planning also requires a high number of staff, which in part is caused by the need to manually consolidate planning figures based on many inconsistent planning sheets. This lack of consistency in liquidity planning is a significant complexity driver. A consultancy project should first look into integrating a planning process and then, based on this, should develop and implement a consistent liquidity planning concept adapted to Media AG across the group.

5.4.2 Project: Optimising liquidity planning

Fig. 5.13 shows which liquidity planning approach was applied to Media AG. This approach comprises three steps: from an analysis of current conditions, through technical design, to implementation of a solution. The first section above outlined how to perform an analysis of current conditions.

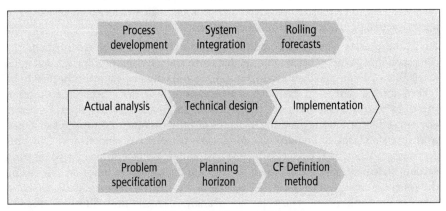

Fig. 5.13: Draft of solution

The second phase, technical design, was devoted to defining the target image, followed by specifying and prioritising areas for action. The main problem faced by the company being advised in terms of liquidity was the absence of a liquidity planning concept, which in turn also resulted in a large number of staff performing liquidity forecasts.

Liquidity forecasts generally distinguish between four different time horizons. The liquidity status has a horizon of only one day and is determined by accessing account information on a day-to-day basis. The second stage is the liquidity forecast, which sets out liquidity transactions to the day for the next three weeks. Liquidity planning depicts the monthly development of incoming and outgoing payments for the upcoming year, and financial planning depicts development over the next five years, giving details for each year. The example in question looked at liquidity planning, i.e. liquidity forecasts for the next twelve months, updated each month. Planning was supplemented by budget/actual comparisons, which is why the focus was also on calculating actual figures.

The purpose of liquidity planning is to determine future cash flows. Cash flows can be determined either directly or indirectly. Using the traditional approach, the indirect method, changes to liquidity are calculated based on the balance sheet and profit & loss statement. This method ultimately means that liquidity planning involves deduced values. It offers the benefit of making comparatively low demands on IT and internal processes, as well as of requiring little time. However, it does not provide much detail, is relatively slow to react to changes and does not focus on actual changes to the cash position. By contrast, the direct method forecasts changes to liquidity based on actual cash transactions. This tends to be more detailed but at the same time is more complex to implement and execute. The direct method of calculating cash flows was selected as this

5 Financial Management and Financial Controlling

offers a more realistic presentation of changes to liquidity and thus more precise details. One further argument in favour of the direct method is that its currency differentiation creates a valid basis for exchange rate hedging.

Combining liquidity planning and the direct cash flow statement thus revealed areas in which the company should take action. These were recording actual payment flows directly and forecasting all payment flows in the company. Both actual figures and the budget were based on the newly defined planning categories. As such, existing planning categories had to be replaced or altered. In addition, logic needed to be developed to allocate actual figures to the planning categories.

First, all processes relating to liquidity within the group had to be recorded and the corresponding payment behaviour, i.e. due dates and payment profiles, needed to be determined. Moreover, all anticipated incoming and outgoing payments needed to be broken down by currency. Examples of payments include: sales turnover, acquisition spending, staff and material costs, tax payments and financial transactions. Processes ensuring efficient and fast planning involving all business functions were implemented to ensure standardised liquidity planning using plan/actual comparisons. This process ensures that actual payments for the past month are determined based on bank account statements and are allocated to the planning categories based on rules using the system. Actual payments are then passed to the different business units, which in turn carry out and comment on a plan/actual analysis. Finally, the rolling budget can be updated – including the findings from plan/actual analyses relating to historic planning quality are used to improve the quality of forecasts. The separate liquidity forecasts for the different business units are then consolidated to create one group-wide liquidity plan. The entire process normally takes approximately 8 working days. **Fig. 5.14** gives an example of the process described above.

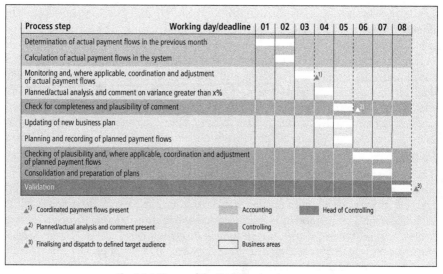

Fig. 5.14: Stages of the liquidity planning process

The process described was integrated into the existing system landscape to ensure that it is implemented efficiently (cf. **Fig. 5.15**). As a result, the different departments, such as Sales or Procurement, automatically reported their calculated and expected cash flows via the system. System homogeneity across all business units from financial accounting through to liquidity planning helped reduce process costs further. For instance, the master data for the different business units is now managed centrally to avoid the need for reconciliations.

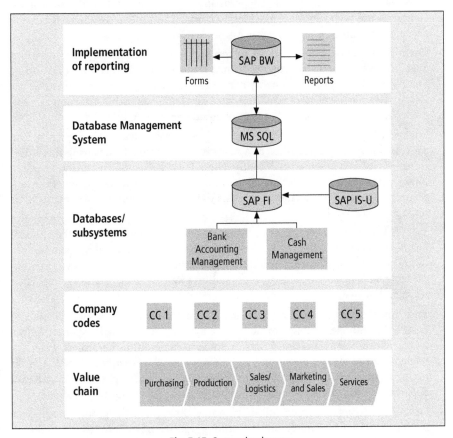

Fig. 5.15: System landscape

In order to ensure that liquidity reports remain accurate and meaningful, they must be updated continuously each month. In addition, the analysis of liquidity planning with actual figures described above and the measures deduced ensures a successive improvement of the liquidity situation.

5.4.3 Lessons learned

In addition to information acquisition, information availability also plays a key role in liquidity planning. This is indirectly linked to the system-based and organisational integration of liquidity planning into business processes. The following seven critical success factors were identified during the course of the project:

- Holistic approach to planning and solutions, and inclusion of all stakeholder groups. This ensured that all of the different needs and requirements of the different business functions and branches were taken into account. This process fostered trust in and acceptance of the new planning process.

- Defining a catalogue of measures to respond quickly to liquidity developments. Scenarios were used to develop predefined measures based on consistent planning and the availability of high-quality planning data. These measures will enable the Treasury Department to respond to future developments within the company and group in a timely manner and to control liquidity accordingly.

- Stringent implementation and execution by the project team. The new planning process was quickly established as a new standard process by ensuring that it was implemented and executed stringently with a focus on solutions. During an initial phase, extensive support was provided in relation to the implementation of the new planning process. This enabled questions to be answered and improvements to be incorporated directly.

- Liquidity reports were prepared with specific recipients in mind so that the different business units were able to identify the possible consequences and opportunities to optimise liquidity planning. In addition, addressing the different recipients within the company directly meant that responsibilities were assigned clearly and reporting was standardised.

- Ensuring IT support. By involving the IT department early on, it was possible to ensure that sufficient capacities were made available to provide IT support for the project. Technical issues could thus be resolved early on in the project. Later on, responsibilities for operations and maintenance could be clearly assigned. Thanks to this process, responsibility for ongoing operations could be passed to the relevant department immediately after implementation had been completed.

- Liquidity forecasts based on rolling planning throughout the group. Group-wide implementation of rolling liquidity planning significantly improved the quality of forecasts. Planning data for all group levels was updated each month, allowing a consistent planning database to be created using a standardised planning process.

- The level of detail of liquidity planning was further improved by including seasonal fluctuations in sales planning. This enables the company to respond to regular fluctuations in liquidity supply in future, thus lowering the costs of liquidity provision further.

The seven success factors listed were essential for ensuring that the Media AG project was implemented successfully, and also contributed to openly communicating successful steps within the company, which in turn promoted employee acceptance and trust. This improved company-wide integration and had a positive impact on the project target of improving the quality of liquidity information and planning processes.

5.5 Design checklist for managers and controllers

 Create a liquidity management system using appropriate, staggered liquidity performance indicators.

 Set up a system for working capital management.

 Define the tasks of finance management and the respective associated finance Controlling tasks and remits.

 Ensure early detection of risks through early warning information.

Further reading

If you would like to find out more about financial management in general, please read:

Eilenberger, G. (2003), Betriebliche Finanzwirtschaft [Corporate Finance], 7th ed., Munich 2003 or

Perridon, L., Steiner, M., Rathgeber, A. (2009), Finanzwirtschaft der Unternehmung [Business Finance], 15th ed., Munich 2009.

If you would like to find out more about financial controlling, please read:

Horváth, P., Gleich, R., Michel, U. (eds., 2011), Finanzcontrolling – Strategische und operative Steuerung der Liquidität [Financial Controlling – Strategic and Operational Liquidity Management], Freiburg im Breisgau 2011 or

Mensch, G. (2008), Finanz-Controlling: Finanzplanung und -kontrolle [Financial Controlling: Financial Planning and Control], 2nd ed., Munich 2008.

6 Management Reporting

6.1 Chapter objectives

Fig. 6.1: Chapter objectives

The objective of this chapter is to introduce the reader to information supply, key figures and reporting as the key phases of effective management reporting. By the end of the chapter, the reader should understand how the supply of information works and be able to form and apply key figures and draft a report.

6.2 Introduction

On one hand, the need for information is triggered by the management process; on the other hand, however, information should also indicate opportunities and warn of risks, i.e. put planning and control into motion. The success of both planning and management reporting as well as the subsequent implementation therefore depends on the systematic provision of information.

It is for this reason that information supply is a key element of successful, forward-looking corporate performance management. The aim is to illustrate current factors of the business model that are critical to success, present management-related financial and non-financial information transparently and, in doing so, make statements on the past and future. The information must be prepared efficiently and presented comprehensibly in short cycles. Overall, requirements are thus growing for the supply of information to give extensive indications of connections and measures to influence them.

There is widespread criticism of management's supply of information.

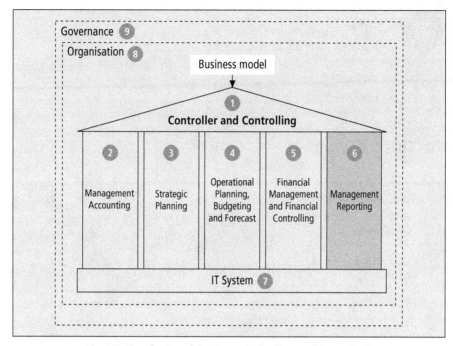

Fig. 6.2: Classification of the chapter in the "House of Controlling"

The main criticisms are:

- The information arrives too late.
- The information is too detailed.
- The information is too extensive.
- The information predominantly focuses on the past.
- The information only contains data that can be quantified.
- The information is not well visualized.
- The individual areas of management receive inconsistent, often even conflicting information.
- Information for future, as yet unknown purposes is inadequate, i.e. the supply of information for strategic planning is often unclear.

In order to rise to these challenges, effective management reporting must be established. This is one of the controller's main tasks.

6.3 Setting up effective management reporting

Planning and control require effective management reporting.

> The purpose of **management reporting** is to supply all the information required for planning and control, with the necessary level of detail and depth, in the right place and at the right time.

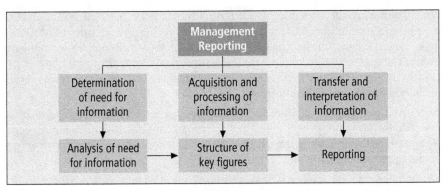

Fig. 6.3: Components of effective management reporting

Effective management reporting has three stages: identifying the need for information, obtaining and preparing the information using key figures, and transmitting and interpreting the information through reporting (see **Fig. 6.3**). These three stages of management reporting are outlined below.

6.3.1 Basis: Effective analysis of need for information

To enable identification of the requirements of the reporting system, the need for information must be analysed. The need for information essentially depends on the tasks that the recipient of the information has to perform. Naturally, tasks and their complexity depend on both the (hierarchical) position of the information recipient and the specifics of the company (see **Fig. 6.4**).

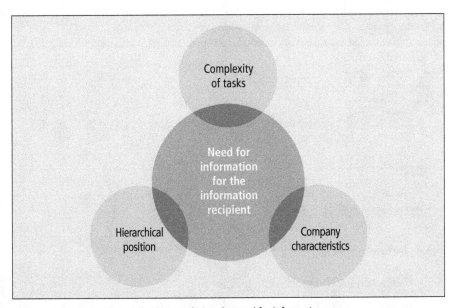

Fig. 6.4: Analysing the need for information

Whilst only a little detailed information is usually required to perform routine tasks at case handler level, the need for more extensive, but more highly aggregated information (e. g. on market conditions) increases at management level, where complex decisions are made. The aggregation of information therefore depends on the recipient's level. Ultimately, the information recipient's personal characteristics also play an important role in determining the need for information (cf. *Weber et al.* 2005, pp. 13 f.).

In reality, however, cases in which the need for information is apparent a priori because the task, the person responsible for it and the context are clearly defined rarely occur. The need for information is usually only identified and modified in stages when formalising plans, budgeting and reporting.

Our starting point for considerations regarding the need for information is the planning and control process. As this process and the context vary greatly from company to company, it is not possible to define a generally applicable framework for the need for information. We have to identify the need for information on an individual company basis. "Derivation" using formal logic, e. g. from the contents of the plan, alone is inadequate.

Many attempts have been made in practice and in literature to describe and systematise the methods of analysing the need for information. A distinction can be made between the following methods in relation to the user's involvement in identifying the need for information:

- **Task analysis** identifies the objective need for information by analysing the information-processing and decision making processes.
- **Document analysis** examines the documents available to a person responsible for a task.
- The **conclusion by analogy method** deduces a user's need for information from that of another user.
- **Observation** places task fulfilment at the centre of the analysis.
- **Interviewing** is the more or less structured questioning of the user.
- In the **questionnaire method**, the questions are asked in writing.
- In the **report method**, the user produces a report on their tasks and the information required for them.

 Which method(s) do you use for your information needs analysis?

It is not possible to recommend one of these methods specifically. Many combinations of them are used when identifying the need for information.

6.3.2 Defining effective key figures

6.3.2.1 Function and categories of key figures

The company's supply of information constitutes an important basis for the quality of planning, the success of implementing plans, high-quality informative accounting and meaningful reporting. The sourcing, preparation and distribution of information within a company is therefore is a critical factor of business success. Managing these processes efficiently and effectively can enable a company to gain a strategic competitive advantage. The value of the information available to the company must therefore be acknowledged. However, the amount of information obtained from internal and external sources and then prepared usually exceeds the capabilities of classic information channels. The challenge thus consists of structuring the information obtained and the necessary access to it. Selecting, preparing and structuring the information is therefore at the centre of information sourcing. The controller's role here involves both selecting the management-related information from the range of information available and preparing this for the management of the company.

One fundamental problem of information preparation is condensing information in a useful, meaningful way. For this reason, pieces of information are consolidated into key figures, so that details of business affairs are given in this summarised format. **Fig. 6.5** illustrates the categories of key figures.

As key figures are very versatile, there are barely any areas of business that are not linked to them. Accordingly, the functions and areas of application are therefore versatile too. The most important functions of key figures and key figures systems are:

- Support for planning, management and control at all levels of the hierarchy,
- Tool for internal (inter/intracompany comparison or benchmarking) and external (tax audit) company analysis, and
- Component of information systems for all levels of the hierarchy.

There are three aspects that are of particular importance: Key figures as a means of decision-making support on site (in the workplace) as well as for management, corporate governance and Controlling. These aspects are supplemented by the function of early recognition.

Key figures fulfil their role of assisting with decision-making through the selection and preparation of the operating information relevant to the decision. The decision-maker receives either a consolidated, systematic edit of the information available (managers) and is therefore able to evaluate the alternatives and make decisions. And/or he/she receives – as is increasingly common in modern companies with a stronger focus on employees – simple, self-explanatory information on key figures for self-monitoring on site (case handler or employee level).

The latter requires concrete planned values (= key figures), for example, in the form of targets. These are either specified by managers or set by these managers together with those below them. Linking key figures and budget values can make an important contribution to the coordination of various business divisions.

The Controlling function of the key figures (systems) is fulfilled through comparative calculations in which actual figures (actual values) are compared with the relevant planned figures (target values). If the comparative calculation relates to the same object (e. g. revenue) but to different periods, this is known as a time comparison. A control calculation within one time period with different objects is known as an object comparison.

A time comparison of the relevant values is of crucial importance to aid early recognition with key figures. In key figures systems that are structured like pyramids, the likelihood of great, latent opportunities and risks is identified in the bottom part of the pyramid, i. e. in the less aggregated levels.

One important form of early recognition is forecasts. In forecasting, the target/actual comparison is expanded to include a target/forecast comparison. While target/actual comparisons only provide information on events that have already occurred and their results, forecasts of actual values at the end of the period or project provide early insight into impending deviations ("forecast" figures) that would otherwise only become apparent at a later date (e. g. at the end of the period or project) in target/actual comparisons.

Forecasting and clarifying the development of key figures in several planning periods are generally good methods of early recognition. Today, this form of early recognition (forecasting) is integrated into the planning and reporting systems of Controlling concepts. However, the period for which forecasts have the capacity for early recognition differs by performance indicator and industry. Numerous key figures systems are referred to in literature (cf. **Fig. 6.5**).

Key figures are either original figures (e. g. prices or quantities), derived figures (e. g. totals, differences) or ratios (e. g. item/period). They should be understood as a computational means of quantifying information for various decision-making scenarios.

> The fundamental principle of **key figures** is the consolidation of individual pieces of information to enable complex issues and interrelationships to be illustrated using a benchmark.

At the same time, this is associated with the risk that heavily consolidating information into one key figure could result in important details of the situation being depicted getting lost and thus of it no longer being possible to answer the question of the source of changes in this key figure. This risk of information loss can be mitigated by the computational breakdown, substitution or expansion of a key figure:

- Breakdown means breaking down the numerator and/or denominator of a fraction into individual parts or sizes (e. g. breaking down the key figure "sales/year") into the key figures "sales product A/year" or "sales product A/month").
- In a substitution, the numerator and/or denominator are substituted for another quantity (e. g. "sales quantity x price" instead of "sales").
- In expansion, the initial key figure in the numerator and/or denominator is expanded by the same quantity (e. g. "profit/total capital" results, when expanded by the factor "sales", in the key figures "profit/sales" [=sales-related return on investment] and "sales/total capital" [=capital turnover rate]).

It is important that key figures are annotated for the recipients, so that they can assess the key figure and its significance correctly. The old controller principle applies: "Every figure needs a comment".

Are all the important key figures provided with comments in your company?

Systematisation feature	Types of management key figures						
Operational functions	Key figures from the division						
	Procure-ment	Warehouse Manage-ment	Produc-tion	Sales	Human Re-sources	Financial Manage-ment	Annual financial statements
Statistical and methodical factors	Absolute figures				Ratios		
	Individual figures	Totals	Difference	Average values	Relation numbers	Structural numbers	Index numbers
Quantitative structure	Overall sizes				Partial sizes		
Temporal structure	Date values				Period values		
Content-related structure	Values				Volumes		
Learning value	Key figures with						
	independent learning value				dependent learning value		
Sources in Accounting	Key figures from						
	Balance sheet	Financial Accounting		Income and earnings statement and cost accounting		Statistics	
Economic principle element	Usage values			Results	Standards from relationships between usage values and results		
Area of statement	Overall operational key figures				Plant-related operational key figures		
Planning perspectives	Target key figures (forward-looking)				Actual key figures (backward-looking)		
Number of participating companies	Single plant-related operational key figures		Group key figures		Industry key figures (indicative numbers)		Overall operational key figures
Scope of determination	Standard key figures				Single plant-related key figures		
Plant performance	Key figures for the pre-investment appraisal				Key figures regarding financial security		

Fig. 6.5: Types of management key figures

ZVEI / BWA		Key figure no. 103
Title	**Cash flow as % of total capital** *(on yearly basis)*	
Application	**Cash flow as % of total capital** Measurement of "cash flow" of average "total capital" employed: Including in particular to determine the extent in which financial means are generated from the result for the period in question, depreciation, change in the special item with an equity portion and change in the pension provision for investments in order to service debts and distribute profits; Including in particular for comparison with Return on Investment *(key figure 102).*	

Formula

$$= \frac{\text{Cash flow} \cdot 100}{\text{Average total capital employed}} \times \frac{360}{\text{Period under review } \textit{(in days)}}$$

Formula content

Numerator: **Cash flow** according to Section 275 (2) HGB *(total cost method)*
According to Section 275 (2) HGB *(cost of sales method)*

Annual net profit/net loss [1]

+ Depreciation during the financial year on assets and, where applicable, on capitalised startup and business expansion expenses according to assets analysis

+ Special item with an equity portion (in accordance with Section 273 HGB) *(closing balance – opening balance)*

+ Pension provisions *(closing balance – opening balance)*

= Cash flow[2]

Denominator: **Average total capital employed**
(= average total assets employed) according to Section 266 HGB

Balance sheet total [1]	Average
./. Subscribed capital unpaid [3] *(Assets side prior to fixed assets)*	$\dfrac{\text{Opening balance} + \text{Closing balance}}{2}$
./. Capitalised startup and business expansion expenses [4] *(Assets side prior to fixed assets)*	
./. Allowances posted as liabilities [5]	Period under review *(in days)*
+ Advance payments received on orders [6]	1 year = 360 days
= Total capital (= total assets)	1 month = 30 days

Notes

1) For companies that have concluded a profit transfer agreement with a controlling company, the amount reported in accordance with Section 277 (3) HGB shall be regarded as the result for the period in question.

2) With regard to international comparisons, income tax according to Section 275 (2) Item 18 HGB (total cost method and/or Section 275 (3) Item 17 HGB (cost of sales method) must be added to the cash flow.

3) See also Section 272 (1) HGB

4) See also Section 269 HGB

5) e.g. special depreciation in accordance with Section 281 (1) HGB

6) if deducted from inventories in the balance sheet

Fig. 6.6: Example of a key performance indicator definition sheet from the German Electrical and Electronic Manufacturers' Association (Zentralverband Elektrotechnik- und Elektronikindustrie, ZVEI)

Key figures vary in significance for company success. It is important to identify the key figures that play a key role in success: These are the Key Performance Indicators (KPI). For a copper processing firm, for example, this is the price of copper per ton.

Key performance indicators must be defined consistently within a company. It is recommended to compile an information sheet defining every key performance indicator (cf. **Fig. 6.6**)

6.3.2.2 Key figures systems

To increase the information value of individual key figures, they are integrated into a key figures system. Key figures systems thus depict an organised collection of key figures that are related to each other and, in this way, provide information on an issue. There are two forms of key figures systems. Computational systems mathematically link key figures up with each other and thus enable a computational breakdown. However, it is often not possible to consolidate key figures that have different logical connections through mathematical linking. In classification systems, therefore, different key figures that are logically related to each other are allocated to a specific area of key figures (e.g. liquidity ratios) and recorded individually.

The following design features must be observed when structuring key figures systems:

- Key figures must be quantifiable values, i.e. they must be (clearly) measurable in units of money or quantity.
- Conflicting relationships between the individual key figures should be avoided in a key figures system. This relates to classification systems in particular.
- Key figures may relate to both past and future circumstances. In comparative calculations, the key figures must be from the same time period.
- The structure of a key figures system may not be altered randomly to guarantee that results can be compared over a longer period of time.
- The calculation of every individual key figure is subject to the requirement for economic efficiency. This means that the costs of supplying and preparing the information relative to the benefits of the information must be reasonable.
- Key figures systems should illustrate the essentials in a consolidated form and still be complete.
- It must be possible to work with key figures systems efficiently, i.e. the core part of the figures may only contain values that the recipient uses regularly, while special parts of the key figures system may be provided as required.

Do you also compare your key figures over time?

In principle, a distinction can be made between key figures systems with an operating or strategic focus. The DuPont system (operative focus) and the Balanced Scorecard (BSC) (strategic focus) are outlined in more detail below.

The DuPont Ratio System of Financial Control is one of the most well-known key figures systems and was developed in 1919 by the chemical company DuPont as the "DuPont Ratio System of Financial Control".

The fundamental principle of this key figures system is that a company's aim should not be to maximise profit as an absolute value, but should focus on its relative size (= return on investment or "ROI").

ROI is calculated as follows:

$$ROI = \frac{Profit}{Total\ capital} \times 100$$

This value is defined as a key performance indicator in the DuPont system and is broken down into further individual key figures. This computational breakdown of the highest target value enables a systematic analysis of the key factors influencing the company's result. **Fig. 6.7** illustrates this relationship.

Various arguments regarding the advantages and disadvantages of the ROI concept are made in literature:

The following are given as advantages of the DuPont system:

- It takes the company's profitability target into account;
- It can also be applied to decentralised company divisions;
- It enables long-term comparisons of these subdivision solutions.

The following are given as criticisms of the ROI concept:

- The individual figure ROI does not indicate whether the numerator or denominator of the fraction has changed;
- Division-based ROI figures can lead to suboptimal results;
- The tendency to seek short-term profit maximisation is reinforced because expenditure on research, for example, is not included in the ROI figure.

Due to the disadvantages of ROI, it is only used in companies as a key performance indicator in exceptional cases. Figures such as return on capital employed (ROCE) are more widespread, as is the use of value-based performance indicators such as economic value added (EVA®) (cf. section 3.3.4.2).

6.3.2.3 The measurement parameter system of a Balanced Scorecard

As described in Section 3.3.5, the Balanced Scorecard (BSC) is a key instrument for strategy development and implementation.

One key requirement of a **BSC concept** is that the implementation of a BSC's strategic objectives must be quantifiable. For this purpose, it is necessary to define a system of key figures that are suitable for strategic management which can be linked up with each other in a strategy map (cf. *Kaplan, Norton* 2004, p. 27). In the context of a BSC, these key figures are called "measures".

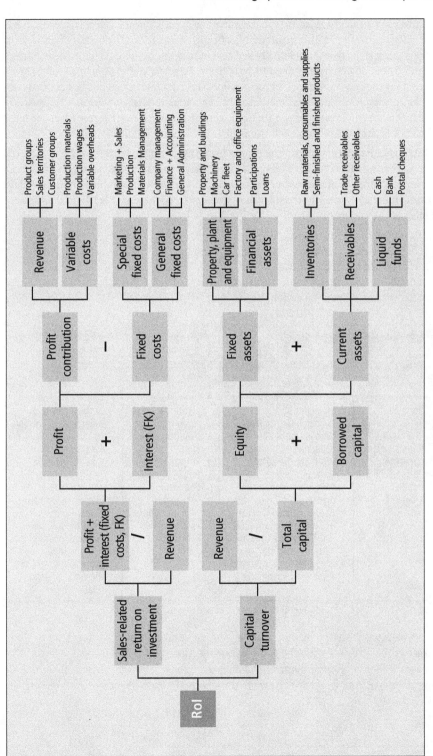

Fig. 6.7: The DuPont ratio system

6 Management Reporting

Ideally, each strategic objective is determined by exactly one measure. However, this is not always possible. To minimise complexity and ensure focus, the number of measures per strategic objective should be limited to a maximum of three. If more measures are required, the objective may need to be split up. Experience has shown that it is more likely that too many rather than too few measures will be selected. **Fig. 6.8** illustrates the key principles for defining measures. In particular, the issue of whether the measure will influence employee behaviour must be considered when selecting measures, as must illustrating the level of target achievement as precisely as possible.

Ultimately, the integrability of measures into a reporting system must be considered when defining them. We have identified five criteria that initially play a secondary role in the derivation of measures but are of greater importance for implementation. These criteria must be taken into consideration when making the final decision for or against a measure at the latest:

- Existence of the measure,
- Costs of the measure,
- Acceptance of the measure,
- Possibility of formalising the measure and
- setting the frequency at which the measure will be recorded.

Formalisation	Availability	Implementation (if measure previously unavailable)	Sensitivity (optional)
• Mathematical formula • Description of the measure (notes on the measure) • Responsibility for performance	• Is the measure currently measured? • Is actual data available? • Who is responsible for collecting it? • What are the data sources? • Frequency of measurement? • Are there historical values (time comparisons)? • Is the measure used in current reporting? • Is budget data available? • Are there benchmarks?	• Does implementing it make sense from cost/benefit perspectives? • Project schedule for implementation incl. – person responsible – time needed – budget	• Can development of the measure be influenced decisively by those responsible for the objective? • Can the measure be influenced in the short term (1 yr) or just in the long term (2 yrs)? • Does the measure correlate positively with the measures preceding it, i. e., are there cause/effect relationships?

Fig. 6.8: Principles of defining measures

Every selected measure must be precisely defined and documented to ensure ongoing target review, always with the same data collection and key figure calculation. The measures should be documented in a table, arranged by strategic objective. **Fig. 6.9** below gives an example of the definition of individual measures (cf. *Horváth & Partners* 2007, pp. 202 ff.).

Key figures examples for the processes and potential perspectives of a BSC

Objective	Measure	Defining the measure	Data source
• High process quality	• Costs of night work	• Absolute amount of night work costs	• Additional costs report
• Short processing time • Low costs	• Ø Total processing time for preparing an offer • Ø Production duration factor • Ø Duration factor Development • Personnel utilisation rate • Machine utilisation rate • Bidding costs	• Ø Time required from receipt of customer enquiry to submission of an offer • Processing time/order throughput time • Processing time/ throughput time • Order-related hours as proportion of the maximum available working hours • Utilisation of machines as % of target utilisation • Costs of preparing an offer/sales	• Distribution statistics • SAP PS and PP report • Proof of productivity and completeness • SAP order information sheet
• Adequate employee qualifications and capital resources • High employee motivation	• Rate of coverage of employee qualifications • Investment rate • Employee satisfaction index • Sickness rate	• Target/actual comparison between employee qualifications and job specification profile • Investment volume/imputed • Allowance for depreciation • Calculate index based on employee survey • Ø Sick days per employee	• Target-setting meetings • Investment planning, expense distribution sheet • Employee survey • Personnel statistics
• Innovative and problem-solving capacity	• Number of implemented suggestions for improvement • Development projects' sales share	• Number of implemented suggestions for improvement • Development costs as proportion of total sales	• Operating statistics suggestion scheme • Sales statistics

Fig. 6.9: Example of defining measures

Do you also use qualitative information to support decision-making?

6.3.3 Designing effective reporting

One important planning objective is improving corporate performance management. Targets for every area of responsibility are derived from planning in the form of concrete planned figures. The control effect is achieved by comparing planned values with actual values or forecast values. Analysing deviations gives indications of their causes and for initiating corrective actions.

Preparing information and transmitting it to the relevant report recipients in the form of reports is a key reporting responsibility. The reports should make clear to what extent the goals set based on plans have been met in the individual divisions and where further action needs to be taken. Reports may not be an end in themselves; they must enable the recipient of the information to make management decisions on the basis of the reports and put these decisions into action. The results should be analysed by Controlling and the department together to ensure acceptance of the results of the analysis and the performance of measures.

Controlling's responsibilities include defining reporting and coordinating the compiling of reports. The controller must ensure that

- the right information
- of the right depth
- is available on the right date,
- in the right place and
- in the right form.

The following aspects are discussed in more detail below:

- Design
- Hierarchy
- Frequency

In terms of content, reports communicate information on planning and control. So that reports satisfy their control purpose, three criteria must be observed when designing a report:

- Reports must compare three categories of information: planned (target), actual and expected (forecast),
- provide a cause analysis for the information provided ("no figure without a comment"), and
- clarify the effect of deviations on results.

The structure of the content of reports must also be identical to that of the plans. This is the only way of obtaining meaningful information from the comparison of actual and planned figures. Highlighting the relevant information is one of the most difficult tasks. Information means purposeful knowledge, i.e. the purpose, not the quantity, determines the informative value. The quality of decisions depends not on the number of available pieces of information but on the number of relevant pieces of information. Relevant pieces of information are often lost in the plethora of information available. This phenomenon of a superfluity of irrelevant information with a simultaneous lack of relevant information is also referred to as "scarcity in abundance" or as an "information dilemma" for short.

"Deviation thresholds" can be used to highlight the essential parts of the reported information. This means that in plans for individual reporting items, fluctuation margins that are considered "normal" or random are determined. Only deviations beyond the threshold are reported and specifically identified.

The advantage of this measure is that important developments are not lost in a flood of information, but management's attention is specifically drawn to problem areas. Functional knowledge is required to define thresholds. Specifying and setting these limits is sometimes very complex. One rule for controllers is to primarily concentrate on the exceptions.

In this regard, a distinction must first be made between standard and ad hoc reports. Standard reports are basic reports that are standardised in terms of content and form, which the information recipient receives at predefined time intervals. Standard reports can thus be standardised and institutionalised. By contrast, ad hoc reports are based on specific individual cases. Regular reports take into account the basic need for information in the areas of responsibility. They are activating in nature: they require and demand action. On the other hand, ad hoc reports are created because of special events and situations. They may be initiated by Controlling or other departments. Thanks to the increasing development of IT systems, the information recipient today is more and more able to generate the information they individually require themselves in the form of ad hoc reports.

As already explained, reports should generally contain forecast values as well as actual and target values. This is because the target/actual comparison is able to illustrate deviations between planned and actual figures and their causes very effectively. It therefore lays the foundations for future improvements. However, this information is only suitable for management interventions to a limited extent. This is because the target/actual comparison is based on the past; the business transactions have already taken place.

By contrast, a forecast "predicts" the anticipated actual value at the end of the period based on the current state of knowledge on the date of the report. This means that, even at a very early stage, there is information on how individual reporting items are expected to look at the end of the period without further intervention. Forecasting allows more time to respond and increases the probability of measures being effective.

In recent years, Performance Cockpits® have become a popular way of visualising important management information (cf. **Fig. 6.10**). Performance Cockpits® are a sophisticated form of the performance management and reporting system;

- are systematically adapted to the information recipient's operating and strategic performance management requirements,
- segment and illustrate the fundamental management issues, and
- aim to optimise the quality of decisions by way of technical and organisational integration.

HORVÁTH & PARTNERS
MANAGEMENT CONSULTANTS

I.g. Other Financial key figures vs. Budget

"Action Title: Clear Message on main developments and essential effects "

Group — Other Financial Key Figures — December 2016

€ in million	YTD Actual	YTD +/- Budget	Full Year FC	Full Year +/- Budget
Turnover	10.000	+1.000	40.000	+4.000
Adjusted EBITDA	5.000	+500	20.000	+2.000
Adjusted EBIT	2.500	+250	10.000	+1.000
Net Interest	1.000	+100	4.000	+400
Non Operating Earnings	-2.000	-200	-8.000	-400
EBT	800	+80	3.200	+320
Operating Cash Flow	600	+60	2.400	+240
CAPEX	500	+50	2.000	+200
Free Cash Flow	100	+10	400	+40

* xxx

Group — Sales Volumes — December 2016

Volume	YTD Actual	YTD +/- Budget	Full Year FC	Full Year +/- Budget
Product 1	50.000	+2.500	200.000	+4.000
Product 2	40.000	+2.000	160.000	+3.200
Product 3	30.000	+1.500	120.000	+2.400
Product 4	20.000	+1.000	80.000	+1.600

* xxx

Comments +/- Budget (YTD and Full Year)

Financial Key Figures	YTD	Full Year
Net Interest	+ €100m	+ €400m
• Interest share in addition to provisions	+ €80m	- €350m
• Lower results from special funds	- €5m	- €45m
• Release of interest provision '06	+ €5m	+ €5m
Non-operating earnings	- €200m	- €400m
• Realized earnings from special funds	- €100m	- €200m
• Gains on disposal of assets	- €150m	- €300m
• Market valuation of derivatives	+ €50m	+ €100m
Operating Cashflow	+ €60m	+ €240m
• Lower income tax payments	+ €40m	+ €200m

Sales Volumes

• Product 1: Sales increased despite negative market development, mainly as a result of increased after sales and promotion activities. This trend is expected to continue over the full year.

• Product 2: Sales decreased as a result of market entry of competitor XY. However, this trend is expected to reverse over the remaining year, resulting from the expected increase in the customer base of the B2B segment in CEE countries.

Fig. 6.10: Illustration of a control cockpit/practical example

The key components of a Performance Cockpit® are the tailored management information obtained by focusing the content, the specific arrangement thereof, the targeted use of supplementary forms of illustration and recourse to extensive, flexible IT functionalities. Even the improved capability of IT systems (business intelligence) has contributed to making efficient front-end solutions possible. Depiction here is based on the presentation format. Current trends such as mobile reporting clearly demonstrate this necessity.

Illustrating several important KPIs gives the information recipient an adequate picture of their area of responsibility and the interrelationships between the performance indicators depicted. With knowledge of the interdependencies, developments can be recognised earlier. Cockpits with 8 to 12 important pieces of controlling information have therefore proven to be successful. They give the information recipient an adequate picture of their area of responsibility. The illustration features all key figures with a traffic light for up-to-date evaluation and a trend arrow for the anticipated development. Three to four key figures are also illustrated with detailed information such as their chronological sequences or the exact position of predefined limits.

Advantages gained from the Cockpit concept:

- Important information at a glance
- No distraction by unimportant details
- Graphic preparation to support decision-making
- Well-rounded management information
- Interrelationships between key figures quickly become apparent
- Focus on deviation information, absolute values as a drill-down

Is it clear in your company who delivers which input information, and when, and who receives the output information?

The likelihood of control measures being successful is highly dependent on the date from which information is available. A fundamental quality characteristic of the reporting system is therefore how up-to-date reports are when they are made available to the responsible persons. In case of doubt, speed should be given preference over excessive accuracy, which prevents deviation information being made available as fast as possible.

Focusing on the recipient is particularly important for an effective report. This primarily means filtering and consolidating information based on the recipient's needs. Consolidating pieces of information results in report hierarchies that take the relevant recipient's field of activity into account. It would thus be unreasonable to shower management with pieces of information that analyse the deviations of one cost type in one production cost centre. Information in reports for management must instead be consolidated in such a way that they enable a quick overview of the development of the entire company. If necessary, further detailed information on individual report items can then be obtained. **Fig. 6.11** illustrates the report contents for various hierarchy levels as an example.

Are the key figures prepared according to the needs of the recipients (for planning, budgeting and reporting) in your company?

Besides focusing on the individual recipient, it is essential to observe departmental standardisation too. This guarantees that the same circumstances and information are illustrated consistently, which makes communication easier. Another way of encouraging the acceptance of reports is visualisation using graphical illustrations. Graphical illustrations are often clearer than mere numerical tables and are absorbed by the recipient significantly more quickly.

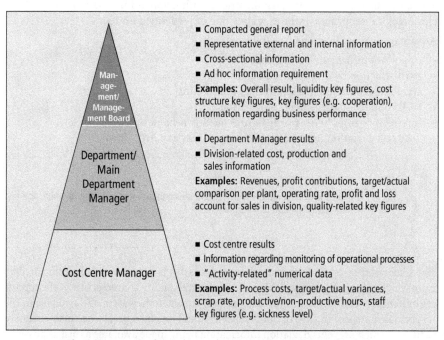

Fig. 6.11: Reporting hierarchies and corresponding reporting information

6.3.4 Current trends in management reporting

It is management reporting's duty to provide report recipients with information in such a way that they are able to make the right decisions on time. To be able to best fulfil this duty, now and in the future, reporting has to continually develop in line with new requirements. This results in content-related and design-related issues on the one hand and issues regarding technical realisation on the other (**Fig. 6.12**). Trends and challenges in management reporting are examined in more detail below.

Content-related and structural trends	Technical trends
■ Expansion of future purchases	■ Big Data
■ Integration of external factors	■ Mobile Reporting
■ Lean Reporting	■ Self-Service Reporting

Fig. 6.12: Top trends in management reporting

Both the company itself and reporting are facing conditions that are changing at increasing rate. An examination of reports from previous years only finds that the content at that time was not, in most cases, compatible with current control requirements, but also that the nature and form of the report have been almost completely transformed. New trends are triggered by environmental changes and technological innovations, and thus pose new challenges for the controller. For example, a broader focus on the future has been on every controller's agenda for several years. This is closely associated with the integration of external indicators into reports. The intention is to form a connection between these indicators and financial and non-financial indicators. If this challenge is mastered, there will be benefits both for the informative value of reporting due to the opportunity of market comparison and for the early recognition of the need for action due to the extended time horizon. Therefore, key figures models that have previously been used must be reviewed and improved by setting the goal of better early recognition and forecasting.

Although previously mainly responsible for the increase in efficiency of another department, the controller must now ask themselves whether the potential to increase efficiency perhaps lies in the evolved structures and established processes. Therefore, the aim of "lean reporting" is to make the creation of reports fast, automated and easy. The controller also plays a different role here. Instead of laboriously examining and working on volumes of data and producing reports, the controller can, thanks to the high standardisation and automation of all activities, including analysis, interpretation and annotation, concentrate on these ennobling tasks.

This goes hand-in-hand with high expectations of a suitable IT solution and of the controller's ability to fulfil their role as "business partner".

Technical conditions in reporting change regularly, almost completely. The three most important current issues include the field of "big data". Experts believe that a company's ability to utilise increasingly bigger and less structured volumes of data in corporate governance in an optimum way will be crucial for its success in the future. This requires suitable strategies, options for application and technical aids to be available.

Mobile reporting – which involves the preparation and evaluation of reports and data, regardless of time and place – is another issue. As approximately one quarter of all companies are currently in the process of setting up mobile reporting, this practice will soon be much more widespread. At the moment, the difficulties here lie in developing a clear strategy as well as in actually making full use of the technical opportunities that are available. Special reporting applications ("apps") are expected to increasingly enable intuitive evaluation, direct annotation and web-based collaboration based on the reports in the future.

The third important development is "self-service BI" or "self-service reporting", with which the recipient can produce reports themselves as required. This can be expanded to the extent that the report recipient themselves takes the place of the author, thus bringing standard reporting down to the necessary minimum.

The developments influencing management reporting today and in the future do not end with the three challenges just mentioned. Increasingly, the flexibility of reporting is subject to demands for it to be possible to promptly adapt the creation of reports to internal and external developments. This includes, for example,

- the depiction of organisational changes,
- the acquisition and divestment of company divisions,
- changes in the customer base, or
- the addition of new key figures and content.

6.4 Practical example

6.4.1 Handels GmbH

Handels GmbH is a German grocery retailer with a comprehensive cross-border network comprising more than 1000 branches. The company focuses on a discount-based product portfolio, which includes both food and non-food products. Food prices, which have already had a tendency to fall for some time, increased the need for efficient management reporting tailored to the information required for Controlling, on the one hand to counteract the increasing cost pressure through transparency and on the other hand to enable the right control signals to be given. The previous method of reporting, which was characterised by a balance between financial and non-financial key figures and too much detail, could not meet these requirements properly. Additionally, the reports were sometimes compiled individually by the relevant national subsidiaries and therefore could not be used for a transnational comparison of performance. For this reason, a consistent key figures system tailored to Controlling requirements and with standardised reports (standard reporting) had to be set up.

6.4.2 Project: Development of a key figures system with standardised reports

As already indicated in the first section, management's supply of information was improved and sustainably guaranteed by consistent, balanced and recipient-orientated management reporting. To this end, a process comprising four phases was selected: (1) analysis phase, (2) key figures design phase, (3) process design phase and (4) implementation phase. Based on the starting point described at the beginning and the customer's requirements profile, the key figures design phase in particular was of key importance. For this reason, the second phase will be addressed in greater detail below. However, this does not mean that the other phases do not make a fundamental contribution to the success of the management reporting method introduced. For example, the visualisation and preparation of the key figures tailored to the report recipient's needs significantly increased the recipient's receptiveness.

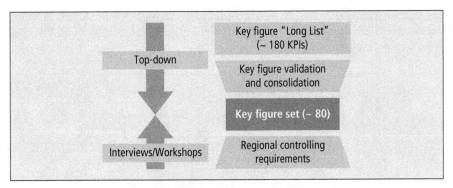

Fig. 6.13: Process of developing the sets of key figures

Two things were important while designing the key figures: The first was defining the requirements and criteria for future key figures together with the wider management team. For example, all future key figures had to be measurable, able to be influenced, of assistance for decision-making and relevant to performance. A "long list", which contains approximately 180 key figures, was then produced. To ensure that the ability of future report recipients (information recipients) to take action and make decisions is not impaired by a level of information that is too granular, the key figures identified ("long list") were validated and consolidated over the course of six workshops, which both representatives of the company's headquarters and representatives of the national subsidiaries took part in (see **Fig. 6.13**). The final set of key figures contained approximately 80 key figures, although not every key figure was reported to every report recipient (see next section).

The second criterion that was observed during the key figures design phase was the scalability of the sets of key figures that were produced (cf. **Fig. 6.14**). This meant that based on the information level (level 1, level 2 and level 3), standard reporting only contained selected key figures. For example, "level 1" reporting only contained the most important key figures and those relevant to the controlling of the entire company. "Level 1" reporting was tailored to the top management level's information requirements and therefore predominantly reported highly consolidated key figures (e. g. ROCE, EBITA, net sales, etc.) in order to illustrate complex business information at a glance. Besides the advantages outlined above, the consolidation of information is also associated with the risk of losing valuable detailed information. However, it became clear during the workshops held that it is precisely this detailed information, together with other information, that is needed for controlling in other parts of the company. These specific key figures did not meet the top management level's information requirements but did meet those of the relevant functional managers. On this basis, reporting for the "Logistics" division contains function-specific key figures that are tailored to the functional process, such as "transport costs per km" or "on time".

After the key figures were agreed upon and assigned to the various report recipients (report level), the key figures concept developed was embedded in a reporting process. Besides the report creation process, the future reporting dashboard and report layout were developed and arranged during this process design phase. The new reporting method was then rolled out across the company and implemented IT-wise. At the end of the project, the company had a management reporting system that was harmonised both hierarchically and globally, which, thanks to the key figures tailored to controlling requirements and the business model, depicted the right financial and non-financial information transparently.

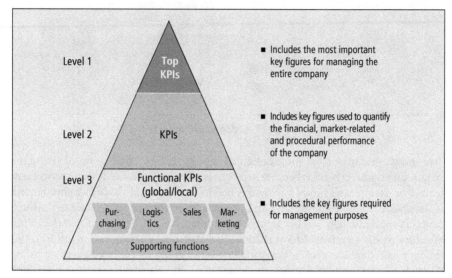

Fig. 6.14: Reporting pyramid

6.4.3 Lessons learned

Retrospectively, it is clear that three factors in particular influenced the success of the project.

- Clearly defined project framework and objectives: The project framework, which was clearly defined from the start, meant that the project team was able to focus on handling the issues and was not constantly faced with new challenges.

- Two-dimensional process: The two-dimensional process, particularly in the design phase, also led to very high acceptance of the project work. Every stakeholder was able to participate in the project through various workshops and influence the result with their input.

- Scalable implementation: As shown in **Fig. 6.13**, the new reporting system is based on the report pyramid, which means that every level is a self-contained report package. This meant that it could be implemented sequentially and the organisation could be introduced to the new reporting concept gradually through change management.

6.5 Design checklist for managers and controllers

 Provide comments for all numbers and key figures.

 Differentiate between need for information and need for decision-making.

 Prepare reporting to suit the needs of the respective recipients.

 Do not change the structure of your key figure system arbitrarily. Only then can you ensure comparability in the long term.

 Consider plan (target), actual and forecast (to be) in the management reports.

 Use quantifiable values as key figures wherever possible.

 Compare your key figures over time.

Further reading

If you would like to find out more about management reporting in general, please read:

Gleich, R., Horváth, P., Michel, U. (eds., 2008), Management Reporting – Grundlagen, Praxis und Perspektiven [Management Reporting – Principles, Practice and Perspectives], Freiburg *et al.* 2008 or

6 Management Reporting

Niebecker, J., Kirchmann, M. (2011), Group Reporting und Konsolidierung: Optimierung der internen und externen Berichterstattung, Ansätze zur Prozessverbesserung, effiziente Unterstützung der Berichtsprozesse [Group Reporting and Consolidation: Optimising internal and external reporting, approaches to process improvement, efficient support for reporting processes], Stuttgart 2011.

If you would like to find out more about the issues of key figures and reporting, please read:

Reichmann, T. (2016), Controlling mit Kennzahlen und Managementberichten [Controlling with key figures and management reports], 9th ed., Munich 2016.

7 IT System

7.1 Chapter objectives

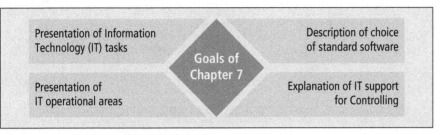

Fig. 7.1: Chapter objectives

Chapter 7 outlines the importance of Information Technology (IT) as a tool supporting the Controller. On reaching the end of the chapter, readers should understand the importance and tasks of a functional IT system in the context of effective controlling, as well as the challenges involved.

7.2 Introduction

During planning, controlling and information supply, large volumes of data are processed, condensed, compared and analysed. In the absence of IT, these tasks would become almost impossible. IT systems enable the Controller to improve information supply (e. g. by quickly compiling analyses) and offer effective support for planning and control functions.

Two main aspects can be identified in relation to using IT in the company:

- IT supports Controlling (e. g. in accounting)
- Controlling coordinates IT (see "IT Controlling")

Rapid IT developments can lead to increasing coordination problems, e. g. due to organisational adjustments. In terms of recent developments, "digitisation" is one such topic.

The focus of the following section will not be on IT Controlling nor on the coordination problems caused by IT. Instead, it will investigate the importance of using IT to perform controlling tasks.

IT can be used to improve and simplify both the quality of the information provided and the results of planning and control as well as their process (e. g. through automated reporting systems or IT-supported planning models).

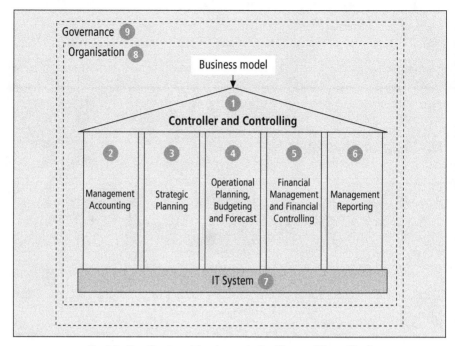

Fig. 7.2: Classification of the chapter in the "House of Controlling"

In practice, the growing popularity of IT means that Controllers must have an even better grasp of IT issues and IT know-how.

The following section starts by outlining which corporate departments use IT and what process is used to select standard software. It then continues by describing IT support in Controlling in more detail.

7.2.1 Using IT in operations

IT has become indispensable in companies. Especially in larger companies, it would no longer be possible to process the data volumes concerned without IT support. IT is increasingly used to support management processes and hence for non-standardised tasks. Its aim is to support management in all information, communication and problem-solving processes.

Fig. 7.3 presents the operational areas in which IT systems are used, split into operative systems, management systems, electronic information exchange systems and cross-sectional systems (cf. *Mertens* 2013, p. 19).

Operative systems can be split into administrative and material planning systems. Administrative (e. g. accounting etc.) systems are used to calculate mass data and manage inventories. Material planning systems (e. g. cost calculations, production planning and control systems etc.) can be used to prepare short-term planning decisions. Operative systems can thus display and support order processing in relation to goods, information and cash flows. Operative systems can be split further, into industry-neutral and industry-specific applications. Given high formal requirements, industry-neutral appli-

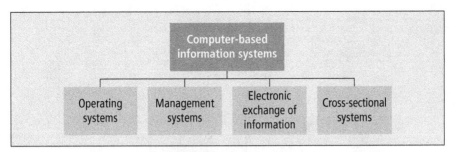

Fig. 7.3: Classification of IT-supported information systems by purpose

cations dominate financial accounting and payroll and wage calculations, as well as invoicing and procurement. A wide range of standard software is available for these tasks. Office communication systems, such as email, are also largely industry-independent. Industry-specific applications fulfil special tasks within an industry, such as Computer Integrated Manufacturing (CIM) solutions in the manufacturing industry (cf. *Mertens et al.* 2012, pp. 100 et seq.).

Management systems are used to prepare for and support decision-making by upper management and typically a distinction is made between planning systems and management information systems.

By now, it can be assumed that company-internal IT systems are broadly used. In the area of electronic information exchange, therefore, cross-company applications and applications linking different companies (e. g. Electronic Data Interchange (EDI), Electronic Business (E-Business), virtual market places or collaborative software) are essential.

Further development of electronic information exchange, particularly the spread of the internet, has created additional options for using cross-company information and communication. Electronic processing of business processes is summarised under the term "E-Business". In particular, the features of E-Business include networking between companies, new types of collaboration and communication with suppliers and customers, creating new products and services, and mobile information exchange. As, in a literal sense, some applications are related to retail, E-Business is often equated with the restrictive concept of E-Commerce.

Fig. 7.4 allocates the main operative E-Business applications to the different stages of the value chain. SCM (Supply Chain Management) systems focus on the interaction between all companies involved in creating a product in order to optimise the entire supply chain from the raw material producer to the end customer. By contrast, E-Procurement systems as business-to-business applications support the procurement of goods and services. CRM systems (Customer Relationship Management) at the business-to-consumer interface support the documentation, management and evaluation of customer relationships, as well as customer care.

Application systems which can be used at all operative workspaces and which can be accessed via interfaces from administrative and material planning/management systems are called cross-sectional systems. These include office systems, multimedia systems and knowledge-based systems (e. g. expert systems). If an integrated system supports all company-internal functions of administration, material planning and management, this is called an ERP System (Enterprise Resource Planning).

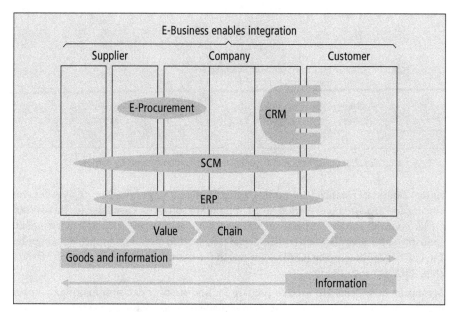

Fig. 7.4: E-Business and added value (*Kemper, Lee* 2002, p. 14)

7.2.2 Standard software selection process

When selecting a suitable IT solution, it is generally always possible to develop software internally or to introduce standard software .

A **standard Controlling software** will have the following features:

(1) firmly defined scope of functions,

(2) general usability (company-independent),

(3) fixed prices,

(4) minimal programme adjustments.

Since the standard software currently available tends to be highly mature, we advise against developing software internally. Evaluations should consider not just costs, time and quality, but also future availability and solution dependence/flexibility. High licence costs and maintenance fees are normally balanced out long-term by lower administration and service costs as well as manufacturer developments covered by the maintenance costs.

Since integrated, company-wide software packages (e. g. SAP) are increasingly widespread, one further question has gained in importance: how to select the right integrated IT platform module or purchase the right specialised third-party provider product. To this end, the opposing targets of achieving a high level of integration and of meeting the specified requirements must be weighed up.

In the selection process, it is the Controller's responsibility to formulate the technical requirements of an IT solution. This IT solution must then be selected in consultation with the IT Department. Generally speaking, while the users must choose a business management software, a pure focus on user needs only has been shown to be uneconomic as there is the risk that too many solutions might end up being used. As a result, many companies are currently focused on harmonising their IT applications and on phasing out isolated applications. Before launching the selection process per se, the market should be explored in order to reduce the list of available products ("long list") to those alternatives which are actually suited to the company ("short list"). Clearly defined and gathered criteria can be applied to achieve this (price, system requirements, etc.).

The selection process per se then comprises the following steps:

1. Defining and grouping company-specific requirements
2. Determining whether the suitable products meet the requirements and cost restrictions
3. Eliminating criteria which all suitable products meet to a comparable extent
4. Eliminating criteria not relevant to the decision
5. Weighting of requirements and requirement groups
6. Evaluating the extent to which requirements are met
7. Ranking alternatives
8. Selecting participants for a so-called "showcase"
9. Breaking down the evaluation as part of the "showcase"
10. Selecting the most economic alternative

 How is the selection process for standard software designed in your company?

In theory, there is a number of other methods and processes, whereby a distinction can primarily be made between more or less objective or subjective processes. The main benefit of the software selection process described above lies in the fact that the relevant criteria are successively reduced in the course of the selection process.

Project experience has shown that software manufacturers increasingly add non-essential performance features to their products (so-called "delighters"), such that the performance profile can often far exceed the requirements profile. When the process described here is used, performance features can either be added to the requirements profile or removed from the evaluation if competing products have comparable functionalities. It is often precisely these features which turn out to be decisive in terms of selecting software, subject to a thorough examination of the relevance of these functionalities.

7.3 Designing effective IT support for Controlling

IT support for Controlling can take many forms. These are presented below (see **Fig. 7.5**).

- IT support must first of all include management accounting systems (see 7.3.1 Principles of IT Support).
- To these are added planning and control as well as data analysis (see 7.3.2 IT Support through Planning, Control and Data Analysis).
- Controlling processes are automated using IT systems (see 7.3.3 Automating Controlling Processes).

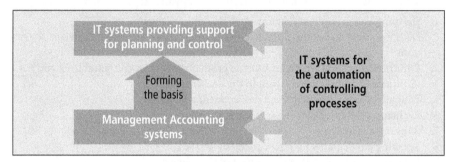

Fig. 7.5: IT support for Controlling

7.3.1 Principles of IT Support

Management accounting (comprising accounts, as well as cost and profit accounting, cf. Chapter 2 on Management Accounting) is one of the most important and most comprehensive areas of IT within Controlling.

Where operative processes in management accounting are automated, this significantly increases efficiency and makes standardised tasks easier for staff to perform. Sub-areas of financial accounting include: accounts payable, accounts receivable and general ledger accounting. These are closely linked to each other as well as to other preceding and successive tasks (e. g. invoicing, inventory management and payroll). General ledger accounting accesses data from the other areas to create ledger sheets, accounting statements (e. g. balance sheet, income statement) and special-purpose statements. This requires an integrated system to ensure efficient use, with sub-systems coordinating and receiving the data that they require directly from the relevant departments. For instance, this means that ledger accounting records any nominal account bookings posted in relation to payments and invoices once only, before automatically posting them to the relevant nominal accounts area. **Fig. 7.6** shows the relationships between the individual sub-systems.

Cost and profit accounting includes cost type, cost centre and cost object accounting, preliminary costing and the operating income statement. Cost accounting almost exclusively uses actual data from other sub-systems, such as the general ledger or production control. This also requires integrated systems. Ideally, IT-supported cost and profit accounting only requires manual data as planning data and for error and reconciliation processes. IT-supported cost centre accounting is largely executed based on manual procedures. System integration makes it possible to display not just cost but also usage and

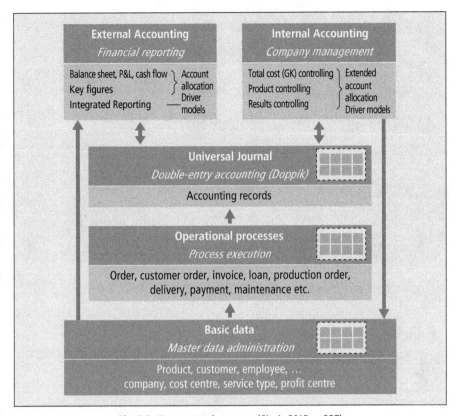

Fig. 7.6: IT-support sub-systems (*Sinzig* 2015, p. 237)

performance deviations and as such to make information available to deviation analysis. IT-supported preliminary costing calculates manufacturing costs by accessing saved bills of material, work schedules and actual costs for each output unit (e. g. each minute of production), costing individual components and then adding these up to make up the finished product. IT-supported historical costing calculates the expenses incurred by individual cost objects based on material transactions from operating data capture and payroll payslips in the system.

ERP (Enterprise Resource Planning) systems support all the main functions of administration, material planning and management. This term was coined in the USA and was based on the idea that the administration functions frequently added to extended Manufacturing Resource Planning systems were cost accounting, financial accounting and HR. Especially in manufacturing companies, this term is equivalent to integrated standard software. We are only dealing with a modern application landscape if recent applications from the areas of Customer Relationship Management or Supply Chain Management are added to ERP systems. However, such tailored company applications can often be time-consuming and expensive. ERP systems, such as the software system SAP ERP, were developed over time. Historically, it had only been possible to process internal company processes. Adding functionalities created programmes able to handle business processes across companies, e. g. using the internet. **Fig. 7.7** shows the scope of SAP ERP. This supports all operating functions.

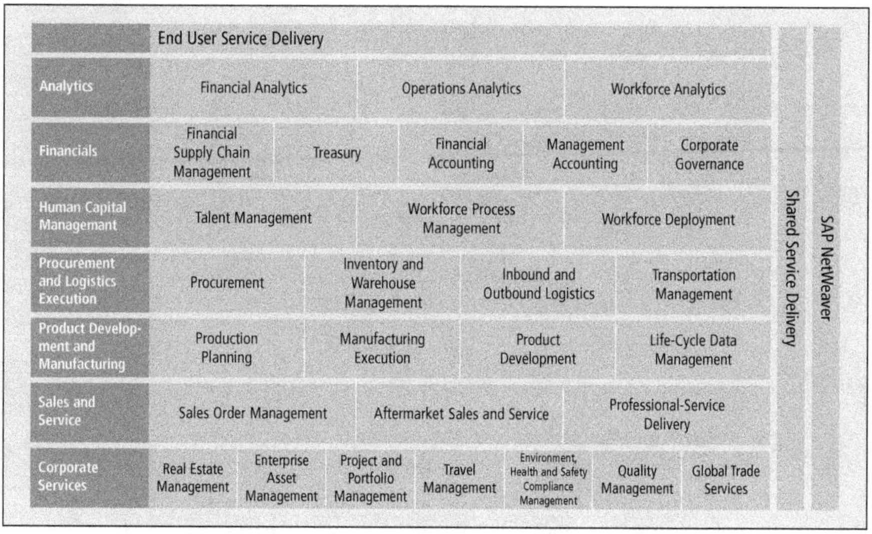

End User Service Delivery						
Analytics	Financial Analytics		Operations Analytics		Workforce Analytics	
Financials	Financial Supply Chain Management	Treasury	Financial Accounting	Management Accounting	Corporate Governance	
Human Capital Management	Talent Management		Workforce Process Management		Workforce Deployment	
Procurement and Logistics Execution	Procurement		Inventory and Warehouse Management	Inbound and Outbound Logistics	Transportation Management	
Product Development and Manufacturing	Production Planning		Manufacturing Execution	Product Development	Life-Cycle Data Management	
Sales and Service	Sales Order Management		Aftermarket Sales and Service		Professional-Service Delivery	
Corporate Services	Real Estate Management	Enterprise Asset Management	Project and Portfolio Management	Travel Management	Environment, Health and Safety Compliance Management	Quality Management	Global Trade Services

(right-side vertical labels: Shared Service Delivery | SAP NetWeaver)

Fig. 7.7: Functional scope of SAP ERP (*Friedl, Hilz, Pedell* 2012, p. 8)

Do you use an integrated ERP system?

7.3.2 IT Support for Planning, Control and Data Analysis

In planning and control, IT is not yet used to the same extent as for management accounting. This is primarily because this area uses qualitative information and planning cannot easily be standardised.

As a result, IT support for planning is strongly focused on operations, e. g. production planning or the annual budget. It is mostly limited to analysing data, developing models and executing model experiments. IT also offers major benefits for strategic planning. This is particularly true where alternatives and scenarios are simulated using company models ("what if" analysis), graphical evaluations and database queries. In this way, it becomes possible to support the planning process in relation to information supply, decision-making preparation and communication.

Since corporate planning requires information from operative IT systems, workstation PCs are normally connected to central servers and databases via a network. This allows data from central databases to be queried locally. This data can then be processed further (e. g. a company's Cost Planning department might use SAP ERP with the CCA (Cost Center Accounting) module) and forwarded (cf. *Mertens, Meier* 2009, p. 197).

The ever-larger data volumes processed by Controlling mean that IT has become indispensable for reporting . We need IT to make information relevant to decision-making in a timely manner and suitable format. Reporting systems enable IT-supported control by comparing budget and actual data. The employees responsible need only be notified of any unusual data constellation applying the principle of "Information by Exception" to avoid information overload. To this end, special filter techniques are applied to the entire data volume (cf. *Mertens, Bissantz, Hagedorn* 1995): thresholds (triggered if limits are exceeded), rankings (creation of orders), navigation within hierarchies (created by combining the threshold and ranking methods) and identification of data patterns (this attempts to find a group of data in the data volume which is "conspicuous" in the same way). So-called expertise systems provide the greatest support in the context of control. These analyse an existing data volume using an expert system and attempt to find the cause and effect of deviations. The Controller is then informed of the result in the form of so-called expertise consisting of tables, graphs and explanatory text (cf. *Mertens, Meier* 2009). Since IT-supported control systems receive actual data from existing accounting systems, invoicing and planning systems must be closely coordinated.

One increasingly important task of IT-supported control involves supplying the company's control bodies with the relevant information. Currently, such control bodies, e.g. the Supervisory Boards, are largely dependent on company management for their information, in spite of the fact that company management is precisely who they are responsible for monitoring. This necessitates concepts on how to make information available automatically in order to enable business activities to be monitored and evaluated.

Increasing use of IT also changes the requirements of Planning and Control employees. It is likely that future developments will involve more flexible planning systems and greater use of expert systems in the field of budget/actual deviation analysis for IT-supported control systems.

In recent years, the term "Business Intelligence" has increased in importance. This describes systematic data analysis processes (including data provision, preparation, evaluation and presentation). Their aim is to offer new findings to support and improve business decision-making. With this in mind, analytical processes in software applications are used to evaluate company-internal and external data (e.g. relating to customers or competitors) to gain the desired findings. The analysis results can help, for example, to minimise risks, make processes more efficient or create more profitable customer relationships. *Kemper, Mehanna, Unger* (2004, p. 7) use the term Business Intelligence to describe an "integrated, company-specific, IT-based overall approach to business decision-making support". **Fig. 7.8** sets out the framework for "Business Intelligence".

Data provision makes available consistent, unified data from operative information and communication systems. Common data management concepts include Data Warehouses and Data Marts. Operational Data Store is a special data pool which also provides data for specific evaluation and application purposes. Information generation uses analysis systems enabling graphical analysis of the database. This primarily employs Online Analytical Processing (OLAP) and Data Mining concepts. Information is then saved to ensure that the findings gained from the analysis continue to be available to the relevant decision-makers.

The majority of IT-supported Controlling systems in use today are based on one or more such Business Intelligence technologies, or at least use centralised data provision for analyses.

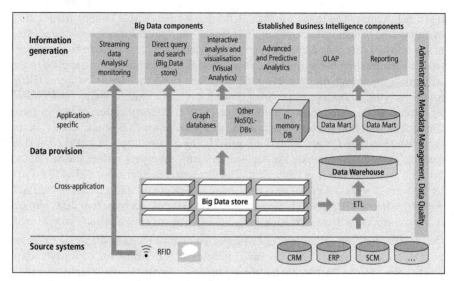

Fig. 7.8: Architecture framework for Business Intelligence (*Baars, Kemper* 2015, p. 226)

Further development of Business Intelligence is discussed using the term "Big Data". Big Data refers to the scope and the unstructured nature of data. Nowadays, only a small percentage (approximately 5 %) of this data volume is specifically analysed and used.

The innovative value of IT solutions dealing with Big Data comes from the following features:

- **Volume:** As implied by the term "Big Data", this includes large data volumes as well as many smaller data volumes analysed together (cf. *Zacher* 2012, p. 2).
- **Variety:** One of the main challenges of Big Data lies not in the large data volumes themselves but in the wide variety of data. The data originates from company-internal and external sources and can be structured (relational databases etc.), partially structured (log files) and unstructured (texts online, video streams, audio files etc.) (cf. *Matzer* 2013, p. 18).
- **Velocity:** Constantly changing data with limited validity require real-time data generation and processing (cf. *Matzer* 2013, p. 18).
- **Veracity:** It is important to ensure that the data is seen to be credible (cf. *Neely* 2013; *Redman* 2013). This is particularly key for Controllers who are regarded as "controlling the figures".

Big Data has diverse use potential. *Davenport* (2014, pp. 73 et seq.) distinguishes between the following use categories:

- Cost reductions
- Quick decisions
- Improved decisions
- Product and service innovations

IT-supported evaluation of Big Data also makes sense in relation to the Planning and Control system. Important topics include: risk assessment, forecasts, scenarios and early detection. The latter points in particular are currently receiving special attention under the term "Predictive Analytics". "Predictive Analytics" investigate what might happen in the future. Approaches such as Data Mining, Text Mining and Prediction in particular are used here.

Do you know how Big Data could benefit your organisation?

7.3.3 Automation of Controlling Processes

For a long time, rationalisation approaches focused on production and ignored administration, even though only 10-20 % of a processing operation tended to generate value. The remainder is made up of unproductive waiting, transport and storage times. Therefore, so-called workflow management system were developed in order to create more effective and efficient processes in administration.

Since many business processes are either based on a division of labour, are repeated or have a clear structure, these can be broken down into individual activities. Activities can only be performed once the activity preceding them in a workflow has been completed. Workflow management systems are software systems whose purpose is to break down activities into individual steps (cf. *Laudon, Laudon, Schoder* 2010, pp. 713 et seq.). Its tools comprise the application software used during processing steps, document management systems to provide the necessary documents, group-related support systems and communication by email between the different processing roles. Workflow Management (WfM) focuses on process control i.e. on performing business processes based on specified models.

In contrast to traditional office communication, WfM is active. It controls and monitors the procedures. WfM software independently chooses the best path for a process based on the conditions specified and then passes on tasks to the employees and roles responsible in accordance with deadlines. Automatic reminders, resubmissions and forwarding avoids delays during processing. Each processing stage is sent the interim products created by the preceding role. This greatly reduces processing times. WfM systems are particularly suited to supporting processes which require great detail, such as applications for business trips or procurement. Partially structured processes, such as complaint processing, are more demanding, especially where these require the option to change process specification during operations (cf. *Mertens* 2013, p. 30).

WfM is particularly useful for paper-intensive business processes which the roles involved must perform at different times and in different locations. WfM systems can support not just standard tasks (e. g. invoice capture) but also complex, irregular ad hoc processes.

WfM can also be used in Controlling as problems must often be solved by several individuals and extensive coordination processes are required. Budgeting is one example of an area in which WfM can support Controlling.

In addition, WfM harbours great information potential for company management and Controlling. Controllers know where a document is located at all times and whether it has been processed, saved or forwarded. WfM provides the process status and overall process data (time required, number of employees and processing steps, process order, expected completion date, etc.) for each ongoing process. Once the process status has been determined, suitable measures such as resubmission to the clerk, consultation or forwarding can be added. After the process has been completed, Controlling can use the recorded process data to analyse the process and identify the need/potential for improvement.

7.4 Practical example

7.4.1 Industrielle Dienstleistungen GmbH and Anlagenbau AG

The project examples described below aim to show the contribution that a consistent company-wide accounts and cost centre plan can make to improving the quality and comparability of financial and non-financial information, and how this can be integrated into the IT architecture.

Both are examples of manufacturing companies with more than 10,000 employees. One of these is in the services industry. In the last few years, Industrielle Dienstleistungen GmbH has undergone strong inorganic growth (through acquisitions) and now comprises more than 400 fully consolidated companies. The other is Anlagenbau AG. Both companies are undergoing a structural reorientation and must learn to handle heterogeneous business structures and different infrastructures, such as in relation to IT architecture. In addition, both companies are facing changing information requirements – driven by a changing market and competitor situation and ever more complex accounting standards – and the task of ensuring transparency and comparability of result, profitability and liquidity figures. Based on these framework conditions, they must increase the transparency and comparability of the different companies' financial data, harmonise internal and external information requirements and integrate the developed concepts into the existing IT structure.

7.4.2 Project: Linking the Chart of Accounts and Cost Centre Plan

The section below shows how chart of accounts and cost centre plans can be linked up with the aim of safeguarding the transparency required of external (P&L based on the total cost method) and internal reporting (P&L based on the cost of sales method) using integrated accounting. The chart of accounts is at the heart of integrated accounting and as such also of harmonised reporting. All value-adding business processes trigger bookings and as such transactions on the accounts defined in the chart of accounts. Both internal and external information requirements must be taken into account when booking/posting such transactions to accounting objects (cost centres, PSP elements, orders etc.), and these must already be considered when designing both the chart of accounts (What transaction detail should be recorded?) and the cost centre plan (How

Account no.		Description	Cost of sales (general)	Pools for (multi-)project management	Machinery cost centres/ vehicle pools	Operational Purchasing	Work preparation	Commercial project execution, project support	Technical infrastructure	Occupational health and safety	Separate project cost centres (major projects)	Warehouse and Logistics	Employee pools, production employees	Planning/deployment control	Separate production buildings	Quality assurance (only operational part)	Technical offices	Workshops	Allocation cost centres, cost of sales
#601000000	2	Revenues																	
#601100000	3	Overall performance																	
#601110000	4	Revenues from projects																	
#601120000	4	Revenues from supply of services and goods																	
#601130000	4	Arge result																	
#602000000	3	Other revenues																	
#604000000	3	Inventory changes																	
#605000000	3	Capitalised work																	
#605100000	4	Other capitalised work (as adjustment item)																	
#606000000	2	Other operating income																	
#606010000	3	Income from the disposal of intangible assets	x	x	x	x	x	x	x	x	x	x	x	x	x	x	x	x	x
#606020000	3	Income from the disposal of tangible assets																	
#606021000	4	Income from the sale of property and buildings	x	x	x	x	x	x	x	x	x	x	x	x	x	x	x	x	x
#606022000	4	Other income from the disposal of tangible assets	x	x	x	x	x	x	x	x	x	x	x	x	x	x	x	x	x
#606030000	3	Income from the write-back of other provisions	1	1	1	1	1	1	1	1	1	1	1	1	1	1	1	1	
#606040000	3	Income from the revaluation of trade receivables	x	x	x	x	x	x	x	x	x	x	x	x	x	x	x	x	x
#606050000	3	Income from the revaluation of other receivables (excluding trade receivables) and other	x	x	x	x	x	x	x	x	x	x	x	x	x	x	x	x	x
#606060000	3	Income from subsidies/debt waivers (on both sides)	x	x	x	x	x	x	x	x	x	x	x	x	x	x	x	x	x
#606070000	3	Compensation claim, unless revenue or production process	x	x	x	x	x	x	x	x	x	x	x	x	x	x	x	x	x
#606080000	3	Any other operating income	1	1	1	1	1	1	1	1	1	1	1	1	1	1	1	1	
#606090000	3	Income from the subsequent adjustment of contingent purchase price payment by companies	x	x	x	x	x	x	x	x	x	x	x	x	x	x	x	x	x
#606100000	3	Other income from the appreciation in value																	
#601000000	4	Income from the appreciation in value of intangible assets	x	x	x	x	x	x	x	x	x	x	x	x	x	x	x	x	x

Accounts structure — Account allocation information

Fig. 7.9: Account allocation matrix

should the recorded transactions be allocated?). Both projects display and specify the interaction between the chart of accounts and the cost centre plan as an accounts matrix developed with the different departments during the course of the project (see **Fig. 7.9**). Accounts are allocated to functional areas in order to show what types of bookings must be allocated to what cost centres.

This ensures that internal and external reporting are standardised as required, in addition to the effect that standardisation has on account allocations and hence on improving cost accounting transparency. The chart of accounts is structured by cost type allowing a P&L to be deduced based on the total cost method. By contrast, the cost centre framework is structured by the functional areas Production (cost of sales), Distribution and Management to facilitate Management Reporting by allowing a P&L to be deduced based on the cost-of-sales method. For instance, any travel costs incurred are allocated to the cost type Travel Costs in line with the total cost method, while using the cost-of-sales method would result in travel costs to be allocated to the functional area incurring them. In other words, a well-designed chart of accounts and cost centre plan, where this is also closely linked to the two sets of rules, can act as a reliable, sufficiently detailed source of information and ensure that information is adapted to the relevant controls.

Both projects can generally make use of one of two solutions, the "OneERP" approach and the "Group Control" approach (cf. **Fig. 7.10**).

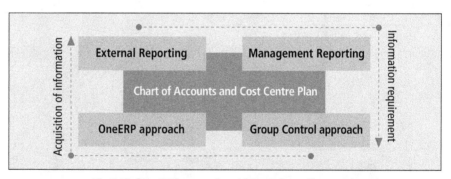

Fig. 7.10: "OneERP" approach and "Group Control" approach

These two solutions differ based on the degree of standardisation, the scope of company specifications and the control requirement chosen. Whereas the "OneERP" solution focuses on ensuring that processes, systems and operative business management are consistent, the "Group Control" approach strives for minimum standards and to harmonise internal and external reporting. For the chart of accounts, this means that the "OneERP" approach involves developing a company-wide, operative chart of accounts, whereas the "Group Control" approach stipulates a minimum structure based on an "accounts framework". The operative chart of accounts organised in the companies must then be mapped using the minimum structure specified by the accounts framework. A distinction must be made between "mandatory accounts" (minimum content requirements, must be included in the operative chart of accounts as a general ledger account), "optional accounts" (minimum content requirements, but do not have to be included in the operative chart of accounts via general ledger accounts), and "recommendations" (optional suggestions to provide further details). To give an example, the group accounts framework splits staff costs into wages and salaries. The operative chart of accounts must also include such a split. The mandatory accounts must be defined such that all information required for the information supply system can be made available to a sufficient level of detail.

A company's initial situation and control requirement determines which approach is most suited to a particular company. Industrielle Dienstleistungen GmbH strictly applies the "Group Control" approach to the project. In the case of Anlagenbau AG, different factors including the existing IT architecture and the intended harmonisation level meant that a combination of the two approaches was most suitable. Whereas all non-SAP companies are using a "Group Control" approach, SAP companies are aiming at a "OneERP" solution. The section below sets out how exactly to implement the "OneERP" solution. In particular, the focus is on system implementation. As described above, the "OneERP" solution aims at harmonising the ERP systems as much as possible. For the project, this means that the results areas and master data from the charts of accounts and cost centre groups must be merged (e. g. from general ledger accounts, cost centres, service types, statistical KPIs). Data harmonisation and IT integration comprise four steps:

1. Creating a mapping template
2. Developing operative target structures for the relevant master data categories
3. Testing the developed structures
4. "GoLive"

The templates are used to define and document the standards stipulated by group headquarters and to set minimum structures for their implementation. The cost framework described above is an example of such a template. These minimum structures are then operationalised together with the pilot companies. An operative chart of accounts can then be deduced from the accounts framework and pilot companies, which can then be saved in the IT system for all companies.

This is technically implemented together with SAP System Landscape Optimization (SLO). A database conversion of all the relevant master data mentioned above is used as the implementation method. This searches for the numerical keys of the relevant master data in the databases using SLO conversion packages and rewrites them in accordance with the mapping tables. The implementation process is executed in five phases in order to prepare, provide quality assurance and identify weaknesses in the mapping. The first four implementation phases are so-called test cycles whose scope and test intensity will increase throughout its course. A test cycle simulates actual implementation, i. e. database conversion, in a physically separate test system. To this end, a copy of the production system from a specific date is used to test the mappings for completeness, validity and freedom from errors based on the given master data level using SLO conversion packages.

After verifying the quality of the master data mappings and ensuring that the conversion packages are fully functional, the final step involves converting the production system. The system can go live in the course of one weekend during which the technical departments involved and the IT department can also perform final approval tests.

7.4.3 Lessons learned

Besides determining the information requirement and information supply, it is crucial to guarantee the availability of information and thus, indirectly, the integration of sets of rules into the system and organisation. The projects revealed that seven factors in particular are highly important to guarantee sustainable system integration:

- **Early involvement** of technical departments and companies during the design phase. Involving the relevant companies early on increases the likelihood that the change will be accepted, and involving the relevant technical departments provides the technical knowledge required to optimally design rules which can be easily implemented. During the initial design phase, only selected companies (pilot companies) must be involved in order to keep coordination and consultation costs at a reasonable level and nevertheless ensure sufficient involvement.

- The concepts **must be developed and documented in detail.** Practical guidelines must be compiled based on the consultations with the relevant pilot companies and technical departments. It must be possible to apply the guidelines directly to practical examples to ensure that they aid full documentation while simplifying day-to-day work with the new concepts.

- The new standards and concepts must be **published and marketed appropriately.** An intranet platform must be set up for the projects in order to provide recipients with any project contents that are developed. Publishing the documents centrally ensures that only the most recent version of the documents can be accessed via the intranet (Single Point of Truth) and that the company does not use several versions. In addition, search functions and keyword-based display enable users to work with the contents and guidelines quickly and in a user-friendly environment.

- **Implementing an extensive pilot project.** It is not only important to involve the pilot companies early on; they must also be involved in the "right" way. To achieve this, standardised templates should be developed in structured workshops. The templates can be used to identify areas in which action may be required, and these can then be assigned to the categories "Accounts structure" or "Cost centre structure" and processed. Such an extensive pilot project can reduce problems (normally caused by a broad roll-out) by approximately 80 %. This both increases acceptance and helps to create more mature concepts.

- **Consistent and close implementation support** by the core project team. Consistent and close support during implementation also helps to ensure that a change is integrated successfully. When new concepts and processes are initially implemented, this can be simplified and improved by e. g. setting up phone support, providing a "starter kit" and subsequently holding workshops in which issues are discussed and suggestions for improvements can be recorded.

- **Ongoing follow-up and integration monitoring.** Integration is also aided by creating commitments. Reviews can be used to create such commitments. Checklists should be employed to regularly investigate such issues as "Which companies have not yet become involved?" or "Where does data quality still need to be improved?". This type of internal audit helps to check the standards set beyond the boundaries of the project and to adjust them if necessary.

- **Early involvement of the IT department.** Involving the IT department early on ensures that it is given sufficient time to become a reliable contact for technical and maintenance-related questions. This also allows "technical" responsibility to be passed on to line managers much more quickly, as the department can take on operative tasks from the beginning. Close involvement early on can also help to create technical understanding so that technical requirements can be implemented more quickly and easily.

All seven success factors contribute to effective communication and subsequent implementation of the developed concepts into the organisation. This in turn means that the employees affected are more likely to accept and trust them. This is the only way to fully integrate the concepts into the organisation and IT and to execute the intended project target of improving the quality and comparability of financial and non-financial information.

7.5 Design checklist for managers and controllers

Document how IT is used in your company.

Make sure you update regularly.

Document the potentials Big Data could generate in your organisation.

Develop concrete information support for management from that.

Draw up a road map for the further development of IT use in your company.

Ensure your use of IT is profitable.

Define clear responsibilities for IT at all levels within your company.

Further reading

If you would like to learn more about IT support in the context of Controlling, please read:

Gadatsch, A. (2012), IT-Controlling – Praxiswissen für IT -Controller und Chief-Information-Officer [IT Controlling – Practical Knowledge for IT Controllers and Chief Information Officers], Wiesbaden 2012.

If you would like to learn more about IT support in the context of value creation, please read:

Meier, A., Stormer, H., Gosselin, E. (2012), eBusiness & eCommerce: Management der digitalen Wertschöpfungskette [eBusiness & eCommerce: Management of the Digital Value Chain], 3rd ed., Berlin 2012

or

Krcmar, H. (2015), Informationsmanagement [Information Management], 6th ed., Munich 2015.

8 Controlling Organisation

8.1 Chapter objectives

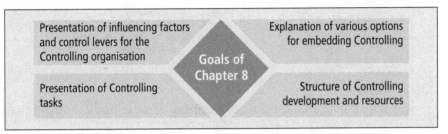

Presentation of influencing factors and control levers for the Controlling organisation	Goals of Chapter 8	Explanation of various options for embedding Controlling
Presentation of Controlling tasks		Structure of Controlling development and resources

Fig. 8.1: Chapter objectives

Chapter 8 deals with the overall organisation of Controlling. Various control levers and design methods will be addressed. By the end of the chapter, the reader should understand which possible arrangements there are for an effective Controlling organisation.

8.2 Introduction

Every CFO and commercial manager has to address the issue of which type of Controlling organisation, and with which associated Controlling resources, is right for their company. Key issues include

- whether the mix of centralised and decentralised controllers is the right one,
- how the organisation of Controlling can be ideally arranged using the "dotted line", and
- whether all promising resources and qualifications are available.

In line with the importance of Controlling duties for the company, the Controlling function must be embedded in the company organisationally. An effective Controlling organisation is characterised by the following factors:

- Alignment of the controller organisation with the organisation as a whole
- Definition of clear tasks and skills specifications
- Definition of clear regulations on the interaction between the manager and the controller
- Clear internal organisation of the controller service
- Concrete adaptation to the development of the company

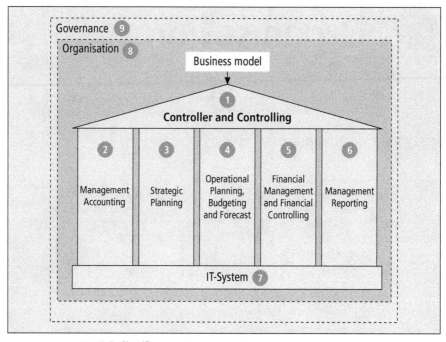

Fig. 8.2: Classification of the chapter in the "House of Controlling"

Based on the company's management model and the management's claim to leadership, the embedding of Controlling into the company, the structure of the Controlling division, Controlling's field of activities and the Controlling resources must be defined to ensure an adequate Controlling organisation (cf. Fig. 8.3).

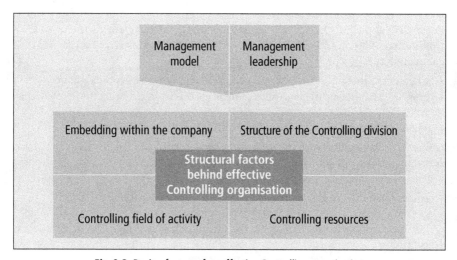

Fig. 8.3: Design factors of an effective Controlling organisation

The influencing factors and levers mentioned are explained in detail below.

8.3 Design of an effective Controlling organisation

8.3.1 Factors influencing the Controlling organisation

The starting point for the Controlling organisation is essentially the management's control model and the highest management level's claim to leadership (management board, executive board or group holding) of the other management levels (division managers, department managers or managers of subsidiaries).

With regard to the management model, the question arises of which dimensions management of the company will be based on. If the company is to be managed by region, division or product, for example, an effective Controlling organisation is also defined by these dimensions.

Management's claim to leadership determines which interests Controlling must represent in the company as a whole. Only when the claim to leadership is clear can the other design parameters of the Controlling organisation be defined. This is illustrated by Company Controlling's tasks (**Fig. 8.4**).

A financial holding company's claim to leadership, for example, is thus limited to influence over finance-related management decisions (e.g. allocation of resources, organisation of the investment portfolio, profitability targets). By contrast, a parent company has predominant, extensive influence over all management decisions (e.g. strategy formulation, operating measures). For the Controlling of a financial holding company, this means, for example, that comprehensive duties have to be implemented in the Investment Appraisal division, while the Controlling of a parent company depicts comprehensive duties in the division of corporate planning and result consolidation.

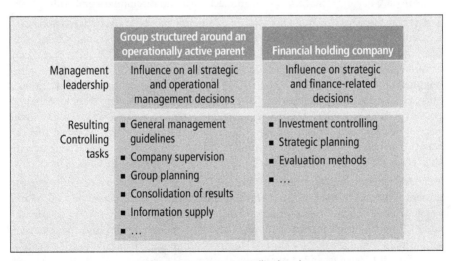

	Group structured around an operationally active parent	Financial holding company
Management leadership	Influence on all strategic and operational management decisions	Influence on strategic and finance-related decisions
Resulting Controlling tasks	■ General management guidelines ■ Company supervision ■ Group planning ■ Consolidation of results ■ Information supply ■ …	■ Investment controlling ■ Strategic planning ■ Evaluation methods ■ …

Fig. 8.4: Corporate Controlling's tasks

Besides the management model and the claim to leadership, there are other influencing variables, such as company size, that affect Controlling organisation (**Fig. 8.5**).

Influencing factor	Effect
Company size	Degree of centralisation of Controlling
Service performance technology	Degree of specialisation of controllers
Legal form (e. g. Aktiengesellschaft)	Scale of regulations to be taken into account
Information processing technology	Degree of automation, quality of forecasting
Capital market, procurement market (e. g. market fluctuations)	Necessity to perform risk assessments

Fig. 8.5: Factors influencing the organisation of Controlling

The critical influencing factors must be considered on a case-by-case basis. The controller must focus on these influencing factors.

 Which critical influencing factors can be differentiated in your company?

8.3.2 Embedding Controlling into the company

The fundamental design factors of embedding the Controlling organisation into the company are departmental allocation and technical and disciplinary embedding.

With regard to departmental allocation, a distinction can be made between allocating Controlling to the office of the CFO (Chief Financial Officer) or the commercial manager and allocating it to the office of the CEO (Chief Executive Officer). Significant advantages can be gained from allocating Controlling to the CFO's office by pooling commercial resources in one division of the company. Short communication channels and decision-making processes can be attained and synergies, e. g. from external accounting, can be leveraged. Additional benefits lie in one consistent database and in the pooling of expertise. If Controlling is allocated to the CEO's office, however, this can lead to conflicts between Controlling and the various finance functions. The reason for this is that an "all-encompassing role", such as that performed by the CFO, is ineffective.

Besides departmental allocation, it is necessary to appoint the Head of Controlling to a corresponding high management level to ensure the modern perception of the role of Controlling as a business partner and the management's right hand. Only assigning Controlling to a high management level grants it enough weight and the necessary authority to enable it to act on an equal footing to management, as its sparring partner. Therefore, it is recommended to appoint the Head of Central Controlling to the first, or at least the second, management level.

The organisation of most companies is also characterised by the coexistence of staff functions and line functions (**Fig. 8.6**). Before controller positions can be created, it must be decided in principle whether Controlling's area of activity can be performed better in a staff function or organisational unit with line competence.

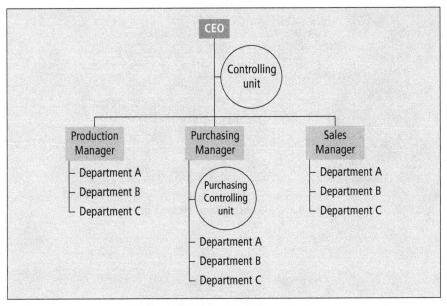

Fig. 8.6: Example of a staff/line organisation

Clear regulations on the authority to give instructions, i.e. subordinate line functions are under the disciplinary authority of superordinate positions, are characteristics of line functions.

Staff functions do not have any power to make decisions or give instructions to line functions. Their primary role is to assist the line function that they are affiliated with by providing advice, preparing for decisions and performing other services. Typical examples of staff functions include legal departments, public relations activities or auditing. As Controlling is understood to be a special kind of management support, creating a Controlling staff function, which is allocated to the highest management level, is often the most suitable way of embedding a results-orientated mindset into the company hierarchy.

The final decision relating to embedding Controlling into the company relates to the difference between a decentralised and a centralised Controlling organisation and the combined form of that, the "Dotted Line Organisation".

The strict decentralisation of decisions in large companies results in the corresponding decentralisation of Controlling. As a result, specialisation is highly varied. There are primarily three categories of decentralised controllers: functional controllers, divisional controllers and regional controllers (see **Fig. 8.7**).

The decentralised Controlling organisation is characterised by the technical and disciplinary subordination of decentralised Controlling under the business divisions (cf. **Fig. 8.8**). Decentralised Controlling is therefore directly integrated into the relevant decentralised organisational unit. The relationship between centralised and decentralised Controlling is merely informal. The decentralised Controlling organisation promotes trust and good cooperation between divisional management and decentralised Controlling. However, there is the risk that, if the level of decentralisation is too high, the

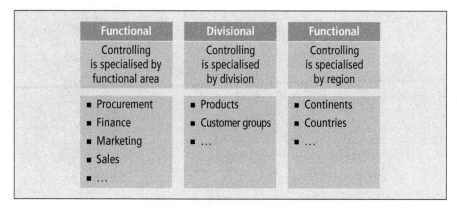

Fig. 8.7: Categories of decentralised controllers

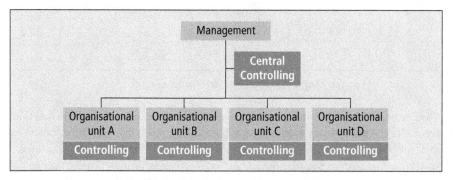

Fig. 8.8: Decentralised controlling organisation

overall Controlling concept (uniform systems, methods, instruments) will be neglected, sectionalism will increase and the decentralised controller will lose their required distance from line activities. This ultimately leads to great potential for synergies and efficiency remaining unexploited.

If Controlling is organised centrally, this means that Controlling by the departments is subordinate to centralised Controlling, in both technical and disciplinary terms (cf. **Fig. 8.9**). The maximum spatial allocation of decentralised Controlling to the departments with simultaneous disciplinary independence gives Controlling a very high level of independence from the managers of the departments. The centralised Controlling organisation also enables Controlling competence to be pooled and Controlling processes and procedures to be standardised. New Controlling concepts can be implemented more quickly and information flows smoothly. However, there is the risk of low acceptance of Controlling in the individual departments and an "information blockade" in relation to centralised Controlling.

The "Dotted Line Organisation" is a combination of centralised and decentralised Controlling organisation (cf. **Fig. 8.10**). This will be illustrated using the example of a departmental controller. On the one hand, the departmental controller is subordinate to the department manager, i. e. he/she receives instructions from him/her on which specific tasks he/she must perform. The departmental control may need special instruments for these tasks under certain circumstances (e. g. for investment appraisal). To ensure that he/she performs the investment appraisal process correctly in technical terms, he/she is also bound by the central controller's technical instructions. This is known as a so-called "dotted line organisation". This form of organisation combines many of the advantages of decentralised and centralised organisation. However, the centralised controller often has a conflict of interest if the department manager's guidelines are not in keeping with those of the centralised controller. In such cases, it is often helpful to allocate responsibility for specific tasks.

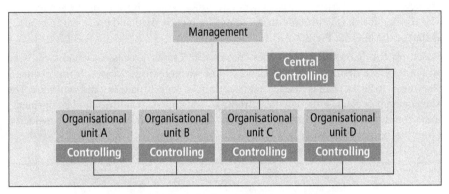

Fig. 8.9: Centralised controlling organisation

8.3.3 Controlling's tasks

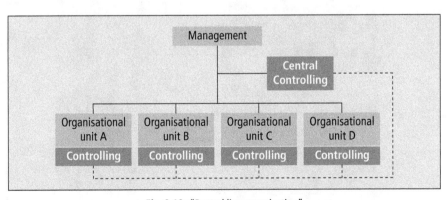

Fig. 8.10: "Dotted line organisation"

Up to this point, discussions on the possible organisational arrangements of Controlling have primarily focused on structural issues. However, how Controlling tasks are synchronised with each other and with other processes within the company is crucial for the efficiency of Controlling. Therefore, process organisation must be considered at least equal to the structural organisation of Controlling. Process orientation in Controlling is taken into account by laying down routine Controlling processes. The focus is on those processes that are particularly resource-intensive or significant for corporate management such as the planning process, internal accounting or reporting. The benefit of a process-orientated perspective of Controlling tasks generally lies in the logical illustration of Controlling tasks, responsibilities, the input required to perform them and, to increase efficiency, the fulfilment of Controlling tasks. This perspective requires controllers to organise themselves based on the processes that are aimed at Controlling's "customers".

8.3.3.1 Process-orientated Controlling organisation

Today, various standard process models have proven to be successful in providing a framework for performance assessment and process optimisation for the sequence of Controlling tasks. One process model that is frequently used and prevalent in practice is that of the IGC (cf. **Fig. 8.7**).

Based on the "Controlling" business process, ten main processes, which are listed in **Fig. 8.11**, are defined at process level 2. The seven main processes, from "Strategic Planning" to "Risk Management", are traditional Controlling tasks and activities. The three main processes "Functional Controlling", "Business Consulting and Management" and "Development of Organisation, Process, Instruments and Systems" are considered "interdisciplinary processes".

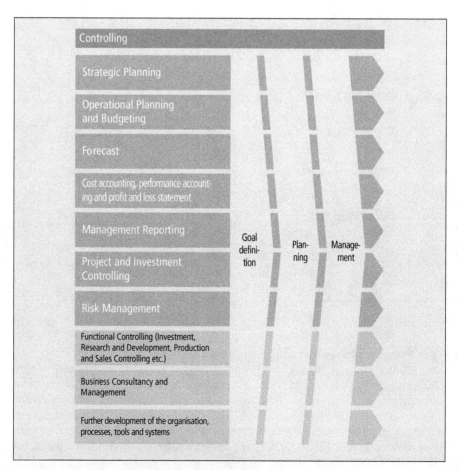

Fig. 8.11: IGC process model (cf. *IGC* 2011, p. 15)

"Functional Controlling" largely contains the first seven process-orientated main processes in a functionally specific way. "Business consulting and management" accounts for the results of the other main processes within the company, among other things. "Development of organisation, processes, instruments and systems" concerns, among other things, the optimisation of all other main processes.

On process level 3 of the Controlling process model, the sub-processes that correspond to each main process are defined. **Fig. 8.12** gives examples of the sub-processes for the main process "Management reporting". Besides the sub-processes associated with the main process, information is provided on the start and end of the process and on the necessary input and the output produced.

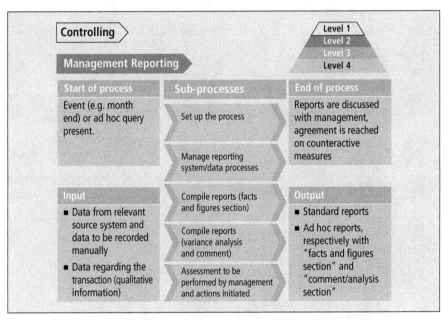

Fig. 8.12: From sub-processes to the main process "Management reporting"
(cf. *IGC* 2011, p. 34)

On process level 4 of the Controlling process model, the relevant activities for each sub-process are defined. **Fig. 8.13** gives examples of the activities for two sub-processes from the main process "Management reporting".

Which controlling activities are already organised along process lines in your company?

8 Controlling Organisation

Process orientation has significant effects on the controller's tasks, organisation and tools:

- Tasks: The sharp distinction between the controller and the manager is mitigated. The controller is involved in the creation of the process.
- Organisation: The controller area itself is structured by process. "Customers" and "products" are key Controlling terms.
- Tools: The supply of information focuses on key performance indicators that those involved in the process can apply directly; i.e. in addition to values, (customer-orientated) time, quality and quantity values are also important.

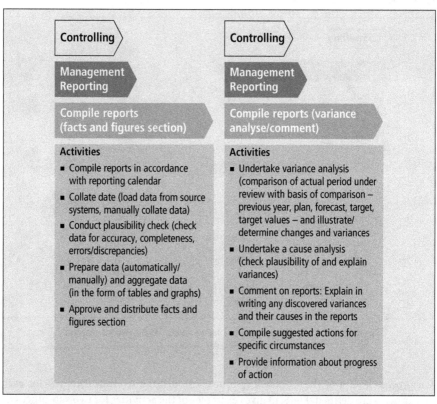

Fig. 8.13: Activities for two sub-processes from the main process "Management reporting" (cf. *IGC* 2011, p. 53)

As the process-orientated Controlling organisation has to be established in most companies first, the controller is often its initiator and facilitator. In such cases, his/her tasks exceed participating in creation of the process (cf. **Fig. 8.14**).

Various environmental developments mean that controllers' tasks have become increasingly automated and standardised cf. *Gleich, Grönke, Schmidt* 2014 in this regard). For example, activities such as data collection and preparation are increasingly automated using integrated systems.

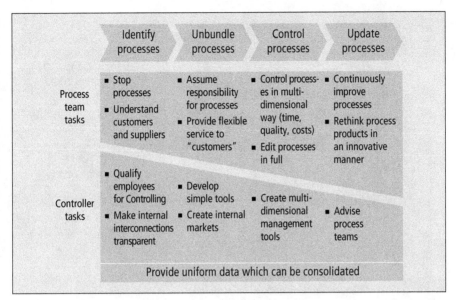

Fig. 8.14: Steps towards process-orientated Controlling

Due to the increasing decline of such routine tasks, controllers are increasingly required to perform demanding activities to support decision-making. At the same time, questions regarding the realisation of effectiveness ("doing the right things") and efficiency ("doing things right") improvements are also being asked in the Controlling division. Controlling is now under similar cost pressure to all other areas of a company's overheads.

For the purpose of effective Controlling, all Controlling activities should solely comprise those that lead to a specific output, i. e. that are aimed at both Controlling products (e. g. reports) and the transformation process "input to output" (e. g. producing reports). The focus should also be on the evaluation and communication of the output or the results, i. e. advising internal customers and managers (e. g. risk analyses).

Activities and processes (contributing, planning, consulting, producing, calculating, designing, etc.) mostly lead to results and output (reports, analyses, expertise, concepts, systems, etc.) whose design and quality are evaluated by their recipients, i. e. Controlling's (internal) customers.

This requires the controller and, in particular, the managers of the controller functions to

- consistently define their own processes and products,
- create starting points for measuring and developing their product and process performance (and thus measuring their own efficiency too),
- have knowledge of their internal customers (i. e. the manager) and their requirements as well as
- understand the necessary competences of resources and select and develop personnel on this basis (cf. *Gleich, Lauber* 2013).

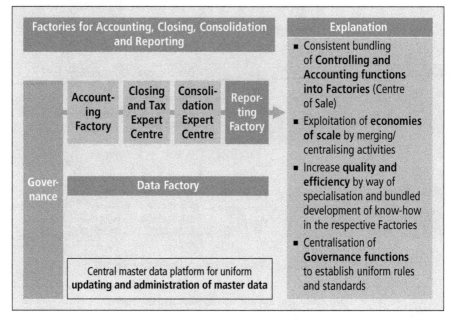

Fig. 8.15: Outsourcing selected Controlling processes

Controlling can address discussions regarding increasing effectiveness and efficiency by setting up shared service centres.

8.3.3.2 Controlling Shared Service Centre

Selected Controlling processes have already been outsourced for a long time under the heading "Controlling Shared Service Centre". So, for example, a "Reporting Factory" is understood to mean the standardisation and centralisation of reporting processes, which then routinely execute a precisely defined workflow (processing rule) "at the push of a button" (cf. **Fig. 8.15**).

The structure of a Controlling Shared Service Centre is based on the analysis and subsequent classification of Controlling tasks as repetitive and non-repetitive Controlling tasks (cf. **Fig. 8.16**). Repetitive Controlling tasks are pooled in a Controlling Shared Service Centre. With regard to the reporting process, this includes tasks such as collecting and structuring data, producing reports – with a quality assessment, if necessary – and distributing and providing reports to the relevant recipients on time. Other typical activities for a Controlling Shared Service Centre are planning and forecasting. Non-repetitive activities such as analysing and annotating reports and ad hoc reports are the responsibility of corporate Controlling, which can establish itself as a real business partner and adviser to management.

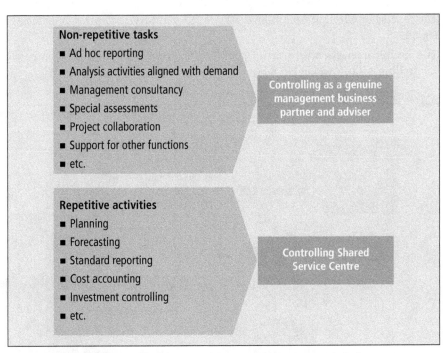

Fig. 8.16: Controlling tasks (based on *Burmeister, Temmel* 2007)

In contrast to a pure central Controlling department, a Controlling Shared Service Centre is characterised by the following features:

- There is a catalogue of clearly defined services.
- There are clearly defined customer relationships, which include service agreements and transfer prices.
- Various service levels and their possible uses are specified in the form of service level agreements (SLAs).
- Performance assessment is carried out transparently based on defined KPIs and/or by performance comparisons with alternative (external) providers.
- In some cases, internal customers are under no obligation to contract and there is therefore a competitive environment.

A distinction is made between a Controlling Centre of Scale and a Controlling Centre of Excellence. A Controlling Centre of Scale comprises repetitive and standardised volume-related activities with a focus on producing and providing information. The aim is to achieve economies of scale by utilising synergies. Examples of volume-related tasks in reporting include reporting figures, producing standard reports and producing monthly target/actual comparisons. By contrast, the aim of a Controlling Centre of Excellence is to realise the advantages of specialisation instead. This means that this type of Shared Service Centre pools tasks that are required in different company divisions but that occur relatively rarely and, at the same time, require more in-depth technical expertise. Examples of excellence functions are investment controlling and setting transfer prices.

8 Controlling Organisation

The process of selecting Controlling tasks for Shared Service Centres is defined in **Fig. 8.17.**

The possible interaction between a Controlling Shared Service Centre and corporate Controlling is illustrated in **Fig. 8.18.**

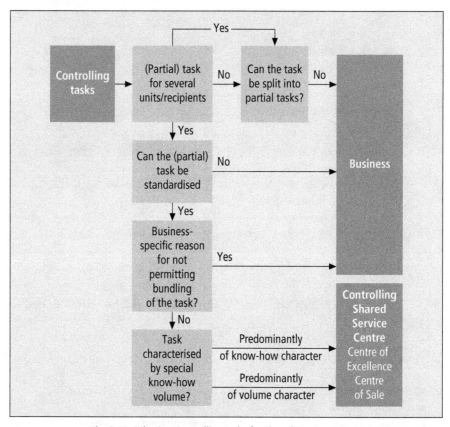

Fig. 8.17: Selecting Controlling tasks for Shared Service Centres

Setting up Controlling Shared Service Centres is associated with commercial advantages. Pooling repetitive activities and the associated learning and experience curve effects decreases the costs of carrying out a process or an activity individually. The available capacity is better utilised, which is tantamount to a decrease in fixed costs.

Challenges arise in particular from the IT requirements that have to be met for a Controlling Shared Service Centre. This includes, among other things, integrated, uniform company-wide Controlling applications as well as centralised data storage and uniform data availability.

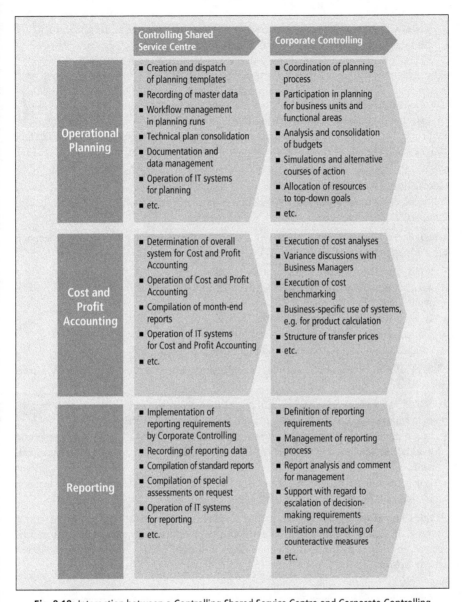

Fig. 8.18: Interaction between a Controlling Shared Service Centre and Corporate Controlling

8.3.3.3 Specialist Controlling tasks

In recent years, Controlling tasks and instruments geared towards purely financial matters were also transferred to non-financial matters as standard. Current examples of these Controlling specialisations are Green Controlling, Innovation Controlling and Marketing Controlling.

Just like other Controlling concepts, Sustainability Controlling is intended to protect managers' supply of information, whereby only the conventional Controlling instruments can be used (cf. *Schaltegger, Zvezdov* 2012, p. 67 and *Gleich, Bartels, Breisig* 2012).

> **Sustainable corporate management** requires economic, social and environmental challenges to be taken into consideration at the same time (cf. *Epstein, Buhovac* 2014). Sustainability Controlling assists sustainability management with this task.

The environmental aspect has been the object of special attention in recent years as part of sustainability initiatives: "Increasingly, companies are recognising that giving processes, products and services an environmental focus reduces costs on the one hand and taps into new sales and innovation potential on the other hand" (*Isensee, Michel* 2011, p. 436).

For us, focusing on the environmental aspect of Sustainability Controlling – i. e. "Green Controlling" – is predominantly for practical reasons (*Horváth, Berlin* 2016), because it is hard to work on all aspects of Sustainability Controlling, which is potentially very complex, at the same time.

Green Controlling tasks include the following six points, which relate to environmental effects and products (*ICV* 2014, p. 47):

- Analysing the relevance and creation of transparency,
- Identifying opportunities and risks,
- Assisting with defining targets and strategies,
- Integrating it into planning and decision-making processes,
- Continuously measuring and managing targets, and
- Integrating it into controlling and reporting processes.

This results in the "green controller"'s main groups of tasks (cited in *Isensee, Michel* 2011, p. 437):

- "Assisting with green strategy and target formation by identifying success factors, benchmarking, and performing market and competition analyses,
- green measuring, managing and evaluating by developing suitable key figures and evaluation benchmarks (e. g. green KPIs and environmental investment assessment) and
- green consulting, sensitisation and supporting key players within the company, e. g. by demonstrating and scrutinising environmental/economic relationships."

Besides Sustainability Controlling, the controlling of innovations has increasingly become the focus of innovation experts and controllers in recent years. This can be seen in an increasing number of publications (e. g. *Möller, Menninger, Robers* 2011 and *Gleich, Schimank* 2015).

> "In contrast to measuring R&D performance, **Innovation Controlling** deals with the integrated management of innovative activities between various business units and thus serves as a way of supporting the management and communicating (*Gassmann, Perez-Freije* 2011, S. 394).

It is becoming more and more important to plan and manage company-wide innovation projects as well as innovation and research and development activities in a structured way, to manage innovation portfolios successfully or to define and implement innovation strategies. This concerns both manufacturing companies as well as companies in the services industry. Companies are increasingly being distinguished by their ability to innovate quickly, efficiently and successfully. As a result, Innovation Controlling as part of innovation management is becoming more and more relevant. Below, it will first be demonstrated how innovations can be managed and controlled, and how internal Innovation Controlling can be viewed.

Innovation facilitates sustainable growth and is thus a source of commercial success. Innovation management should ensure that innovative achievement does not just remain an accidental, one-off undertaking. On the one hand, innovation should be structured as a routine process by standardising innovative activities through sequential phases. On the other hand, it is necessary to involve all relevant players within the company in this process. However, innovations are characterised by a high level of novelty, as certain features are unknown before starting the project due to its forward-looking nature. Innovation management thus faces risks, uncertainty and complexity as well as external influences such as the increasing lack of resources, intensity of competition and growing customer and market requirements. It is therefore necessary to assist with innovation management when carrying out your tasks. Innovation Controlling incorporates this support role and aims to increase the effectiveness and efficiency of innovation management.

As it is a relatively new area of Controlling, however, there is still a certain degree of uncertainty relating to the organisation of this sub-discipline. On the one hand, the features and characteristics of Innovation Controlling are unclear; on the other hand, companies are not able to make a precise statement on the quality of their Innovation Controlling.

Innovation Controlling is generally understood to be a service function of innovation management with no decision-making authority. Instead, it has to facilitate the decision-making process, provide recommendations for action and review the decisions made.

The aim of Innovation Controlling is therefore to increase the effectiveness and efficiency of innovative activities. The former guarantees that the company's targets are met through the "right" innovation projects ("doing the right things"). The latter ensures that the means employed to achieve targets are put to optimum use ("doing things right").

Innovation Controlling performs various tasks as part of innovative activities in order to fulfil its supportive role. The following three key groups of tasks can be identified (cf. **Fig. 8.19**):

- Planning support ensures that for the purpose of results-orientated coordination, decisions are aligned with each other in such a way that innovation targets are met. In addition, it should identify both risks and complexity within innovative activities.
- Information support should cover innovation management's information needs and make the decision-making process easier. For this purpose, Innovation Controlling must first identify this need, then generate data and information and prepare these in a way that supports the management system in a productive way.
- As a counterpart to planning, it is necessary to safeguard the controls – the comparison of targets and actual circumstances – within innovative activities. Quantitative as well as qualitative targets must be taken into account. As a performance measurement, Innovation Controlling thus exceeds the traditional understanding of financial and results-orientated controlling.

8 Controlling Organisation

Finally, in addition to Sustainability and Innovation Controlling, Marketing Controlling is another traditional Controlling specialism.

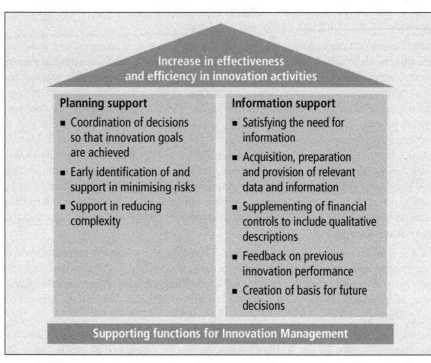

Fig. 8.19: Groups of Innovation Controlling tasks (according to *Munck, Chouliares, Gleich* 2014, p. 110)

Marketing Controlling does not just relate to typical accounting tasks and instruments but also to the structure and control of all planning, decision-making and controlling instruments that assist with the process of customer orientation. This includes consulting and coordination tasks in strategic and operational marketing planning as well as retrospective analyses of success.

Fig. 8.20 illustrates the process of marketing planning and control for various things, differentiated by strategic marketing planning and budgeting and operational marketing planning and budgeting. At the core is marketing mix planning from the top down, which leads to both long-term and strategic components as well as operational action planning.

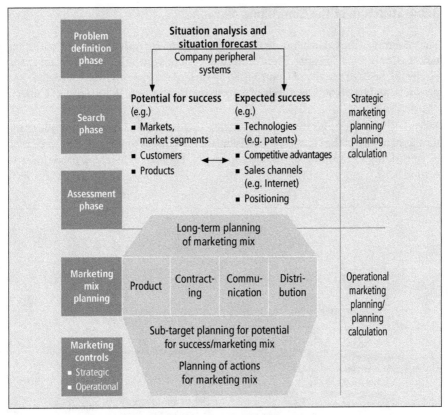

Fig. 8.20: The process of marketing planning and control (*Link, Weiser* 2011, p. 48)

Cooperation with Controlling occurs during marketing planning in relation to, for example,

- sales programme planning,
- setting prices and terms,
- selecting customers and customer groups,
- defining the markets and sub-markets to be supplied,
- defining distribution channels, and
- defining the various marketing activities.

Besides planning management, Controlling within the company is largely devoted to information management. Controlling gets information systems up and running, develops them further and ensures that they are used efficiently. For the connection between marketing and controlling, this means that Controlling is jointly responsible for creating, processing and handling data.

A marketing information system may comprise the following expansion stages:

- Marketing statistics,
- Marketing costs and operational accounting,
- Field sales reporting,
- Sales planning and a
- Market research system.

8 Controlling Organisation

8.3.4 Structure of the Controlling division

The structure of the Controlling division defines the internal distribution of Controlling tasks to Controlling positions. The Controlling positions can be broken down, for example, by the fields of activity of Controlling, by various business divisions or regions and products, and based on a synthesis of various approaches, e. g. in the form of a matrix organisation.

Essentially, the questions that arise in relation to technical and disciplinary allocation for the structure of the Controlling division are the same as those that arise in relation to embedding Controlling into the company (cf. **Fig. 8.21**). Therefore, please refer to section 8.3.2.

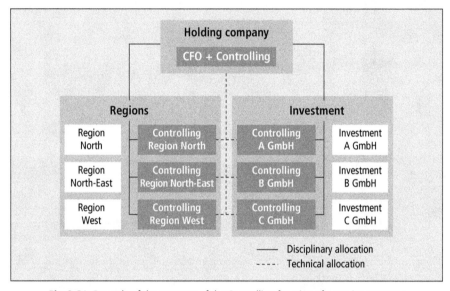

Fig. 8.21: Example of the structure of the Controlling function of a service company

Besides the actual task of organising the structure of the Controlling function, the issue of the organisation of the entire CFO function is increasingly coming under scrutiny. Under the heading "The CFO of the Future", various requirements have been discussed and posited, all of which feature

- a greater focus on the future,
- increasing value orientation,
- additional control with non-financial key indicators, and
- a focus on the core (Controlling) business.

The Controller's self-awareness is redefined and expanded to include the directions of impact mentioned. In response to criticism of only producing backward-looking financial information that only satisfies the management's information needs in some cases, various types of controller have been defined, which describe the stages of development of a controller's self-awareness at the same time. In its classic form, the controller is considered a goalkeeper, who largely stands on the line – motionless and defensive – and only reacts to attacks. By contrast, a modern and forward-looking controller is described as a business partner who, as a partner on an equal footing, proactively supports management by providing forward-looking information and tools and also provides stimuli and ideas for managing the company.

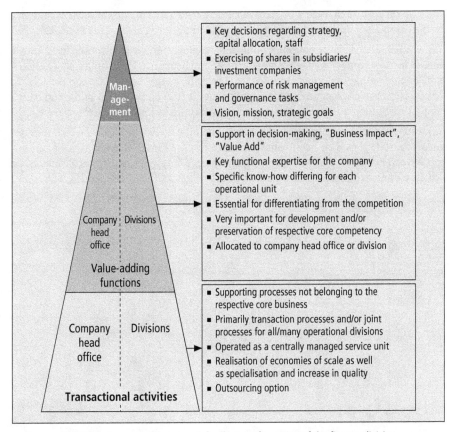

Fig. 8.22: Conceptual framework for the transformation of the finance division

Fig. 8.22 illustrates the conceptual framework with three different levels, which constitutes the basis for the transformation of the finance division and groups the possible courses of action in relation to increasing efficiency and effectiveness.

The requirement for a focus on the key (Controlling) business is aimed at increasing efficiency and effectiveness in the finance division itself, while previously the Controlling function in particular had the task of supplying the divisions of the company with management information simply for evaluating and facilitating this rationalisation, e. g. in procurement, production, logistics and sales. One approach to this is, as already mentioned above, the Controlling Shared Service Centre.

8 Controlling Organisation

8.3.5 Controlling resources

With regard to the provision of resources for the organisation of Controlling, there are issues regarding the optimum number of controllers in a company as well as their qualification profiles.

Various surveys, such as that by Horváth & Partners' CFO panel, show that as the size of the company increases, the number of Controlling staff does too (cf. **Fig. 8.23**).

Recommendations on the optimum number of employees in the Controlling function are ideally derived from best practice comparisons and benchmarking studies. It is essential here to ensure that the input variables for Controlling organisation are comparable. To be specific, besides company size this also concerns the comparability of the company's management model as well as the management's claim to leadership (cf. section 8.3.1).

In connection with the structure of Controlling there is also the issue of which requirements must be placed on a controller depending on their tasks and which skills controllers have to exhibit. A competence model for controllers gives rise to four role models on which various requirements are placed (see *Gleich und Lauber* 2013, cf. **Fig. 24**):

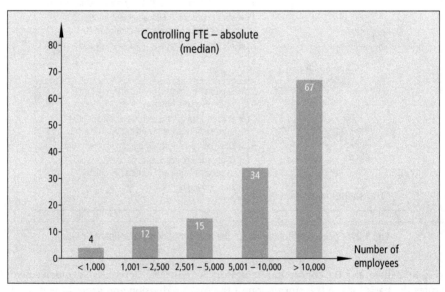

Fig. 8.23: Number of employees in Controlling depending on company size
(source: *Horváth & Partners*, CFO Panel 2016)

- The controller as an analyst/information specialist who evaluates information and prepares it for the recipients, i. e. the management
- The controller as the economic conscience for whom the operational monitoring of performance indicators is a priority
- The controller as a business partner/consultant to the management who actively supports the management in decision-making processes on the basis of valid information
- The controller as a change agent who initiates processes of change within the company on his/her own initiative

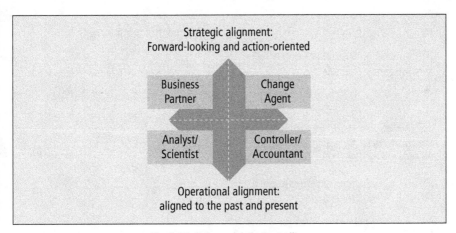

Fig. 8.24: Role models in Controlling

Fig. 8.25 gives an overview of the competence profiles of the various role models for a controller.

Besides the job specifications for the four roles, the competence model illustrates a development process that extends from the analyst to the controller and via the business partner to the change agent. The development process constitutes an increase in requirements in all relevant fields of competence. The only exception is the methodical field of competence, as it is of similar importance for the business partner and change agent. The highest increase in requirements lies in the development from controller to business partner, which is associated with significant requirements in terms of training for additional social and personal skills.

Based on the competence model, companies can organise the personnel development of controllers more effectively by consistently monitoring the competences that are critical to success throughout employees' life cycles, from approaching potential Controlling employees to succession planning. This ensures that a consistent understanding of job specifications can be developed within a company.

How is the organisational integration of controller services regulated in your company?

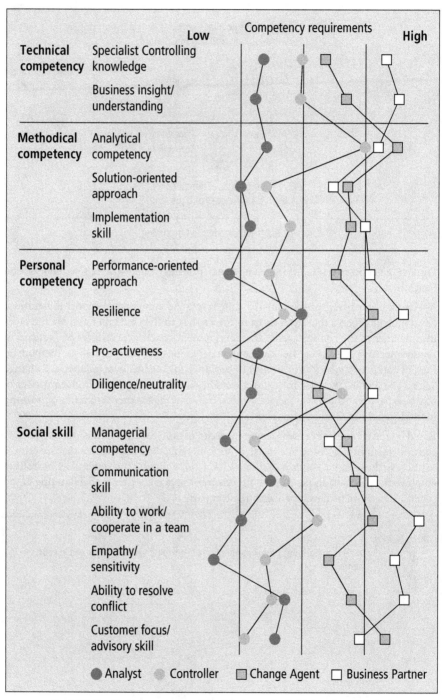

Fig. 8.25: Detailed competence profile of the controller (*Gleich und Lauber* 2013)

8.4 Practical example

8.4.1 Travel SE

The group is a tour operator active throughout Europe with several fixed and online retail brands for different holiday preferences. The group also has its own hotels and its own airline. The group started out as two almost functionally independent financial organisations with different local cultures. It became apparent that there were some significant differences in commercial processes, different system landscapes, different competency requirements and profiles, and only rudimentary overarching group-wide standards. The understanding of the CFO function's role as a consultant to management was generally not well-developed either.

8.4.2 Project: Development of a CFO organisation across different locations

Below, it will be demonstrated how the group's financial organisation was realigned to ensure effective, efficient performance in the CFO function (cf. **Fig. 8.26**). Controlling should be aligned with the business model and its role as a forward-looking business partner thus reinforced. The functions Accounting, Controlling, Treasury and Finance Business Solutions were designed in detail in order to achieve targets; only Controlling will be discussed specifically.

The organisation was realigned based on the dimensions CFO Agenda and Governance, Roles and Responsibilities, Management Principles and Management Instruments, Organisational Structure and Processes, as well as Employees and Resources (cf. **Fig. 8.27**).

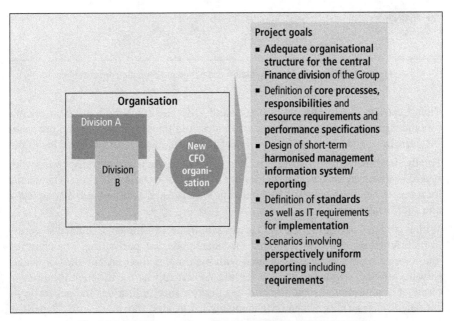

Fig. 8.26: Development of an efficient and effective CFO organisation

The analysis of the dimension CFO Agenda and Governance shows that there was no consistent, uniform governance in the group, but that this was only embedded into fundamental features decentrally. Potential for optimisation was exhibited in internal customer orientation through focusing and needs orientation.

The dimensions Roles and Responsibilities exhibited a lack of role-specific competences. A comparison of the locations found differences in the breadth and depth of the functions' value chains. The performance portfolio within the locations exhibited a lack of definition.

The analysis of the dimensions Management Principles and Management Instruments found that reporting lines did not follow the organisational structure, commercial management levels were sometimes operationally integrated and multiple roles were often carried out by the same person.

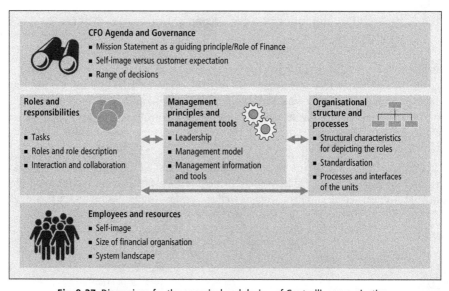

Fig. 8.27: Dimensions for the appraisal and design of Controlling organisations

The dimension Organisational Structure and Processes exhibited a different organisational structure based on the business model. Additionally, there were no processes that were independent of the business model and harmonised across different locations.

Finally, the dimension Employees and Resources exhibited a lack of transparency with regard to where competences were found, as well as little communication between the locations. A heterogeneous system landscape with isolated solutions led to complexity and additional outlay.

With regard to Controlling, the CFO organisation had a customer-orientated structure in its original state. It only exhibited inadequate business partnering. The planning and forecasting process was associated with high outlay (bottom-up) and was rarely forward-looking. Reporting was not defined consistently across different locations in terms of organisational structure and key performance indicators, and generating a consistent, overarching view of the company led to high transition costs. Repetitive tasks took up a significant amount of the time available. The allocation of tasks among internal customers was non-transparent.

An analysis of the dimensions found clear areas of action going forward:

- **Integrated organisational structure:** Derivation of an integrated and harmonised organisational structure across all locations with clear management and reporting lines.
- **Role model implementation:** Pooling of roles in individual components of the organisational structure, derivation of a defined and role-based performance portfolio, and embedding of customer orientation into the business partner's role.
- **Centrally embedded governance:** Organisational embedding of the policy role in order to guarantee centralised, consistent governance for the group.
- **Harmonisation and standardisation of processes:** Harmonisation and standardisation of processes in consideration of the specifics of the business model and exploitation of efficiency potential by way of automation.
- **Integrated system landscape:** Creation of the most consistent system landscape possible as the basis for further harmonisation and standardisation.
- **Perfectly fitting competence profiles:** Transparent definition of job specifications based on consistent and comparable performance specifications and development of adequate personnel development paths.

The new CFO organisation was developed and dimensioned in a structured way (cf. **Fig. 8.28**). The first step was to establish requirements for the targeted design of the organisation. The second step was then to allocate the performance specification, defined by organisational unit, as well as the roles and responsibilities. The third step involved a scenario-based derivation of an adequate organisational structure for the central finance division. Decentralised templates were also developed. As a fourth step, resource requirements were defined and savings potential was identified. Finally, in the fifth step, means of achieving targets and measures were developed.

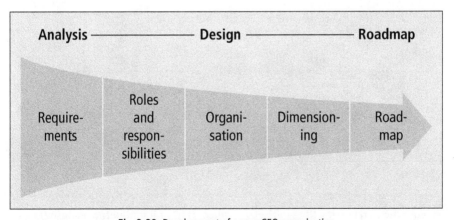

Fig. 8.28: Development of a new CFO organisation

In the new CFO organisation, roles and responsibilities are clearly defined and reporting lines are reduced (cf. **Fig. 8.29**). The efficient and effective CFO organisation is characterised by:

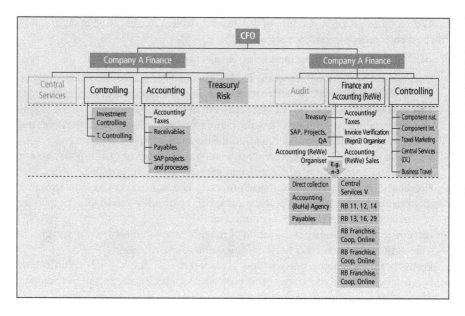

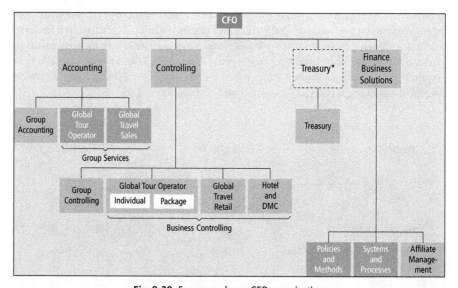

Fig. 8.29: Former and new CFO organisation

- Four direct reporting lines to the CFO (plus a staff unit for internal auditing),
- a CFO organisation across all locations,
- overarching governance, and
- a clear allocation of roles and responsibilities.

While creating the initial organisation, the foundations for further efficiency measures were laid.

8.4.3 Lessons learned

During the course of the project, it became apparent that the following four factors in particular had an influence on the successful completion of the project:

- **Communicating punctually:** Communicating punctually allowed possible solutions to be developed promptly in the project team. This enabled adherence with the project schedule at all times and the punctual presentation of interim results.
- **Taking a change approach:** An extensive change approach allowed long-standing structures to be scrutinised and discussed openly. This approach was particularly valuable when involving employees in the solution process and identifying innovative solutions.
- **Making sound arguments:** When implementing the approach, good arguments were key to convincing employees and the project team of an overall solution. It was only in this way that it was possible to implement it smoothly.
- **Top-level management commitment:** Even from the beginning of the project, top-level management was completely behind the project. This enabled prompt decisions and also helped to convince employees of the project.

8.5 Organisational checklist for managers and controllers

Define and document the expenses and competences of your controller services.

Ensure your controllers are clearly designated as business partners in the organisation.

Organise your Controlling predominantly with a process orientation.

Ensure the internal organisation of controller services is clearly structured.

Develop a roadmap for automating the tasks of controllers.

Further reading

If you would like to know more about the organisation of Controlling in practice, please read:

Gleich, R., Michel, U. (eds., 2007), Organisation des Controlling – Grundlagen, Praxisbeispiele und Perspektiven [Organisation of Controlling – Principles, Practical Examples and Perspectives], Freiburg 2007

or:

Temmel, P. (2011), Organisation des Controllings als Managementfunktion – Gestaltungsfunktionen, Erfolgsdeterminanten und Nutzungsimplikationen [Organisation of Controlling as a Management Function – Design Functions, Success Factors and Usage Implications], Wiesbaden 2011.

If you would like to know more about the IGC process model, please read:

IGC International Group of Controlling (2011), Controlling-Prozessmodell – Ein Leitfaden für die Beschreibung und Gestaltung von Controlling-Prozessen [Controlling Process Model – Guidelines for Describing and Designing Controlling Processes], Freiburg 2011.

9 Governance

9.1 Chapter objectives

Fig. 9.1: Chapter objectives

Chapter 9 sets out the regulatory framework for Controlling based on the legal, organisational and information rules on monitoring corporate events, rule compliance and handling risks. This is the object of the governance system. This chapter is aimed at introducing the reader to the Internal Control System, Internal Audit and Risk Management/Controlling as the three key Controlling-related sub-sections of an effective governance system. On finishing this chapter, readers will understand the functions and tasks of these sub-sections and their relationship to Controlling. This chapter also presents a practical example to illustrate a risk management and governance system.

9.2 Introduction

> A company needs a regulatory framework in order to manage, monitor and observe all the relevant rules and regulations. Governance systems are concerned with how to design such a regulatory framework. The focus of **Corporate Governance** is not just on internal structures but on external relationships with all of the company's stakeholders (e.g. customers, suppliers. etc.).

A distinction can be made between three major corporate governance areas:
- Designing the management structure using "checks and balances" (e.g. interactions between the Board of Directors and the Supervisory Board)
- Monitoring all activities to protect company assets.

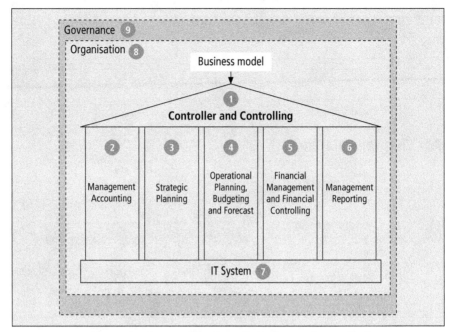

Fig. 9.2: Classification of the chapter in the "House of Controlling"

Monitoring is of key importance for Controlling. Its main aims are defining tasks and coordination.

Corporate Governance regulations in Germany particularly include the Stock Corporation Act (AktG), the Limited Liability Companies Act (GmbHG), the Corporate Sector Supervision and Transparency Act (KonTraG) and the German Corporate Governance Code (DCGK). This Code contains recommendations and suggestions making it easier to apply than the laws mentioned ("Soft Law").

The topic of "Corporate Governance" can be understood as a principal agent problem. It results from the fact that the company's owners ("shareholders") as well as other interest groups ("stakeholders") do not manage the company themselves, i.e. shareholders and stakeholders are "principals", with company management acting as the "agent". The relationships between these two groups are characterised by an asymmetrical information split (company management tends to have more information about the company's activities, or information which becomes relevant earlier, than the principals). Governance systems are focused on reducing such information asymmetries and are aimed at therefore balancing out information inequalities between the interest groups (cf. *von Werder* 2009).

The very general definitions of corporate governance make it difficult to define monitoring aspects and specify sub-areas. The now frequently used "Three Lines of Defence" model presents a clearer system of governance (cf. *The Institute of Auditors* 2013 and **Fig. 9.3**):

- The "First Line of Defence" comprises operational internal controls based on processes for which operative management is responsible.

- The "Second Line of Defence" describes control and monitoring systems covering several processes, such as Controlling, risk management, quality assurance, etc. for which separate organisational units are responsible.
- The "Third Line of Defence" is internal audit, which monitors the "performance" of the first two lines of defence independently of processes.

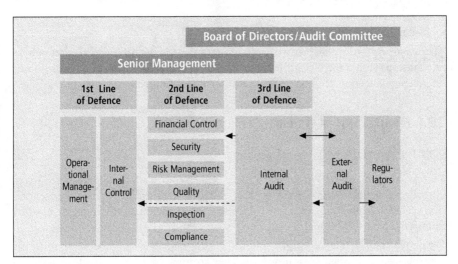

Fig. 9.3: "Three Lines of Defence" model (*The Institute of Internal Auditors* 2013, p. 2)

These three lines of defence are supplemented by external auditors and supervisory bodies. Clearly, the different functions must coordinate and communicate in order to avoid redundant work or security gaps (cf. *Hampel, Bünis* 2013, pp. 599 et seq.).

It is worth noting that small to medium-sized enterprises will not be able to assign separate organisational units to perform these tasks. However, it is more important that the tasks are performed systematically – albeit in a simplified process.

 Is there a "Three Lines of Defence" system in your company?

In the following section, we will analyse the relationships with the Controller/the Controlling department. Therefore, the focus is on the monitoring function of a governance system.

9.3 Designing an effective monitoring system

Governance literature tends to use the term "monitoring" to describe three overlapping areas (cf. **Fig. 9.4**):

- Internal control system,
- Internal audit, and
- Risk management.

The remainder of this chapter will present these areas in detail. It will also set out the relationships with Controlling/the Controller. The three areas to be examined are based on independent concepts, some of which also contain Controlling elements.

9.3.1 Internal control system

9.3.1.1 Internal control system function

The management process includes planning-related controls. These controls are aimed at ensuring that planning is implemented. The specific control types used are comparisons. These comparisons are aimed at implementing planning requirements in order to improve future planning.

While planning-related controls are used in the management process, monitoring controls form part of business processes. They are aimed at ensuring that rules are observed and potentially damaging actions are prevented. This tends to be called "Internal Control" or "Internal Control System".

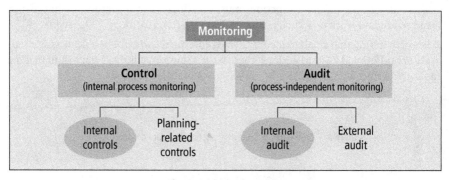

Fig. 9.4: Monitoring topics

One extensive internal control concept comes from the USA. According to this concept, all company-internal monitoring activities are treated as a unit called "Internal Control".

German authors tend to use the term "internal control system" (ICS); however, the concept of Internal Control goes far beyond regular controls.

The Internal Control concept arose out of practical need as a response to the major fraud and embezzlement scandals in the US economy of the 1930s. Internal Control sets out four objectives:

- safeguarding assets,
- measures to ensure reliable and precise accountancy figures,
- promoting efficient operations, and
- supporting compliance with the business policy.

The media, process and methods required to achieve these targets must be determined and coordinated.

Such controls are inseparably linked to the Controller's work. By definition, designing and continually coordinating the planning and control system requires planning-related controls. Where internal controls relate to the control system, they also form part of Controlling. They are used to reduce information asymmetries resulting from the Principal-Agent relationship and ensure rule compliance in company management. It is often impossible to separate planning-related controls and internal controls (e.g. when ensuring that information is complete and correct). Controls must be used to ensure that assets are safeguarded and data is protected and secured in all processes.

Are sufficient internal controls integrated in all the business processes in your company?

9.3.1.2 The COSO concept

The "Internal Control" concept underwent further fundamental development in the USA in the 1980s. In 1992, the Committee of Sponsoring Organisations of the Treadway Commission (COSO) published the "Internal Control – Integrated Framework" ("COSO Framework"). A further developed version was presented in 2013 (cf. **Fig. 9.5**). The concept was intended as a guideline for setting up and assessing internal control systems. It now forms part of global auditing standards.

No single specific method can be used to set up and "operate" the internal control system. First, the general rules of organisation and process design are applied. The COSO documents can be used to assist the systematic process. From the Controller's perspective, cost-benefit analysis must be used to determine effectiveness, risks and costs.

The COSO concept distinguishes between three dimensions:

- Dimension I comprises the three levels of "Ensuring the effectiveness and efficiency of all processes" ("Operations"), "Reliability of reports" ("Reporting") and "Ensuring compliance with all applicable laws and regulations" ("Compliance").
- Dimension II contains the five control activity levels. The Control Environment influences the behaviour of all organisational members. Risk Assessment supports management in assessing risks. Control Activities ensure a target focus. Information and Communication guarantees adequate information supply. Monitoring Activities check that all the relevant processes are monitored constantly.
- Dimension III describes the control objects of the company as a whole down to the individual functions.

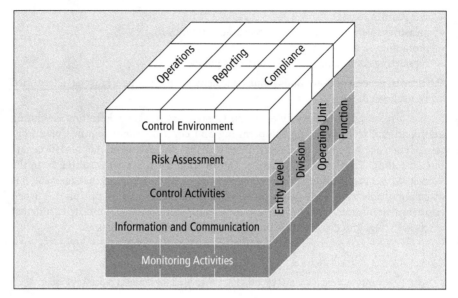

Fig. 9.5: Controls and audit (*COSO* 2013, p. 6)

The COSO documents contain a detailed description of all dimensions and stages, design principles and review procedures.

The COSO cube is ideal for evaluating a Controlling system in relation to control and compliance aspects. "Controlling" and "Internal Control" are two sides of the same coin. "Controlling" is largely concerned with planning and as such is focused on the future; by contrast, "Internal Control" focuses on control and monitoring aspects.

For Controllers, the Internal Control concept thus provides an important tool to ensure that the control system is reviewed as required and to monitor compliance with rules and regulations.

9.3.2 Internal audit

9.3.2.1 Internal audit function

> **Internal Audit** (IA) is an organisationally independent monitoring tool allocated to company management and acting on its behalf. In smaller companies, company management performs audits itself, perhaps with the help of external auditors.

Secondary literature often equates the term "audit" with "review". Alternatively, "auditing" is also often used. Internal audit is responsible for carrying out process-independent budget/actual comparisons.

Fig. 9.6 highlights the different areas of Audit and Controlling. Two key aspects are important here:

- Controllers tend to focus on planning, whereas Internal Auditors are more interested in whether rules are being observed, and
- Controllers are continuously integrated in the control process, whereas Internal Auditors look into all processes on a case-by-case basis.

Criterion	Criterion	Criterion
Reference to company objectives	direct reference to company objectives	direct reference to company objectives (previously: indirect via risk reduction)
Tasks	information supply, coordination of management sub-systems, rationality assurance	independent objective reviewing and advisory services
Timing	focused on the future	assurance services tend to focus on the past; Internal Consulting tends to focus on the future
Timing of actions	continuous	case-by-case or cyclical
Relationship to monitored processes	process-dependent	process-independent
Relationship to presented data	assumes data is correct	checks whether data is correct
Tools	task-independent combination of tools including partial overlaps	

Fig. 9.6: Internal audit and Controlling (*Berens, Wöhrmann* 2011, p. 612)

A clear distinction can be made in relation to assurance services; where advisory services are provided, these can include some of the same tasks as Controlling.

9.3.2.2 Internal audit method

Internal audit has seen a number of developments over the years:

- Originally, the sole focus of internal audit was on finance ("financial auditing"). With companies growing ever more complex, its tasks now encompass all areas of operations ("operational auditing").
- In the past, internal audit dealt only with operative activities and functions. Today, audit also examines management ("management auditing").
- In the past, internal audit primarily checked that specific information was correct ("case-by-case review"). It has now developed to include reviews of entire systems ("system review") with the aim of improving the system as a whole.
- Previously, the exclusive objective of internal audit was to ensure safety and rule compliance. Nowadays, audit reviews also check for cost-effectiveness.
- Internal audit now sees itself as an internal advisory body.

It is now recognised that effective internal audit must not just focus on specific sub-systems of the company, but should instead also examine the interactions between all of the company's sub-systems.

The US Institute of Internal Auditors has carried out a large-scale survey in order to summarise the most important internal audit approaches in consistent definitions. The results are, amongst other things, the definitions which are still valid today (*The Institute of Internal Auditors* 1975, pp. 51 et seq.):

- **Financial Auditing:** Financial Auditing is an independent review focused on past transactions which is performed by external auditors. This review aims to confirm the compliance, correctness and reliability of financial data to protect assets, verify system suitability and ensure that the system performs the tasks as required (internal audit).

- **Operational Auditing:** Operational Auditing is a future-focused, independent, systematic review performed by an internal auditor. It is aimed at managing company activities and is checked by upper, middle and lower management. The objective of Operational Auditing is to improve company profitability and achieve other company goals, such as agenda targets, social targets and employee development.

- **Management Auditing:** Management Auditing is a future-focused, independent, systematic review of the activities of all management levels performed by internal auditors. This is aimed at improving company profitability and meeting additional company targets by improving management function. This comprises achieving agenda targets, social targets and employee development.

We can distinguish between two internal audit approaches: case-by-case review and system review.

Case-by-case review looks at individual results generated by information processing procedures. In particular, it is focused on management accounts figures. Therefore, the term "financial auditing" can be largely equated with case-by-case reviews.

Case-by-case review objects describe the legal provisions and the principles of true and fair accounting and balancing of accounts. These are also supplemented by internal guidelines and codes.

Several important decisions must be made regarding the review methods used when performing case-by-case reviews (cf. *Institut der Wirtschaftsprüfer* 2012):

- **Formal vs. material reviews:** A formal review establishes whether external regulations are being observed. For instance, it checks whether transactions are fully recorded, processed correctly and assigned to the correct accounts in accordance with GAAP. Material reviews investigate whether processes have the correct content and whether they are cost-effective.

- **Full vs. sample reviews:** Full reviews investigate all transactions and processes within a defined period and/or area. However, full testing tends to be an exception. Given the scope and complexity of areas and departments, sample testing is normally used. Different selection procedures can be used to select the sample to be tested.

- **Progressive vs. retrograde reviews:** Progressive reviews check that inputs are consistent from the first record across all accounting steps until the final aggregate posting (e. g. balance sheet for the year). Retrograde reviews take the opposite approach by tracing items from the aggregate posting back to the individual transaction.

- **Direct vs. indirect reviews:** Direct reviews deal directly with individual transactions and processes. This is the approach used for most tests. Indirect reviews enable auditors to obtain information about specific circumstances (e.g. scrap rates) by comparing figures and investigating their relationships. This method is also called plausibility testing.

Nowadays, case-by-case reviews are often performed automatically. A number of software solutions are offered with this in mind. Software solutions designed for testing can be used to this end, and software (e.g. service programs) developed for other purposes can also help with specific tests.

By contrast to case-by-case reviews, system reviews do not check whether specific information is correct. Instead, they comprehensively check whole systems with the aim of improving them. The term "operational auditing" can be used more or less analogous to "system review". The term "management auditing" also includes a system review focused on actions by management.

As companies grow more complex, reviews must offer more than mere management accounting and must also provide information on system functionality. This goes beyond the scope of case-by-case reviews. For instance, IT-supported information processing reviews could not reasonably be achieved without system reviews. System reviews cover all the main processes of a company.

To start off "system improvement", the reviewer normally begins by checking the internal control system and control mechanisms. In other words, the reviewer must identify and describe the individual control features and assess control system effectiveness.

Internal audit reviews must be carefully planned and controlled. First, the objects to be reviewed are defined and then a realistic review schedule is compiled. At the same time, staff and material resources must be assigned. Review assignments are normally planned and executed as part of the following phases:

- Review planning
- Review execution
- Reporting
- Follow-up

In order to be effective, Internal Audit must be independent from the rest of the organisation. This ensures that Internal Audit can provide objective, independent review and advisory services. It must therefore be directly organisationally assigned to company management (Board of Directors) as a whole.

Within the organisation, Internal Audit must be situated as close as possible to the area to which it has the closest technical and functional links. This is, without doubt, the Finance department, and the Controller normally reports to the Chief Financial Officer (CFO).

What organisational form does internal auditing have in your company?

9.3.3 Risk management

9.3.3.1 Role of risk management

Risk management and risk controlling start by defining and reaching an understanding of the term "risk" (cf. *Diederichs* 2012, p. 8).

> Business Administration broadly defines risk as the deviation of future develop-ments from expected developments or objectives. This comprises both negative deviations, i. e. uncertain losses (down-side risk), and positive deviations, i. e. unforeseeable potential for profit (up-side risk). **Risk in a stricter sense** means the risk of losses (see **Fig. 9.7**).

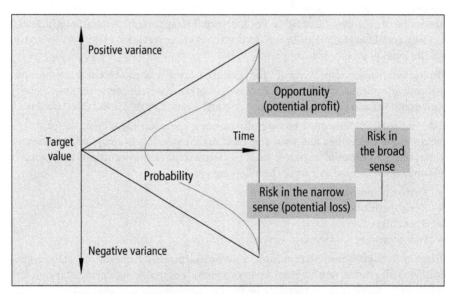

Fig. 9.7: The concept of "risk" (*Diederichs* 2012, p. 9)

Given the fact that all decisions by a company are subject to risks, management invari-ably also involves risk (and opportunities) management. As such, risk management forms part of both the planning and control system and the information supply system.

Controlling provides support during all risk management phases. Overall, the aim is to include risk in the Controlling system. Planning and control as well as information supply must be focused not just on opportunities but also on risks.

An effective risk management process is functionally made up of three phases which must be integrated into the Controlling process:

- risk analysis,
- risk planning and control, and
- risk monitoring.

Is there a systematic risk management process in your company?

The following **Fig. 9.8** provides an overview of these phases and the relevant tools.

The section below contains a brief and concise summary of three phases which make up an effective risk management system.

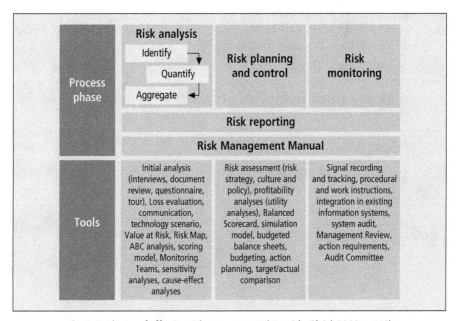

Fig. 9.8: Phases of effective risk management (*Horváth, Gleich* 2000, p. 110)

Which tools of risk management do you use in the individual phases of the risk management process in your company?

9.3.3.2 Risk analysis

Risk analysis starts with identifying the risks. Both a top-down approach initiated by management and a bottom-up approach initiated by the employees can be used for this. Ideally, the two processes should be combined to achieve mixed top-down/bottom-up planning (this tends to be more costly).

Targeted bottom-up analyses supported by top-down identification and evaluation of risks has proven to be sensible and useful when designing an effective risk management system. Such a process also helps to take a holistic view of individual risks.

Checklists and tools can be used to support this process. Checklists are particularly useful for recording all risk types relevant to the company. Many different standard tools are also available for this.

Analyses must first identify and evaluate risks which could significantly influence the company's assets, financial situation and income. However, once risks have been identified, they must be distinguished further. For instance, a distinction should be made between strategic and operative risks. The latter type tend to be easier to identify because strategic risks are often strongly linked to future events.

Given such a strong link to future events, strategic Controlling tools can give important impulses in this area. Examples of tools include: scenario technology, cause-and-effect analyses and monitoring teams to systematically identify strategic risks.

Risk impact and expected probability of occurrence must then be identified for the risks in order to calculate a monetary value. Risk maps are useful for allocating (and subsequently monitoring) risks. One such risk map is shown in **Fig. 9.9**.

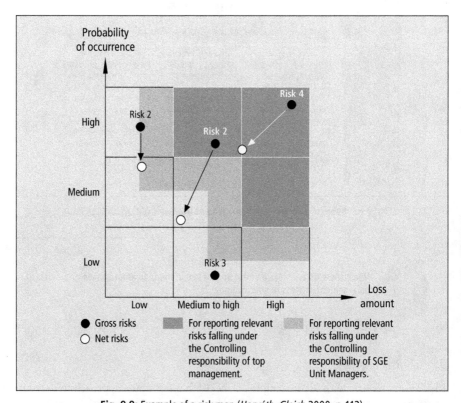

Fig. 9.9: Example of a risk map (*Horváth, Gleich* 2000, p. 112)

A wide range of tools is available to help during the risk analysis phase, from simple estimates to cash value calculations.

Once the volume of individual risks has been determined and a monetary value has been calculated, this information must be aggregated across the company or down to the desired level of detail and presented as a bundle. Only experienced Controllers are able to handle this demanding task of aggregating risk items. Several different tools are available for displaying aggregate risk information. For instance, the use of risk KPIs (e.g. Value at Risk and Return on Risk Adjusted Capital) has proven useful in this context.

9.3.3.3 Risk planning and control

Risk planning and control require a risk strategy in line with the company or business area strategy. The following processes must first be applied to set risk-related objectives. Strategies can incorporate risk aspects implicitly or explicitly (cf. **Fig. 9.10**).

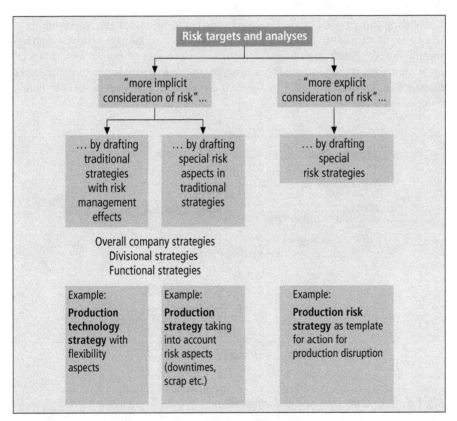

Fig. 9.10: Ways to incorporate risk aspects in formulating a strategy (*Horváth, Gleich* 2000, p. 113)

Risk aspects can be incorporated implicitly by either formulating traditional strategies and including the effects of risks, or integrating risk aspects into the strategy. They can be incorporated explicitly by formulating a specific risk strategy, e.g. at company or department level.

During planning, a decision must be reached as to the level of risk which will be borne, i.e. accepted, in specific business areas or in relation to the company as a whole. Based on this, individual risk planning must look towards mandatory available internal and external early detection updates and incorporate these into the strategic planning process. Risk planning can also make use of simulations to calculate alternative scenarios. Next, the results must be combined in a plan balance sheet. A Balanced Scorecard can be used to strategically deduce the budget. This can be set up as a link to general strategic planning and assist with special planning for opportunities and risk in a business area.

Once the measures required to achieve the strategic objectives have been budgeted for, the risks for each perspective can also be identified and the range of risks for each perspective can be taken into account in the budget. For example, one or more special cost types, "Computational costs of hazards and risks", can be introduced to include risks in the operative control system.

Controlling cannot directly influence risk control itself; this is the responsibility of management. Controlling or the relevant responsible Risk Manager provide management with risk-related target/actual comparisons or additional information. Management must then respond to possible deviations and initiate measures to reduce risks. Management can use the following general response mechanisms or ways to handle risk (see **Fig. 9.11**).

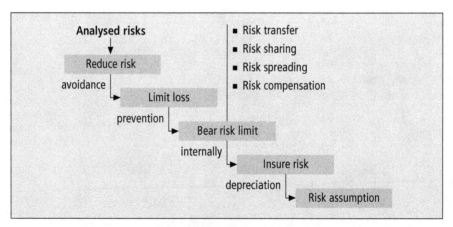

Fig. 9.11: Ways to control risk

9.3.3.4 Risk monitoring and documentation

Risk planning and control are closely linked to monitoring and documentation. Regular, structured risk reporting tailored to the recipients can help to systematically monitor risks. Finally, risk reporting is used to, amongst other things, outline the risks of future developments in the Annual Report as required in accordance with KonTraG.

First, the scope of reporting and the size of the group of recipients should be defined. In this context, it is important to identify what company employees are responsible for handling what risks, such that they should also be informed of risks and risk scope. Normally, this should be the company's managers.

The managers must receive regular updates on the risks defined in the areas for which they are responsible. Regular standard reports can be used here. Ad hoc reports are required if risk-related planned values in an area are exceeded significantly or newly identified significant risks occur.

In addition, thresholds must be defined to decide when top management (Board of Directors, Management Board) must be informed of risk scopes.

The Controller, in their role as the risk manager, must ensure that the way in which management responds to any relevant deviations is documented. The Controller does not monitor the effectiveness of such measures; this is the responsibility of Internal Audit.

9.4 Practical example

9.4.1 Medizintechnik AG

This practical example looks at a European industrial group in the medical technology industry which employs approximately 12,000 staff at around 60 production sites primarily in Europe, North America and Asia. In the 2014 financial year, the group earned a turnover of around EUR 2.0 billion. Approximately two-thirds of this was generated in Europe, with the remainder split across North America, Asia, the Middle East and Africa. The group's corporate structure is managed centrally in four major divisions.

9.4.2 Project: Setting up systematic risk management

Both the Board of Directors and the Supervisory Board were aware of the importance of responsible, transparent corporate leadership and control, and for years they had made efforts to incorporate most principles defined in national law within the company. However, many of the governance structures defined in the last chapter had clearly not been designed properly, nor were they monitored appropriately.

It was also striking that at this time, risk management only played a minor role within the company and no systematic approach was pursued. Nevertheless, the group's global presence has meant that it continually faces numerous risks at an international level. The medical technology market is also characterised by constant price and cost pressure, high regulatory requirements and great pressure to innovate. To counteract these risks, the company was intending to set up systematic risk management as a key component of its business activity, such that it would take on a key role within the group-wide governance system.

Consultancy services were to achieve the following: identify weaknesses, establish an integrated Enterprise Risk Management system, and integrate forecasting and planning processes. This practical example will highlight key practical aspects of designing and implementing an effective risk management and governance system.

When the project started, the industrial group's risk management system used an entirely isolated model which was not at all integrated into the organisation's processes. An initial risk assessment based on target meetings with the technical departments revealed an unstructured, irregular and highly heterogeneous top-down approach when recording, evaluating and quantifying risks. These were largely handled locally, but not aggregated centrally. It also became apparent that process owners often struggled with correctly assessing risks because they often only had insufficient information or only operative information, meaning information relating to individual production sites. Moreover, no consistently communicated or applied risk culture had been established, and opportunity management was not taken into account in the present model. This was ultimately reflected in a missing link to company management such that valuable risk information was not taken into account when reaching decisions.

The project target was to develop and implement a risk management system focused on conscious, controlled risk and opportunities management. In addition, this was to form the basis of the risk-adjusted forecast and planning processes by being integrated into all the relevant company departments. Below it is explained how such an effective Enterprise Risk Management System was designed in practice and what key functions, tasks and relations to forecasting and planning it should have.

The newly developed risk management framework is based on a company-wide risk management process deeply integrated into the organisation. The individual risk life cycle phases (A-D) of risk management (see **Fig. 9.12**) are embedded in the overall company risk strategy and culture and into internal and external industry-specific requirements. The manufacturing group was subject to several external rules in relation to its business activity, particularly regarding the conditions for its products' market entry. Stakeholder analyses were performed for internal requirements to be able to incorporate the different ideas into the new framework design as well as possible. From the start of the project, supporting change management was seen as the organisational "enabler" required to achieve successful integration into the new framework. However, this practical example does not go into further detail regarding change management implementation.

As shown in **Fig. 9.12** and **Fig. 9.13**, Corporate Risk Governance is regarded as an overall framework to enable legal, organisational and information-related monitoring. This must be recorded and set out in a set of rules tailored to the group.

The Management Board is generally the highest instance and above all is considered the recipient of information and the decision-maker for entrepreneurial and risk-related decisions. The usual "Three Lines of Defence" approach was chosen in order to optimally define and delimit the different new Corporate Risk Governance and Risk Management Framework areas. These were used to present and define the key functions of the risk management process, as well as the relevant responsibilities and tools, in a structured way.

The first "Line of Defence" describes operative, applied risk management and as such is the direct responsibility of operative management. As such, the risk owners working in operations are responsible for recording and initially documenting all individual risks in special risk registers. In the course of the project, a risk management software was implemented which allows users to record and initially evaluate risks in a standardised template requiring minimal time. Special risk committees made up of risk owners at department level then discuss any risks that have been recorded and are responsible for updating them and compiling them in the risk register. The risk management software also supports these tasks.

The second "Line of Defence" handles cross-process and thus centralised risk management. The responsible risk coordinators are largely tasked with the management of the

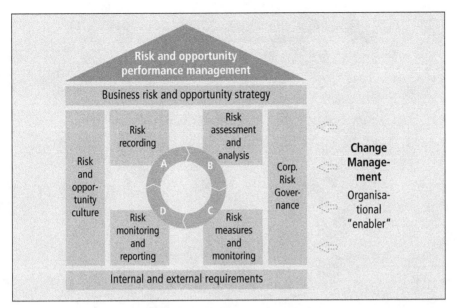

Fig. 9.12: Risk management framework

overall risk management process. These risk coordinators perform a special, important function and as such report directly to company management as one unit. It is important for the four phases of standardised and harmonised risk life cycles to be run through interactively between the first and second "Lines of Defence" (see Fig. 9.13).

The Internal Control System (ICS) and Internal Audit (Group Audit) are so closely linked to risk management that it becomes difficult to make a clear distinction. On the one hand, Group Audit forms part of the internal monitoring system by performing independent checks and supporting management with managing risks and opportunities. On the other hand, an internal control system was built up step-by-step in order to provide better support during early detection, monitoring and preventative risk avoidance. The system is based on the internationally recognised COSO I standards for internal control systems (COSO – Internal-Control-Integrated Framework by the Committee of Sponsoring Organizations of the Treadway Commission). During system design, special attention was paid to balancing out the three factors of risk, countermeasures and management controls, as set controls are required to ensure countermeasures are taken. In addition, proof of effectiveness was specified for all important defined countermeasures and management controls.

The "Three Lines of Defence" approach generally ensures that precisely defined, allocated roles and responsibilities help to integrate the risk management processes at the different organisational levels. Risks are recorded decentrally, but coordinated centrally. This ensures that all significant risks are handled and coordinated comprehensively and consistently, and in a controlled manner.

The section below describes the individual risk life cycle phases in relation to their significance when integrating important risk information into the corporate management process. An appropriate information supply system and a planning and control system needed to be taken into account when designing the individual phases.

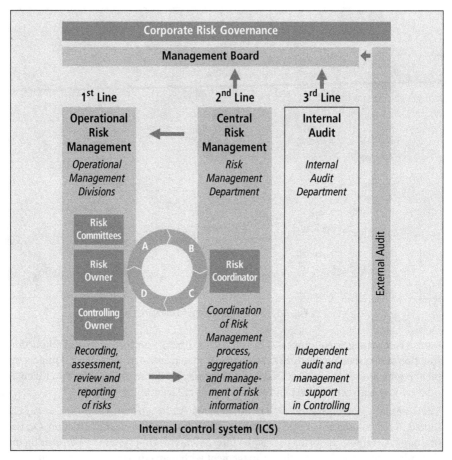

Fig. 9.13: Corporate Risk Governance

As a first step towards "genuine" risk-adjusted company management, the risks identified and evaluated in phases A and B need to be included as events within the planning process. A set of core risks to be incorporated into the planning process was selected together with the industrial group. The risks were described in detail and grouped based on their probability of occurrence, scope and correlations such that concrete factors could be deduced to influence the forecast either positively or negatively. A data interface needed to be set up to allow data to be integrated manually and automatically. The aggregate risk data was also used to improve existing risk reporting. To this end, corresponding reporting processes were defined which were integrated as a key component of the company-wide reporting system and as such sustainably support performance measurement.

9.4.3 Lessons learned

The newly developed and implemented risk management system generated sustainable benefits for the group. The group was able to use structured risk information and optimised planning to create stability in relation to its financing activities in spite of ongoing economic fluctuations and consistent cost and price pressure in the industry. In addition, effective opportunities management was established to enable early detection and consideration of upcoming opportunities such that innovations could be both created and promoted. As such, a basic Enterprise Risk Management System integrated into planning was set up to generate a sustainable competitive edge, which is of key importance especially given the prevailing strong pressure in the medical technology industry. The following success factors played a central role:

- Structuring and documenting the process of optimally integrating risks and opportunities into company-wide control processes using the risk management framework.
- A number of benefits were generated by incorporating critical events and new opportunities in the forecast and planning process. Significant risks were recorded and opportunities identified and a consolidated, extensive company-wide risk portfolio was put together. Dependence on their effects and probabilities of occurrence could thus be included in planning.
- By integrating any identified risks and opportunities in further planning processes, companies are enabled to include findings in future decision-making, react better and manage the relevant processes optimally. Performance-focused, integrated risk and opportunities management can thus enable better decision-making and sustainably increase company value long-term.

9.5 Organisational checklist for managers and controllers

Use the COSO cube to check the state of development of your governance system.

Document your internal controls and all responsibilities in the processes for creating goods and services completely and with no gaps.

Practice and document end-to-end the principle of dual control in all leadership processes.

Define effective principles and guidelines for the cooperation between Controlling and internal audit.

 Tackle all risks systematically through risk analysis, risk planning and risk monitoring.

 Differentiate between internal control and internal audit.

 Adapt your risk tools to suit the different phases of the risk management process.

Further reading

If you would like to find out more about corporate governance in general, please read:

Hommelhoff, P., Hopt, K. J., Werder, A. v. (2009), Handbuch Corporate Governance [Corporate Governance Manual], 2nd ed., Stuttgart 2009.

If you would like to find out more about internal control systems and the COSO concept in particular, please read:

COSO – Committee of Sponsoring Organizations of the Treadway Commission (2013), Internal Control – Integrated Framework – Executive Summary, Durham 2013.

If you would like to find out more about internal audit, please read:

Peemöller, V. (2011), Entwicklungsformen und Entwicklungsstand der Internen Revision [Forms and Status of Internal Audit Development], in: *Freidank, C.-C., Peemöller, V. H. (eds.), Kompendium der Internen Revision [Compendium of Internal Auditing]*, Berlin 2011, pp. 69–92.

10 Trends

The controller's role in the modern sense can now be traced back over one hundred years. It has always involved assisting corporate management for the effective, target-orientated management control of an organisation.

Through the years, the value of the supportive role of the controller has increased – and this also applies in individual companies when structuring controlling:

- In the early stages of development, the controller was rather focused on historical bookkeeping ("registration").
- In the next stage of development, the focus on planning distinguished itself with the support of management-orientated accounting ("navigation").
- Today, the controller is usually responsible for the entire control system, including strategic issues ("business partner").

The controller coordinates planning, management and control. Often, they are – rightly – referred to as the "economic conscience" of the company.

In our opinion, further development of the controller's tasks will be fundamentally influenced and shaped by two complex factors:

- Digitalisation is changing the creation of value and the business models of all organisations fundamentally.
- The pursuit of sustainability puts all organisations' target systems to the test.

Digitalisation largely enables the automated execution of all operative management control processes and, through the analysis of previously inaccessible information ("big data"), creates greater support for management control.

The use of the information that is now available with the help of mathematical and statistical models ("business analytics") presents the controller with new challenges in relation to knowledge and instruments. Controlling's methods and instruments of analysis have, over time, yielded increasingly more detailed findings, but have also become increasingly more complex in their application (cf. **Fig. 10.2**). In the course of development, the basic arithmetic operations have therefore been supplemented by the calculation of compound interest as a "tool" and now by mathematics, using business analytics.

The concept of sustainable economic management involves dealing with target categories that were not previously the object of Controlling. Environmental protection issues and social engagement will be crucial in the future. Target figures and performance indicators in this field will have to be defined in most companies.

For the controller, this does, on the one hand, create new, challenging tasks, while on the other hand, their role comes under dispute by other persons responsible for tasks.

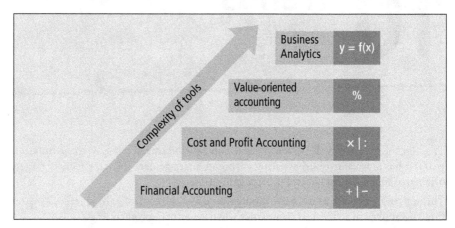

Fig. 10.1: Development of the supportive role of Controlling (*ICV* 2016, p. 57)

- For business analytics, data scientist, with their IT and mathematics knowledge profiles, have often established themselves in larger companies.
- The automation of operational planning, management, reporting and controlling processes enables the company management to perform more "self-controlling" (cf. **Fig. 10.2**).

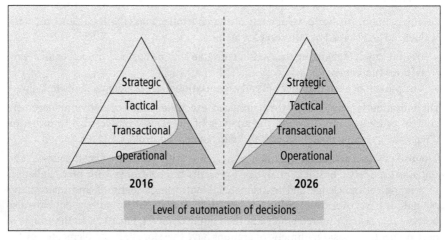

Fig. 10.2: Increasing degree of process automation (*Vocelka* 2016, p. 27)

However: The controller will be urgently needed in the future too.

- They must remain the "economic conscience" of management.
- They must ensure the quality and consistency of information ("single source of truth").
- They are the creator and coordinator of the management control system.

There are exciting, challenging things in store for the controller!

Review your business model regularly.

 Keep up-to-date on new information that could enable you to make more profitable decisions.

 Familiarise yourself with business analytics.

 Integrate non-financial goals into your control system.

List of authors

Goedecke, Axel, Senior Project Manager
  Business Unit Accounting, Treasury and Risk Management
Grönke, Kai, Partner
  Business Unit CFO Strategy and Organization
Horváth, Péter, Prof. Dr. Dr. h.c. mult.
  Chair of Controlling, Universität Stuttgart (retired 2005), Deputy Chairman of the
  Board, Horváth AG, and Founder/Deputy Chairman of the Board, International
  Performance Research Institute gGmbH (IPRI)
Huck, Christian, Principal
  Business Unit Cost and Profit Accounting
Jäck, Klaus Martin, Principal
  Business Unit Risk & Compliance Management
Kappes, Michael, Partner
  Business Unit Planning, Reporting and Consolidation
Kirchberg, Andreas, Principal
  Business Unit CFO Strategy and Organization
Kreuzer, Achim, Principal
  Business Unit Accounting, Treasury and Risk Management
Linsner, René, Partner
  Business Unit Cost and Profit Accounting
Michel, Uwe, Dr., Partner
  Competence Center Controlling & Finance, Member of the Managing Board, Horváth
  AG
Palmer, Daniel, Managing Consultant
  Business Unit Planning, Reporting and Consolidation
Poschadel, Frank, Principal
  Business Unit Cost and Profit Accounting
Ritzmann, Michael
  Managing Consultant, Business Unit Cost and Profit Accounting
Tobias, Stefan, Partner
  Business Unit Planning, Reporting and Consolidation
Vocelka, Alexander, Partner
  Business Unit Risk & Compliance Management
Wenning, Achim, Principal
  Business Unit CFO Strategy and Organization

List of abbreviations

AfA	Absetzung für Abnutzung [allowance for depreciation]
BAB	Betriebsabrechnungsbogen [expense distribution sheet]
BBK	Buchführung, Bilanzierung und Kostenrechnung [bookkeeping, accounting and cost accounting]
BI	Business Intelligence
BDI	Bundesverband der Deutschen Industrie [Federation of Germany Industry]
BEP	Break-even point
BSC	Balanced Scorecard
BW	Business Warehouse
CAM-I	Consortium for Advanced Manufacturing International
CAPM	Capital Asset Pricing Model
CPM	Corporate Performance Management
DB	Deckungsbeitrag [profit contribution]
DCF	Discounted Cash Flow method
DIN	Deutsche Industrie-Norm [German Industry Standard]
DRG	Diagnosis Related Groups
DSWR	Datenverarbeitung Steuern Wirtschaft Recht [Journal]
DP	Data Processing
EB	Endbestand [final balance]
Einr.	Einrichtung [equipment]
ELS	External Logistics System
ERP	Enterprise Resource Planning
EVA®	Economic Value Added
Exp.	Export
FA	Fertigungsauftrag [production order]
FASB	Financial Accounting Standards Board
FCF	Free Cash Flow
FiBu	Finanzbuchhaltung [general accounting]
FK	Fremdkapital [borrowed capital]
R&D	Research and Development
GB	Geschäftsbereich [business area]
GK	Gemeinkosten [overheads]
GKV	Gesamtkostenverfahren [nature of expense method]
GoB	Grundsätze ordnungsmäßiger Buchführung [financial accounting standards]
P&L	Profit and Loss Statement
GWA	Gemeinkostenwertanalyse [overhead cost value analysis]
HGB	Handelsgesetzbuch [German Code of Commerce]
IAS	International Accounting Standards
IASB	International Accounting Standards Board
IFRS	International Financial Reporting Standards
IGC	International Group of Controlling
ILS	Internal Logistics System

List of abbreviations

Inl.	Inland [domestic]
ISM	Integrated Service Management
IT	Information Technology
IV	Informationsversorgung [information supply]
Y	Year
Imp.	Imputed
KGSt	Kommunale Verwaltungsstelle für Verwaltungsvereinfachung [Local administration for administrative simplification]
KHBV	Krankenhaus-Buchführungsverordnung [hospital accounting regulations]
KLR	Kosten- und Leistungsrechnung [cost and profit accounting]
KonTraG	Gesetz zur Kontrolle und Transparenz im Unternehmensbereich [Act on Control and Transparency in the Corporate Sector]
KPI	Key Performance Indicators
lmi	leistungsmengeninduziert [quantity-induced]
lmn	leistungsmengenneutral [quantity-neutral]
L+L	Lieferungen und Leistungen [supplies and services]
Mafo	Marktforschung [market research]
Masch.	Maschine [machine]
ME	Mengeneinheiten [quantity units]
MY	Man-year
NOA	Net Operating Assets
NOPAT	Net Operating Profits After Taxes
NPO	Non-Profit Organisation
NSM	Neues Steuerungsmodell [new management model]
OECD	Organisation for Economic Co-operation and Development
OLAP	Online Analytical Processing
PY	Person-year
Prop.	Proportional
PwC	PricewaterhouseCoopers
Q	Quarter
RoI	Return on Investment
SBK	Systembildende Koordination [system-forming coordination]
SEC	Securities and Exchange Commission
SEM	Strategic Enterprise Management
SHV	Shareholder Value
SKK	Systemkoppelnde Koordination [system-linking coordination]
SOX	Sarbanes-Oxley Act
SSC	Shared Service Center
StuB	Steuern und Bilanzen [taxes and balance sheets]
SVA	Shareholder Value Analysis
SWOT	Strengths Weaknesses Opportunities and Threats analysis
TP	Teilprozess [sub-process]
US-GAAP	US-Generally Accepted Accounting Principles
UKV	Umsatzkostenverfahren [cost of sales method]
Verw.	Verwaltung [administration]

VS	Vorstand [Management Board]
VU	Versicherungsunternehmen [insurance company]
WISU	Wirtschaftsstudium [the study of economics]
ZB	Zentralbereich [central unit]
ZBB	Zero Base Budgeting
ZE	Zeiteinheiten [time units]

Bibliography

Adam, D. (2000), Investitionscontrolling, 3rd ed., Munich 2000.

Bahlinghorst, A., Sasse, A. (2005), Steigerung des Unternehmenswertes durch strategieorientierte Investitionsplanung, in: Buchführung, Bilanzierung und Kostenrechnung (BBK), 2005, 3, vol. 26, pp. 1135–1144.

Bange, C., Marr, B., Dahnken, O., Narr, J. (2004), Balanced Scorecard – 20 Werkzeuge für das Performance Management, Würzburg 2004.

Baars, H., Kemper, H.-G. (2015), Integration von Big-Data-Kompenenten in die Business Intelligence, in: Controlling 27 (2015) 4, pp. 222–228.

Buchner, H., Kraus, S., Weigand, A. (2000), Anforderungen an die Planung in turbulenten Zeiten, in: Horváth & Partners (Pub.), Früherkennung in der Unternehmenssteuerung, Stuttgart 2000, pp. 127–142.

Bunce, P., Hope, J., Fraser, R. (2002), Beyond Budgeting White Paper, www.bbrt.org, 2002.

Coenenberg, A. G., Fischer, T. M., Günther, T. (2012), Kostenrechnung und Kostenanalyse, Stuttgart 2012.

Coenenberg, A. G., Salfeld, R. (2003), Wertorientierte Unternehmensführung – vom Strategieentwurf zur Implementierung, Stuttgart 2003 (updated edition: *Coenenberg, A. G., Salfeld, R., Schultze, W. (2015)*, Wertorientierte Unternehmensführung – Vom Strategieentwurf zur Implementierung, 3rd ed., Stuttgart 2015).

Currle, M. (2001), Wertmanagement und Performance-Measurement. Konzepte, Kritik und Weiterentwicklungen, in: Bilanz & Buchhaltung 47 (2001) 6, pp. 229–233.

Currle, M., Witzemann, T. (2004), Bonusbanken: Unternehmenswertsteigerung und Managementvergütung langfristig verbinden, in: Controlling 16 (2004) 11, pp. 631–638.

Dahnken, O., Banges, C. (2002), Standards ausgereift und Plattformen flexibel, in: IS-Report 6 (2002) 7, pp. 20–24.

Davenport, T. H. (2014), Big Data at Work: Dispelling the Myths, Uncovering the Opportunities, Boston 2014, pp. 73 ff.

Diederichs, M. (2012), Risikomanagement und Risikocontrolling, Munich 2012.

Eilenberger, G. (2003), Betriebliche Finanzwirtschaft: Einführung in Investition und Finanzierung, Finanzpolitik und Finanzmanagement von Unternehmungen, 7th ed., Munich 2003, p. 69.

Epstein, M., Buhovac, A. (2014), Making Sustainability Work: Best Practices in Managing and Measuring Corporate Social, Environmental, and Economic Impacts, 2nd ed., Sheffield/San Francisco 2014.

Franke, G., Hax, H. (2009), Finanzwirtschaft des Unternehmens und Kapitalmarkt, 6th ed., Berlin/Heidelberg 2009, pp. 124 f.

Friedl, G., Hilz, C., Pedell, B. (2012), Controlling mit SAP®, 6th ed., Wiesbaden 2012.

Gaiser, B., Greiner, O. (2003), Strategiegerechte Planung mit Hilfe der BSC, in: Horváth, P., Gleich, R. (Pub., 2003), Neugestaltung der Unternehmensplanung, Stuttgart 2003, pp. 269–295.

Gaiser, B., Wunder, T. (2004), Strategy Maps und Strategieprozess – Einsatzmöglichkeiten, Nutzen, Erfahrungen, in: Controlling 16 (2004) 8/9, pp. 457–463.

Gassmann, O., Csik, M., Frankenberger, K. (2013), Geschäftsmodelle entwickeln: 55 innovative Konzepte mit dem St. Galler Business Model Navigator, Munich 2013, pp. 6.

Bibliography

Gassmann, O., Perez-Freije, J. (2011), Eingangs-, Prozess- und Ausgangskennzahlen im Innovationscontrolling, in: Controlling & Management 55 (2011) 6, pp. 394–396.

Gladen, W. (2011), Performance Measurement – Controlling mit Kennzahlen, Heidelberg 2011.

Gleich, R. (2001), Prozessorientiertes Performance Measurement – Konzeptidee und Anwendungserfahrungen, in: Der Controlling-Berater (2001) 2, pp. 25–46.

Gleich, R., Bartels, P., Breisig, V. (2012), Nachhaltigkeitscontrolling: Konzepte, Instrumente und Fallbeispiele für die Umsetzung, Freiburg 2012.

Gleich, R., Grönke, K., Schmidt, H. (2014), Prozesse des Controllerbereichs kontinuierlich weiterentwickeln: Konzeptionelle Überlegungen und Praxislösungen am Beispiel des Hauptprozesses „Management Reporting", in: Controlling 26 (2014) 7, pp. 364–372.

Gleich, R., Horváth, P., Michel, U. (2011), Finanz-Controlling – Strategische und operative Steuerung der Liquidität, Freiburg im Breisgau 2011.

Gleich, R., Kopp, J. (2001), Ansätze zur Neugestaltung der Planung und Budgetierung, in: Controlling 13 (2001) 8/9, pp. 429–436.

Gleich, R., Lauber, A. (2013), Ein aktuelles Kompetenzmodell für Contoller, in: Controlling 25 (2013) 10, pp. 512–514.

Gleich, R., Schimank, C. (2015), Innovationscontrolling: Innovationen effektiv steuern und effizient umsetzen, Munich 2015.

Götze, U. (2008), Investitionsrechnung. revised and updated 6th ed., Berlin/Heidelberg 2008.

Greiner, O. (2004), Strategiegerechte Budgetierung, Munich 2004.

Grothe, U., Himmelmann, N., Renner, A., Sasse, A. (2003), Modifizierte Folgekostenrechnung, in: Der Nahverkehr 21 (2003) 4, pp. 60–65.

Hahn, D. (2003), Grenzen der Unternehmensplanung, in: Horváth, P., Gleich, R. (Pub.), Neugestaltung der Unternehmensplanung, Stuttgart 2003, pp. 89–101

Hampel, V., Bünis, M. (2013), Zusammenwirken von Controlling und Interner Revision im Three Lines of Defense-Modell der Unternehmensüberwachung, in: Zeitschrift für Controlling 25 (2013) 11, pp. 596–601.

Hofmann, N., Müller, M., Sasse, A. (2004), Umsatzkostenverfahren nach IFRS: Vorteile aus unternehmensexterner und -interner Sicht, in: Der Controlling-Berater (2004) 3, pp. 193–210.

Hofmann, N., Sasse, A., Hauser, M., Blatzer, B. (2007), Investitions-, Finanz- und Working Capital Management als Stellhebel zur Steigerung der Kapitaleffizienz – Stand und neuere Entwicklungen, in: Controlling (2007) 3, pp. 153–163.

Horváth & Partners (Pub., 2005b), Studie "Best Practice Anreizsysteme 2004", Stuttgart 2005.

Horváth & Partners (Pub., 2005c), Studie "100x Balanced Scorecard 2005", Stuttgart 2005.

Horváth & Partners (Pub., 2007), Balanced Scorecard umsetzen, 4th ed., Stuttgart 2007.

Horváth & Partners (2016), CFO-Panel – Top Performance im CFO-Bereich, Stuttgart 2016.

Horváth, P. (2009), Controlling, 11th ed., Munich 2009.

Horváth, P., Berlin, S. (2016), Green-Controlling-Roadmap – Ansätze in der Unternehmenspraxis, Stuttgart 2016.

Horváth, P., Gleich, R., Seiter, M. (2015), Controlling, 13th ed., Munich 2015.

Horváth, P., Reichmann, T. (Pub., 2003), Vahlens Großes Controllinglexikon, 2nd ed., Munich 2003.

IGC International Group of Controlling (2013), Controller-Leitbild, https://www.igc-controlling.org/fileadmin/pdf/controller-de-2013.pdf, 8 Jun 2013.

IGC International Group of Controlling (Pu., 2011), Controlling-Prozessmodell: ein Leitfaden für die Beschreibung und Gestaltung von Controlling-Prozessen, Freiburg/ Berlin/Munich 2011, pp. 15.

Internationaler Controller Verein (Pub., 2014), Green Controlling. ICV-Leitfaden: Leitfaden für die erfolgreiche Integration ökologischer Zielsetzung in Unternehmensplanung und -steuerung, Freiburg 2014, pp. 47.

Isensee, J., Michel, U. (2011), Green Controlling – Die Rolle des Controllers und aktuelle Entwicklungen in der Praxis, in: Controlling 23 (2011) 8/9, pp. 436–442.

Kaplan, R. S., Norton, D. P. (2004), Strategy Maps, Stuttgart 2004.

Kemper, H.-G., Mehanna, W., Unger, C. (2004), Business Intelligence – Grundlagen und praktische Anwendungen, Wiesbaden 2004, pp. 7.

Kramer, D., Keilus, M. (2006), Rechnungswesen und Controlling im regionalen Umfeld, http://www.fh-trier.de/index.php?id=5389, 5 Nov 2007.

Kruschwitz, L. (2009), Investitionsrechnung. updated 12th ed., Munich 2009.

Laudon, K. C., Laudon, J. P., Schoder, D. (2012), Wirtschaftsinformatik. Eine Einführung, Munich 2010.

Link, J., Weiser, C. (2011), Marketing-Controlling, Munich 2011.

Männel, W. (2000), Rentabilitätsorientiertes Investitionscontrolling nach der Methode des internen Zinssatzes, in: Kostenrechnungspraxis (krp) 44 (2000) 6, pp. 325–341.

Matzer, M. (2013), Kein Hexenwerk: das moderne Orakel. Prognosen für Tests von Szenarien, in: BI-Spektrum (2013) 1, pp. 18–21.

Mayer, R. (1991), Prozeßkostenrechnung und Prozeßkostenmanagement, in: IFUA Horváth & Partner (Pub., 1991), Prozeßkostenmanagement, Munich 1991, pp. 73–100.

Meier, M., Sinzig, W., Mertens, P. (2002), SAP strategic enterprise management business analytics – Integration von strategischer und operativer Unternehmensführung, Berlin/Heidelberg 2002 (updated edition: *Meier, M., Sinzig, W., Mertens, P. (2004),* SAP strategic enterprise management business analytics – Integration von strategischer und operativer Unternehmensführung, improved and expanded 2nd ed., Berlin/Heidelberg 2004).

Mensch, G. (2008), Finanz-Controlling: Finanzplanung und -kontrolle, 2nd ed., Munich 2008.

Mertens, P. (2013), Integrierte Informationsverarbeitung 1: Operative Systeme in der Industrie, 18th ed., Wiesbaden 2013.

Mertens, P., Bissantz, N., Hagedorn, J. (1995), Top-Down Navigation and Knowledge Discovery in SAP Operating Results Data: The BETREX System, in: Managing Information & Communication in a Changing Global Environment, Proceedings of the 1995 Information Resources Management Association International Conference, 21–24 May, Atlanta, Georgia, USA.

Mertens, P., Bodendorf, F., König, W., Schumann, M., Hess, Th., Picot, A. (2012), Grundzüge der Wirtschaftsinformatik, 11th ed., Berlin/ Heidelberg 2012.

Mertens, P., Meier, M. (2009), Integrierte Informationsverarbeitung 2: Planungs- und Kontrollsysteme in der Industrie, Wiesbaden 2009, pp. 197.

Bibliography

Meyer, M., Birl, H., Knollmann, R. (2007), Tätigkeitsfeld und Verbesserungspotenziale des zentralen Investitionscontrolling, in: Controlling (2007) 11, pp. 633–640.

Möller, K., Menninger, J., Robers, D. (2011), Innovationscontrolling. Erfolgreiche Steuerung und Bewertung von Innovationen, Stuttgart 2011.

Müller-Stewens, G., Lechner, C. (2001), Strategisches Management: Wie strategische Initiativen zum Wandel führen, Stuttgart 2001 (updated edition: *Müller-Stewens, G., Lechner, C. (2005)*, Strategisches Management: Wie strategische Initiativen zu Wandel führen, updated 3rd ed., Stuttgart 2005).

Munck, J. C., Chouliaras, E., Gleich, R. (2014), Innovationscontrolling-Audit – Entwicklung und Verprobung eines Konzeptes zur Messung und Bewertung des unternehmensinternen Innovationscontrolling, in: Controlling 26 (2014) 2, pp. 109–115.

Neely, A. (2013), Big Data and Business Model Innovation: The New Wave of Analytics, Stuttgarter Controller Forum, Stuttgart 2013.

Perridon, L., Steiner, M., Rathgeber, A. (2009), Finanzwirtschaft der Unternehmung, 15th ed., Munich 2009, pp.145 f.

Porter, M. E., Heppelmann, J. E. (2014), How Smart, Connected Products are Transforming Competition, in: Harvard Business Review 11 (2014).

Redman, T. C. (2013), Data Credibility Problem. Management – not technology – is the solution, in: Harvard Business Review 10 (2013), pp. 84–88.

Sasse, A. (2003), Investitionsentscheidung, Einsatz der Kapitalwertmethode unter Berücksichtigung von Ertragssteuern, in: Der Controlling-Berater (2003) 2, pp. 119–134.

Ulrich, H., Hill, W., Kunz, B. (1994), Brevier des Rechnungswesens, 8th ed., Bern/Stuttgart 1994.

Voggenreiter, D., Jochen, M. (2002), Der kombinierte Einsatz von Wertmanagement und Balanced Scorecard, in: Controlling 14 (2002) 11, pp. 615–621.

Weber, J., Kaufmann, L., Schneider, Y. (2005), Controlling von Intangibles: Nichtmonetäre Unternehmenswerte aktiv steuern, Reihe Advanced Controlling, vol.48, Weinheim 2005.

Weber, J., Schaler, S., Strangfeld, D. (2005), Berichte für das Top Management, Schriftenreihe Advanced Controlling, vol.43, Weinheim 2005.

Zacher, M. (2012), White Paper: Big Data Analytics in Deutschland 2012, IDC Manufacturing Insights (Pub.), http://www.sas.com/content/dam/SAS/bp_de/doc/whitepaper1/ba-wp-idc-big-data-analytics-2012-1925633.pdf, January 2012, p. 2.

Zvezdov, D., Schaltegger, S. (2012), Nachhaltigkeitscontrolling: mehr als nur ein Konzept?, in: Controlling & Management 56 (2012) 4, pp. 2–4.

Index

Index